Business Travel and Tourism

Business Travel and Tourism

Manoj Sharma

RANDOM

RANDOM PUBLICATIONS

NEW DELHI (INDIA)

Business Travel and Tourism

ISBN 978-93-5111-328-7

Published in 2014 in India by

Reprint 2020

RANDOM PUBLICATIONS
4376-A/4B, Gali Murari Lal, Ansari Road
New Delhi-110 002
Phone : +91-11-43580356, +91-11-23289044
e-mail: randomexports@gmail.com, sales@randompublications.com, info@randompublications.com

Type Setting by : Keystoneprintads, Delhi-110051
Printed at : Mehra Printers, Delhi-110 092

Preface

Business tourism or business travel is when more limited and focused subset of regular tourism. During business tourism, individuals are still working and being paid, but they are doing so away from both their workplace and home. Some definitions of tourism tend to exclude business travel. However, the World Tourism Organization defines tourists as people "traveling to and staying in places outside their usual environment for not more than one consecutive year for leisure, business and other purposes".

Primary business tourism activities include meetings, and attending conferences and exhibitions. Despite the term business in business tourism, when individuals from government or non-profit organizations engage in similar activities, this is still categorized as business tourism. Historically, business tourism, in the form of traveling to, spending money and staying abroad for some time, has a history as long as that of international trade.

In late 20th century, business tourism is seen as a major industry. Compared to regular tourism, business ones involves a smaller section of the population, with different motivations, and additional freedom-of-choice limiting constrains imposed through the business aspects. Destinations of business tourism are much more likely to be areas significantly developed for business purposes. An average business tourist is more wealthy than an average leisure tourist, and is expected to spend more money.

I thank all associates of my group who have helped in the preparation of the book. My individual thanks go to "Random Publications" who have in print the book.

— *Manoj Sharma*

Contents

1

Workforce Planning and Employment for Business Travel

There are a number of dynamics that increasingly make workforce planning and employment critical components of the organization's strategic plan. The United States economy has transitioned from a manufacturing base to a service base and is in the process of transitioning to a knowledge base. As the economy moves along this continuum, the success of the organization is increasingly based on the quality of its human capital, which is defined as the total current and potential capabilities of the organization's workforce. As this transition occurs, organizational strategies increasingly must be developed to develop the organization's primary resource: people. The quality of its human capital will allow an organization to differentiate itself in the market place, much as innovative products and services now do. In fact, for many organizations, human capital will become their core competency—the unique capability that distinguishes them from their competitors. To create this competency, an organization must be able to attract the right kinds of people in the right place at the right time.

The nature of competition has changed and is global. Markets and environments are frequently dynamic and volatile, and organizations have been downsized and right-sized to improve cost efficiencies. Globalization requires the organization to understand multiple cultures and how to attract, retain, and motivate persons from those cultures. The dynamics of the environment often require flexibility and adaptation at the lower levels of the organization. All this affects the workforce planning and employment practices.

Technology has not only changed the way work is done, it has also changed the knowledge, skills, and abilities needed to do the work. Organizations must plan to either attract those with the right skills to the organization or to develop those skills internally. The latter requires hiring individuals who have the capacity to learn and to grow.

Workforce demographics in the United States are changing. The workforce is aging and contains an increasing percentage of both women and members of minority groups. In addition, workers often come to the organization with deficient skill sets. The organization must plan how to replace the impending retirement of the "Baby Boomers" while developing the skills of those that follow. The organization must be actively engaged in planning to determine how to react to the dynamics just discussed to develop an internal workforce that is capable of accomplishing the organization's strategic goals. That is the essence of workforce planning and employment.

Concept and process of Human Resource Planning

Human resources alignment means integrating decisions about people with decisions about the results an organization is trying to obtain. By integrating human resources management (HRM) into the agency planning process, emphasizing human resources (HR) activities that support broad agency mission goals, and building a strong relationship between HR and management, agencies are able to ensure that the management of human resources contributes to mission accomplishment and that managers are held accountable for their HRM decisions. This is especially important in light of the Government Performance and Results Act's (GPRA) push to align all agency activities, including HRM, toward achieving defined agency strategic goals and measuring progress toward those goals.

In fiscal year 1999, the U.S. Office of Personnel Management (OPM) embarked on a special study to determine how much progress Federal agencies have made toward aligning HRM with agency strategic goals in support of HRM accountability and agency mission accomplishment. Our key findings and conclusions are summarized as follows.

Many more agencies than expected include HR representatives in the agency planning process and integrate human resources management goals, objectives, and strategies into agency strategic plans. However, most agencies are still struggling in this area. Therefore, agency executives and HR leaders need to work together to fully integrate HRM into the planning process so that it will become a fundamental, contributing factor to agency planning and success.

Although some agency HR offices have begun focusing on organizational activities that assist agency decision-making, most are still emphasizing internal HR office efficiency efforts. While internal issues are important to the success of any HR programme, HR offices also need to examine the "big picture" and find ways to impact the success of the agency as a whole.

Most agencies are in some way measuring the efficiency and/or effectiveness of the HR function. These measures, however, are generally output-oriented, focus on internal HR processes and activities, and are used to make improvements to HR-specific policies and procedures. As HR refocuses its activities to broader organizational issues, HRM measures also need to be expanded to gauge the impact HRM has on agency goals and mission. Then, the measurement data can be used to inform agency-level decisions.

The relationship between HR and management is becoming more collaborative. HR executives are beginning to earn a seat at the management table. HR offices are becoming more consultative and involved in day-to-day line management activities. Nevertheless, there is still a long way to go if HR is to become a strategic partner at all levels. To do so, HR needs to build its own internal competencies to deal with organizational issues, educate itself on agency and programme missions, and find ways to offer creative and innovative solutions to organizationwide issues.

Although many National Performance Review (now known as the National Partnership for Reinventing Government) initiatives, such as downsizing, reorganizing, streamlining, and delegating HR authorities, were meant to improve HR's ability to focus on organizational issues, they have not taken hold as quickly or thoroughly as hoped. Therefore, HR is still doing most of the process work, and its ability to focus on alignment has been limited. However, as HR's role in agency planning, activities, and decision-making advances — and it is advancing — so too will the alignment of human resources management with agency mission accomplishment.

Alignment

Strategic human resources management...strategic alignment...alignment with mission accomplishment. These are just a few of the terms being used to describe the new, evolving role of Federal human resources management (HRM). What do these terms really mean? If you were to ask agency personnelists, managers, or employees, you would probably get a wide range of answers. So, it's important to establish from the beginning what we are really talking about. Human resources management alignment means to integrate decisions about people with decisions about the results an organization is trying to obtain. Our research indicates that agencies that successfully align human resources management with agency mission accomplishment do so by integrating HRM into the agency planning process, emphasizing HR activities that support mission goals, and building strong HR/management relationships.

In addition to being a vital contributor to agency mission accomplishment, HRM alignment is the ultimate level of HRM accountability, as demonstrated in the Hierarchy of Accountability. While HRM accountability must begin with basic legal compliance, it ultimately encompasses all four levels of the pyramid, including demonstrating how HRM supports achievement of the agency strategic goals.

Why Align?

Why the sudden emphasis on aligning HRM activities with agency mission accomplishment? Basically, it comes down to demonstrating the value of human resources management to the agency. In the past, one of HR's primary roles has been to ensure compliance with laws, rules, and regulations.

Although this is still, and will always be, a necessary function, many recent developments have led to a strong emphasis on results.

The National Performance Review (NPR) took on the task of reinventing government to make it work better, cost less, and get results. NPR mandated many initiatives that changed the focus of HR from just compliance toward results, including downsizing the HR function, delegating HR authorities to line managers, calling for HR to demonstrate its business value, and enhancing customer service. Through these initiatives, management of human resources would become more responsive to mission-related needs because it would take place at the line level, and the HR staff would be able to expend more of its energy on broader organizational issues.

The Government Performance and Results Act (GPRA) of 1993 has also played a large part in focusing agencies on results. The purpose of GPRA is to improve Federal programme effectiveness, accountability, service delivery, decision-making, and internal management, thereby improving confidence in the Federal Government. This is achieved by demonstrating organizational results through strategic planning and performance measures.

Although the primary focus of GPRA is on programmatic functions, agencies are also required to describe how administrative resources, such as HR, are being used to achieve strategic goals. Further, the General Accounting Office (GAO) and the Office of Management and Budget (OMB) have evaluated many of these efforts, and are calling for agencies to improve their discussions of HRM alignment in strategic and annual plans. Therefore, the human resources function is increasingly being aligned to the agency strategic plan, which requires HR to show how it is supporting mission accomplishment.

Alignment has already occurred in other key administrative functions. When Congress developed a statutory framework to introduce performance-based management into the Federal Government, it initiated financial, information technology, and procurement reforms through such mandates as the Chief Financial Officer Act and Information Technology Management Reform Act. Human resources management is the administrative missing link to this comprehensive package.

The private sector has recognized that it is not just financial and technological capital that provide companies with the competitive edge, but people, or human capital. Without attracting and retaining the right people, in the right jobs, with the right skills and training, an organization cannot succeed. Therefore, people have been recognized as companies' most important asset. As the Federal Government moves toward a performance-based management approach, we, too, need to realize the importance of our human resources. A huge percentage of agencies' budgets is spent on human resources — salaries, benefits, training, work life programmes, etc. Nowhere else do you make that substantial an investment and not measure the return.

Not only do human resources provide the competitive edge, but several recent studies have confirmed that the quality and innovation of HR practices impact business results. These studies were able to draw a correlation between increased quality of HR practices and increased business success. Among other benefits, HR alignment with mission accomplishment increases HR's ability to anticipate its customers' needs, increases the agency's ability to implement strategic business goals, and provides decision-makers with critical resource allocation information. Finally, HR alignment is a vital process to advance agency accountability. By defining, maintaining, and assessing HRM goals and measures, communicating them throughout the agency, and using the information to make management decisions, agencies are able to ensure that the management of human resources contributes to mission accomplishment and that managers are held accountable for their HRM decisions in support of mission accomplishment.

STRATEGIC PLANNING

Agencywide Planning

To some agencies, strategic planning is a way of life. To others, it's an exercise. To almost all, it's a requirement. As part of GPRA, agencies, unless specifically exempted, follow a continuous, three step strategic planning process:

Strategic planning allows agencies to map out where they are, where they want to go, and how they plan to get there. Some agencies adopted the idea of strategic planning even before GPRA was enacted, whereas others are just beginning to understand its potential benefits. The results of the fiscal year 1999 Merit System Principles Questionnaire (MSPQ), an OPM Governmentwide survey of supervisors and employees, show that agencies are beginning to embrace not only the concept, but also the practice, of strategic planning.

HRM Integration in Agency Strategic Plans

The management of agency human resources is an integral part of how an agency is going to achieve its mission goals. Without people, there is no one to do the work. Therefore, integrating HRM into the agency strategic plan is the first step in aligning it with the mission. Even though GAO and OMB are pushing for improvement of HRM alignment discussions in strategic and annual plans, GPRA's primary focus is still on agency programmes, rather than corporate functions. Therefore, we assumed at the beginning of this study that not many agency strategic plans would have addressed HRM's role in mission accomplishment. We were pleasantly surprised. Out of the 31 strategic plans reviewed, 87 per cent had addressed HRM in some way. Below is a breakdown of how integration between HRM and the agency plan is achieved, a count of how many strategic plans have integrated HRM in a particular way, and some examples of actual agency approaches.

Although some agencies are clearly ahead of the pack, integration of HRM in agency plans is still evolving. When looking at the actual placement of strategic plan HRM discussions, they are generally segregated from the programmatic goals, objectives, and strategies. Considering that an agency's mission cannot be achieved without its people, this is an important point. Could this be an indication that human resources management is not yet recognized as a critical contributor to agency mission accomplishment?

In any case, it is clear that though there are some exceptions, as evidenced by some of the examples above full HRM integration into agency strategic plans have not yet been realized. The human resources issues addressed in agency plans provide insight into what aspects of human resources management are most important to agency management. In reviewing the plans, or even just by looking at the examples above, it is clear that diversity, recruitment, retention, employee development, and workforce quality are the major areas of interest. Although these could be looked at as process or output programmes, when they are designed and implemented well, they lead to the ultimate result: the right people, with the right skills, in the right positions to carry out the agency mission.

Agency HRM Strategic Measures

Defining practical, meaningful measures that assess the effectiveness of agency human resources management and its support of mission accomplishment is a topic that agencies have been struggling with. It is easy to measure a process — how long does it take to complete an action? It is easy to measure productivity — how many actions were completed in any given time frame? But how do you measure the outcome of human resources management? How does an agency know if it has the right people, with the right skills, in the right positions to carry out the agency mission? Have any agencies found a way to do this? To help answer these questions, we looked to see if agencies are including HRM measures in their strategic plans, and what types of measures they have identified.

Not surprisingly, 71 per cent of the plans did not identify any HRM measures. Moreover, the meaningfulness and practicality of the 29 per cent of agency identified measures could be stronger. About one-third of the 29 per cent contain measures that are not really measures. They are lists of activities or projects that, when completed, will help to reach the goal. In other words, they are strategies labelled as measures. The other two-thirds of that 29 per cent have fairly good measures that are tied to specific mission or support goals and provide seemingly relevant information. However, even these fairly good measures tend to focus on HR processes (outputs) rather than intended outcomes. For example, some agencies measure the average number of employee training hours to measure workforce skill levels, rather than what skills are actually gained through the training or what skills the workforce actually possesses.

HR Involvement in Agency Strategic Planning

Now that we have seen what types of goals, objectives, strategies, measures, and other forms of HRM integration are present in agency strategic plans, we should look briefly at how these were developed. The legitimacy and ultimate value of these pieces of the plan will depend substantially on where they came from. Historically, members of the HR community have remarked on the difficulty they have had "getting to the table" with top agency management. Rather than being involved in agency planning from the beginning, HR is commonly consulted after decisions have been made in order to help implement any major changes. Considering the invaluable perspective HR has on how decisions will impact agency resources, HR professionals have been frustrated that they are not involved sooner in the planning process.

Therefore, it was surprising when 79 per cent of the agencies we talked to indicated that they do play a role in the overall agency strategic planning process. The roles vary from a peripheral consultant who reviews and comments on preliminary products to an integrated team member who actively helps to identify not only HRM agency strategic goals and objectives, but programmatic goals as well. Two or three of the responding agencies fall in the former category, a handful in the latter, and the rest somewhere in between. Later, we will discuss how some HR officials are able to elevate themselves to agency strategic partner, while most are still struggling to achieve this.

Patent and Trademark Office (PTO): HR's Involvement in Strategic Planning

The PTO's planning process tracks closely. HR, as well as the other administrative functions, is integrally involved in and present during all aspects of planning — the top management discussions, business line planning, and overall ranking and budgetary discussions. The administrative functions serve several purposes: to inform managers what resources are available to them; to determine what resources managers will need; and to discuss the impact programme initiatives will have on the agency.

When it comes to defining actual HRM goals, strategies, and measures, the roles also vary. In general, agencywide HRM-related goals, strategies, and measures are identified by the agency leader or other senior managers with HR collaboration. They decide what is most important to the agency based on the challenges the agency will face in years to come. Some use a more elaborate collaboration approach that involves agency management, HR officials, and other stakeholders, as is demonstrated in the presented examples from the Department of Commerce's Patent and Trademark Office (PTO) and the Department of Veterans Affairs (VA). Then there are the agencies that use the functional strategic planning approach where the HR office is tasked with coming up with the goals, strategies, and measures itself. In these cases, HR generally uses some type of feedback from customers to identify what is important to the agency and should be included in the plan.

Department of Veterans Affairs Collaborative Approach

The Department of Veterans Affairs (VA) Office of Human Resources Management was integrally involved in the Department's strategic planning process. Although the programme offices were the drivers for the strategic goals, the administrative functions were integrally involved in establishing how resources can be attained, retained, and utilized to support the programmes that deliver services to their customer, the veterans. The HR staff worked with programme planners and line managers in an iterative and interactive series of meetings that provided HR with information on the Department's current and future business and corresponding human resource needs. The HR staff was able to translate this information into specific objectives with supporting strategies and performance goals that were incorporated into the VA strategic plan.

To further refine its priorities, HR held a conference attended by approximately 300 people representing its key stakeholder groups departmentwide including: HR professionals, political appointees, headquarters executives, field line managers, staff offices, unions, and veterans. A "real time" strategic planning process that included facilitation, formal presentations, and inter-active discussions led to the identification and prioritization of four critical human resources "strategic opportunities" that must be dealt with if VA is to successfully accomplish its mission. Top management at the conference committed to supporting the pursuit of these strategic opportunities, and, subsequently, teams including field and headquarters, line and staff representatives were formed around these opportunities.

Agency Annual Performance Plans

In addition to reviewing strategic plans, we also reviewed 28 agency annual performance plans to see how HRM is addressed. As mentioned earlier, performance plans are the yearly operational plans defining what the agency will accomplish in that fiscal year that will contribute to the longer-term strategic goals, and how they will measure accomplishment of these performance goals. Seventy-five per cent of the reviewed plans contain both HRM performance goals and measures. This is not surprising because these operational plans tend to be more process and budgets focused than strategic plans and therefore contain more detail about the resources needed to accomplish the performance goals. Therefore, administrative functions, in general, are represented more fully than in the strategic plan.

The development of the performance plan is invariably more functional than overall strategic planning. At most agencies, each programme and administrative function is responsible for defining its own goals and measures which it then forwards to the planning office for coordination into the annual performance plan. As with the strategic plans, the HRM goals, strategies, and measures identified by HR offices tend to focus more on processes or activities than on overall outcomes. These process measures can be helpful, but because operational goals, strategies, and measures.

Human Resources Management Strategic Plan

The Health Care Financing Administration (HCFA) has developed a very noteworthy approach to aligning human resources management with mission accomplishment. HCFA's Human Resources Management Group (HRMG), Learning Resources Group (LRG), and Office of Equal Opportunity and Civil Rights (OEOCR) collaborated to develop a draft Human Resources Strategic Plan that goes beyond each of these individual organization's human resources responsibilities and instead addresses the entire sub-component's human resources management responsibilities. It assigns accountability for specific HRM goals to HRMG, LRG, OEOCR, senior leadership, line managers, employees, the union, and/or other non-HR stakeholders. The HRMG, LRG, and OEOCR worked very closely with the HCFA strategic planning and evaluation office to tie the plan to HCFA's strategic plan.

Specifically, the plan includes challenges that HCFA will face in the future, HRM goals that will support HCFA in meeting those challenges, potential performance indicators and strategies for each goal, the roles and responsibilities of HRMG, LRG, OEOCR, managers, employees, and other stakeholders, and finally how to implement and assess its results, help determine achievement of mission goals, they should focus more on whether or not the intended outcome of the activity was achieved.

HR Strategic Plans

Approximately half of the agencies we talked to have developed separate Human Resources strategic plans. These plans generally serve one of two purposes. Either they provide direction for those agencies that have not integrated HRM into the agency strategic plan, or they are used as implementation plans which support agencywide HRM goals, strategies, and measures.

These plans are particularly important to those agencies that do not integrate HRM into the agencywide plan because it helps them map out where they want the HR programme to go. They seem less important to many of the agencies that have thoroughly integrated HRM into the agency plan. For example, the Social Security Administration (SSA) has not developed a specific HR strategic plan because HR's goals and measures are part of the agencywide approach. Then, there are some agencies that integrate HR extensively into the agency plan, but still prefer to have a separate HR operational plan supporting the agencywide plan, as is often done by other corporate functions such as information technology and financial management.

Most of these plans focus on internal HR office programme activities, rather than on agencywide accountability for the effective use of human resources in accomplishing the mission. Therefore, ownership of the plan belongs to the HR office, not the agency. The Health Care Financing Administration (a sub-component of the Department of Health and Human Services) is an interesting exception to this, as seen in the inset. As with agency strategic plans, the measures identified in HR strategic plans are typically process- oriented and tend to address what steps have been taken to achieve a goal, rather than whether the intended outcome of the goal has been achieved. A little over half of the agencies use management input in developing these plans, generally in the form of previous customer satisfaction surveys.

Strategic planning allows agencies to put down on paper where they are, where they want to go, and how they plan to get there. But the best planning in the world does nothing for an agency if it does not act on those plans. Strategic implementation of human resources management means performing activities that support agency mission accomplishment and measuring how well those activities contribute to achieving agency strategic goals.

Strategic HRM Activities

When we talk about HRM activities, we tend to focus on what the HR office, itself, is doing even though we recognize that supervisors would bear the responsibility of HR decisions in an ideal world. After all, NPR advocated deregulation and delegation and the downsizing and outsourcing of HR office activities so that human resources management could take place at the line level, making it more responsive to mission-related needs. Additionally, the HR staff would be able to devote more time to broader organizational issues, thereby improving its contribution to mission accomplishment.

Unfortunately, deregulation and delegation, as reported in OPM's 1997 special study, Deregulation and Delegation of Human Resources Management Authority in the Federal Government, have not taken hold as quickly or thoroughly as was hoped. HR is still doing most of the HR- related work and is the nerve centre for HRM activities. That is why the focus of this section is on the HR office and what it does to support mission accomplishment. So what are HR's contributions toward mission accomplishment? Although most line managers we interviewed cannot describe precisely which HR activities support specific agency strategic goals, they recognize that they could not accomplish their mission without HR's help. Ironically, the areas most often mentioned by managers as HR's most valued contributions are also the areas they feel need the most improvement: recruitment and staffing, employee development, and employee relations. They would like to see HR become more involved and innovative in these areas, but they also admit that it would be extremely difficult for them to get their jobs done without the help HR already provides.

With this system, HR can immediately identify available deployment candidates for selection as soon as disasters are declared. Additionally, the system allows HR to better identify employee training and promotion needs, match employee expertise with specific disaster site victim needs, and create a selection routine that rotates available employees, thereby avoiding employee burnout. Clearly, staffing, development, and employee relations are important HR activities that make a difference to agency goal accomplishment. However, there are other areas in which HR offices contribute to and align with mission accomplishment, such as the few described below.

Agency Reorganizations: Because of all of the downsizing, streamlining, and budget cuts that have been occurring in recent years, many agencies and sub-components have had to redefine their missions and restructure the programme areas that support those missions. Human resources staffs play key roles in some of these redesign efforts. Managers at the Federal Emergency Management Agency and the Department of Labour's Occupational Safety and Health Administration were particularly complimentary of all of the work the HR staffs did to redeploy and retrain the workforce, provide guidance on organizational development issues, and redesign performance standards.

Workforce Planning: In this time of budget cuts, downsizing, and an aging Federal workforce, workforce planning becomes extremely important to increasing agencies' overall ability to achieve their missions. Although few agencies have strong workforce planning systems in place, some are beginning to take steps in this direction. The Department of the Army has an automated civilian forecasting system that uses 15-year workforce data trends to project future employment patterns, up to 7 years. This is part of a developing workforce planning initiative. SSA has developed a methodology to predict the number of actual

Tracking Strategic Progress

Engineers at NASA's Kennedy Space Centre have designed and implemented an excellent strategic management tool: the Goal Performance Evaluation System. This computer system implemented a major performance management change by linking individual employee performance goals all the way up through the Centre and Agency goals.

The system tracks the status of performance plans, and allows organizations to track results achieved against their mission. Managers can access the system to see what their units and individual employees are contributing toward the agency strategic goals. The system functions as a strategic management tool, an employee performance management system, and a Centre-wide communication tool. Kennedy and Johnson Space Centres have piloted the computer system with very positive results, retirements and is developing a workforce transition plan that will identify current and future required skill sets, determine how the workforce can obtain these skills, and set action plan milestones. Additionally, OPM is in the process of developing a workforce planning model that will assist agencies in this area. Linking Performance Management to Mission Accomplishment: When managers and employees are interviewed, they almost always cite the performance management system as a way they are held accountable for meeting agency goals. So, does this mean performance management systems are aligned with agency strategic goals? In most agencies, the answer is "not yet" — at least not fully. Recently published research has identified over a dozen agencies and agency sub- components that have started to formulate systematic approaches to aligning performance management to strategic goals. Most are starting by linking top management performance plans and contracts to agency goals and rating and rewarding executives based on achievement of those goals.

Many of these agencies are planning to cascade the alignment down to the employee level. OPM's 1999 publication, A Handbook for Measuring Employee Performance: Aligning Employee Performance with Organizational Goals, is a very useful tool to help agencies link employee performance to the goals of the organization and measure employee accomplishments. A couple of agencies actually mandate the linkage of employee level plans to agency goals, while others are using team-based performance management approaches that include performance targets, informal team assessments, and awards that are linked to mission goals. The National Aeronautics and Space Administration (NASA), as shown in the inset, actually has an automated system that assists in the linkage. Nevertheless, as the General Accounting Office (GAO) concluded in its study, Performance Management: Aligning Employee Performance with Agency Goals at Six Results Act Pilots, aligning performance management systems with organizational missions and goals is still a "work in progress."

HR Self-Assessment: A handful of agency and sub-component HR offices are actually assessing how well their programmes align with agency mission accomplishment as part of recently established HR self-assessment programmes. These assessment programmes focus on the compliance of HR activities with law as well as how effectively HR programmes are achieving their objectives in support of mission accomplishment. Because these assessment programmes are fairly new or are in the process of being revamped, it is too soon to tell the success they will have in measuring HR's impact on organizational mission accomplishment.

HRM Measurement

In the end, HR can only determine its value to the organization by measuring it. Earlier in this report, we saw that most agencies had at least defined HR output measures in agency strategic plans, annual performance plans, and/or HR strategic plans. This is an encouraging trend, but we need to look further at whether these measures are actually being tracked and used for decision- making. The best measures in the world are meaningless if not used. HRM measures in the strategic and annual performance plans are usually tracked by the HR office and forwarded to the planning office for distribution and sharing of the information.

A few agencies, such as NASA, SSA, and Education, report actually using the information for decision- making and tracking whether goals are being met. NASA even posts the information on its web page. However, we found that most agencies look at available data without really evaluating how the information can be used to enhance goal attainment. HR staffs find that measures from HR strategic plans tend to be more useful than those in the agency strategic or annual plans, at least at the functional level. As discussed earlier, HR strategic plan measures tend to focus on internal HR programmes, policies, and processes, and can therefore point to deficiencies in these areas.

HR officials can then use this information to make improvements to the problem areas. From an organizational perspective, however, the measures are generally not very helpful in determining achievement of HR goals because they are process rather than outcome oriented. Few agencies have implemented elaborate systems to track HRM goals and measures. Nonetheless, there are quite a few interesting approaches some agencies are using to measure their HRM performance.

Benchmarking is a systematic process of measuring an organization's products, services, and practices against those of a like organization that is a recognized leader in the studied area. Many Federal HR offices are using this practice to identify ways to improve service and align with business results. The most common benchmarking effort Federal HR offices have participated in is the National Academy of Public Administration-Hackett Group HR Benchmarking Study. There are at least 19 Government agencies involved in the benchmarking of 22 HR processes within four areas: administration, risk management, employee development, and decision support. The study also helps to gauge HR alignment through decision support categories such as resource planning, organizational planning, and strategic HR planning. Most participating agencies see the value in the information but have not devised strategies for how to use it.

The Balanced Scorecard in Action

The Veterans Benefits Administration's New York Regional Office implemented a balanced scorecard that uses outcome measures linked to organizational goals at the team, core group, and division-wide levels. The purpose is to determine how successful its operations are and where improvements are needed. This "balanced scorecard" measures five performance areas: customer satisfaction, speed, accuracy, cost-per- claim, and employee development. For each element in the balanced scorecard, teams are awarded points based on how well they are performing, and the scorecard is aligned with individual employee assessments and incentive pay. Veterans' expectations are used to define customer performance targets, and employee measures are derived from climate surveys, team development data, and technical skills inventories. HR has played an important role in designing the balanced scorecard, including developing measures, peer assessments, and other tools, as well as helping managers understand the approach and how to manage under it.

The Balanced Scorecard is a framework many agencies are using to translate strategy into operational terms by measuring a full range of perspectives: financial, customer, internal, and learning and growth. Vice President Gore advocated the use of this type of balanced set of results to evaluate agency performance at the Global Forum on Reinventing Government, January 1999. The scorecard is generally used at the business unit level, as with the Veterans Benefits Administration. To date, most agencies are in the beginning stages of implementing balanced measurement approaches.

Activity Based Costing (ABC) is a method of cost management that determines the true cost, including overhead, for a service or product. Finding the true cost allows agencies to discover cost improvement opportunities, prepare and actualize strategic and operational plans, and improve strategic decision-making. This cost management methodology involves identifying activities, determining activity costs, determining cost drivers, collecting activity data, and calculating the service cost. ABC is being explored by a number of agencies. The Patent and Trademark Office is using ABC agencywide, and the General Services Administration is using it to determine HR costs, as described on the following page.

Measuring True Cost and How to Use It

Both the General Services Administration (GSA) and the Department of Commerce's Patent and Trademark Office (PTO) have successfully used Activity Based Costing (ABC) to determine the true cost of human resources management services. The General Services Administration began tracking HR costs due to customer complaints that services were too expensive. The problem was that no one, including HR, knew the actual cost of HR services. By using Activity Based Costing, GSA was able to compute the HR activity costs and make comparisons to other Government and private sector organizations using the Hackett Benchmarking Study data. HR demonstrated to managers that its costs were actually relatively low, and it had the data to prove it.

The Patent and Trademark Office (PTO) has engaged in agencywide Activity Based Costing. All senior managers were trained in the process, and each functional area, including HR, formed teams to identify activities, activity-based drivers, and primary products. PTO has used the information to close out fiscal year 1998 financial activities and to plan the fiscal year 2000 budget. ABC has helped determine the full cost of agency activities, the proper distribution of costs, and has even influenced service rates. An additional benefit to the system is that it has encouraged strategic thinking. Managers see how much a function, such as HR, costs and starts asking what value that function really adds to the programme. This challenges HR to show its value and return on investment.

The Malcolm Baldrige and the President's Quality Award Criteria are each based on a set of core values and concepts that integrate key business requirements into a results-oriented framework. Using the criteria as a framework for management practices and measurement can help agencies to improve performance, facilitate communication and best practice sharing, and serve as a tool for managing performance, planning, training, and assessment. HR measures are 15 per cent of the total Baldrige framework score. Several agencies, most notably the Department of Navy's Inspector General's Office, have successfully used the criteria to assess agency mission programmes.

STRATEGIC RELATIONSHIPS

The lynchpin that holds all of this planning and implementation together is the relationship between HR executives and staffs and agency management. In the past, there was often much contention between the two groups because of HR's role as "gatekeeper," enforcing the laws, rules, and regulations. Now, with the role of the human resources staff shifting toward achieving organizational results, HR and management need to work together to further HRM's ability to have an impact on agency decisions and achievement of goals. So, let's take a look at how well these relationships have been fostered thus far.

Corporate HR and Top Agency Management

The relationship between corporate HR and top agency management varies greatly by agency. A few agencies, like SSA, NASA, Air Force, and GSA, have been able to develop strong working relationships with management in which HR is a full member of the agency decision-making body. Most other agency HR executives have not been so fortunate. They are generally brought into the agency decision-making process during the implementation phase rather than being consulted in the beginning on how decisions may impact agency human resources or vice versa.

For some agencies, it has been a hard road "getting to the table." For others, it has been more of a natural transition. In exploring how to elevate HR's role to management partner, agencies where this has been achieved attribute their success to a combination of the following factors: Reporting relationships - In agencies where there is a direct reporting relationship between the head of HR and the head of the agency, HR generally has a more visible role in agency decision-making.

Management advocates - In agencies where there is a strong HR advocate in senior management, HR enjoys more involvement in the agency decision-making. Credibility - HR representatives who are formerly programme managers tend to earn more credibility from the other managers. This type of individual knows, first hand, what the programme concerns are and how HR decisions will impact the programme, and can speak the same programmatic language.

The Social Security Administration: How HR Stays at the Table SSA's HR Office has a good record of contributing substance, creativity, and innovative solutions to dealing with agency issues.

For example, when SSA heeded NPR's call to downsize administrative staffs, the HR office devoted substantial time and resourcefulness to redeploying these displaced employees to direct service jobs. For the headquarters employees who did not want to leave the area, HR helped to create a direct service office at headquarters and bring work there. Not only does this demonstrate HR's ingenuity in turbulent times, but it is a fitting example of how SSA values its employees. Traditionally been part of the culture. Therefore, it is natural for the HR leader to have a voice in agency decisions.

Value - In all cases, HR has to bring value to the discussion in order to be considered a member of the management team. If you have little or nothing to offer, you will not keep your seat at the table. Because HR executives have little control over agency reporting relationships, management advocacy, executive appointments, and agency culture, they need to focus their efforts on providing value to agency business discussions. But what kind of value can HR bring to the agency decision-making table? Other corporate functions have no problem demonstrating their value.

The Chief Financial Officer has the money. The Chief Information Officer has the technology. Without money and technology, an organization is severely hindered. But HR has the people, and without the people, the organization has no one to do the work. So why has HR not been able to capitalize on this strength? We were able to identify two reasons.

First, HR has not historically had the statistics or data that can excite management and show how HRM influences agency success. Second, HR has focused on internal operations rather than activities that impact the entire agency. These facts are recognized by the Strategic Human Resources Roundtable, an OPM-sponsored working group of Governmentwide HR Directors that meets periodically to discuss HR's role in GPRA. This group acknowledges that to address these shortcomings, HR needs to ask itself what are the HRM concerns that will gain management's attention, and does HR have the data that can help address those concerns? SSA has done this, as is demonstrated in the above inset.

The HR Office and Line Management

Now that we have explored the relationship between HR executives and top agency managers, we need to look at how the HR office interacts with its line managers and if there has been any movement toward a more cooperative, consultative relationship. HR's role is changing, but is HR changing with it? As discussed earlier, NPR advocated HR delegating, downsizing, and outsourcing so that it could start concentrating on broader organizational issues rather than transactional processes. As we have seen, this is beginning to occur at the corporate level, but what about the line level?

The problem is that delegation to managers has not taken hold very quickly, but HR offices have already been downsized. Therefore, HR is still expected to do the transactional work it did before, while also focusing on broader organizational issues, and doing all of this with an average of 20 per cent less staff. It is not hard to understand why agency HR offices are struggling to redefine their role to strategic partner. Just how far have they gotten?

HR as Consultant: Most agency managers we interviewed acknowledge that their HR office has become more consultative. Rather than telling a manager he/she can or cannot do something, HR professionals are more helpful in finding solutions to HR issues.

HR as Contributor to Mission Accomplishment: These same managers also recognize the importance of the HR office to mission accomplishment. There is so much that HR does for managers in terms of recruitment and staffing, employee development, and employee relations that managers would have difficulty doing it on their own. However, HR does have its limitations, particularly the size of the staff in relation to the amount of work it has to do, its knowledge of the mission, and skill gaps resulting from downsizing.

HR as Strategic Partner: Few, if any, agency managers feel that their HR office is a true strategic partner. Few HR offices are included in business planning from the beginning, generally being brought in to implement a decision that has already been made. For HR to become more involved in line-level decision-making, managers would like the office to: C have greater knowledge of the organizational mission, and C get more involved and innovative in broad, organizational HR issues that impact most on the organization, such as recruitment and workforce and succession planning.

HR has made some headway, as demonstrated in the following NASA example, but clearly has some distance to go in being involved in line management decision-making. Now let's look at the other side of the coin — how managers are involved in making decisions about HR programmes. Most line HR offices involve managers at least at an informal level, generally through satisfaction surveys or informal discussions. A few have HR/ management councils that get together

NASA's Centres Working Together

NASA has 10 field centres, and each of these centres maintains a strong sense of its own identity and purpose and a strong enthusiasm for its mission. At the same time, each centre can identify the linkage to the agency mission.

This sense of empowerment appears to help motivate the centre HR staffs to actively support that identity and purpose. Personnel officers generally participate in deliberations on centre affairs. HR staffs are proactive in their work by making site visits, attending line staff meetings, asking managers for input on HR issues, and briefing managers about changes in HR programmes. Managers are impressed with HR's availability, knowledge, and resourcefulness.

This symbiosis is portrayed well in results from various employee surveys, data trends from the Central Personnel Data File, and third party evaluations of the HR programme. Periodically to discuss human resources issues. This is as close as agencies get to real integration of managers into the HR programme decision-making process. Generally, managers do not feel that they have a large impact on the direction of HR programmes and therefore feel little ownership for them.

Accountability

With the developing relationship between HR and management, both at the top and line levels, along with NPR and GPRA mandates, accountability should become a shared responsibility. Managers are making more and more HRM decisions while the HR staff is becoming more involved in broader organizational issues. This means that both the HR staff and managers are ultimately accountable for effective, legally compliant HRM.

Is this shared accountability occurring in Federal agencies? Approximately half of the responding agencies agree that HRM accountability is shared between the HR staff and managers. Managers are accountable for the business results achieved through good human resources management, the HR staff is accountable for HR compliance, and both are accountable for the overall effectiveness of the agency HRM programme. However, the other half still feels that the ultimate accountability falls on the HR staff. They are the ones responsible if actions are found non-compliant, and little attention is given to whether managers' HRM decisions are an effective use of resources. OPM's HRM Accountability System Development Guide goes into quite a bit of detail on shared accountability and can assist agencies in understanding the concept, determining who is accountable for what, and devising strategies for how to hold them accountable.

Strategic alignment of human resources management has come farther than we expected to find when we embarked on this study. There is definitely a trend toward integrating HR into the business planning process, measuring aspects of human resources management and its contribution to the organizational bottom line, and establishing a collaborative working environment between HR and management. Nevertheless, there are several indications that human resources management is not yet recognized as a critical contributor to agency mission accomplishment. HRM alignment is still evolving, and there are several steps agencies can take to help it along.

Fully integrate human resources management into the business planning process.

Although many more agencies than expected include HR representatives in the agency planning process and integrate human resources goals, objectives, and strategies into agency strategic plans, most are still struggling in this area. Agency executives need to recognize the value that HR can impart to discussions about agency activities, priorities, and goals. In turn, HR leaders need to understand agency mission needs and be able to contribute substantive, creative solutions to meet these needs. Once these realizations occur, HR will no longer be segregated out as a support function but will become an integral, contributing factor to agency planning and success.

Agency Decision-Making

Because of NPR mandates to downsize, streamline, and improve customer service, HR's recent improvement efforts have focused on the efficiency and effectiveness of traditional HR programmes and processes. These are important endeavours. However, in response to GPRA's call to measure performance and demonstrate value, it is time to start concentrating efforts outside of the traditional realm of HR and on to broader organizational issues. When HR demonstrates that it can have an impact on agency direction, then it will gain credibility with agency executives and earn a seat at the table. To generate that type of impact, HR needs to develop strategies based on actual business needs, which will require involving management in the planning process. In addition, it must address Governmentwide concerns about the workforce capabilities of the future, such as workforce planning, succession planning, training needs assessments, skill gap analyses, etc.

Measure HRM Outcomes

HR's role is evolving. Therefore, HRM measures need to evolve as well. As HR becomes more involved in broader organizational activities, HRM measures should evaluate the impact these activities have on the organization as a whole. At this point, measures typically focus on outputs and processes and are generally internalized to the HR function or office. The data are used mostly to make improvements to HR-specific policies and procedures. While this kind of measurement is important, measures should also focus on organizational outcomes. Information from these measures should then be used to inform agencywide decisions and find solutions to agencywide concerns.

Advance the collaborative working environment between HR and management.

To facilitate all of the changes recommended above, HR has to have a strong, collaborative working relationship with top agency and line management. Since there is no tradition in most agencies of HR as strategic partner, much depends on personal relationships established by HR officials with top managers and key line managers. Meanwhile, HR and agency management need each other more than ever. Authorities are being delegated to line managers, HR staffs are being downsized, and top agency management is being asked to show how its resources are being used to support mission accomplishment. HR must be able to make the case that everyone in the agency, from the agency leader down to the HR function, must share accountability for ensuring that the use of human resources not only complies with Federal laws, rules, and regulations, but adds to the success of the agency.

This shared accountability is beginning to occur. HR management is beginning to earn a seat at the table. HR line offices are becoming more consultative and involved in day to day management activities. Nevertheless, there is still a long way to go in becoming strategic partners. First, HR needs to build its own internal competencies to deal with organizational issues, change, and strategizing. Further, it needs to educate itself on agency and programme missions in order to understand what is important to those organizations and be able to offer creative and innovative alternatives and solutions to organizationwide issues. Finally, it must continually assert the absolute criticality of effective HRM to organizational success.

This all looks so easy on paper. Do this, do that, and you will be aligned with the mission and able to demonstrate your contribution toward it. Obviously, it is not that easy. Private sector, public sector, and some Federal entities have been struggling with this issue even before GPRA was enacted — and that works to our advantage. There is a wealth of information out there that can help — hundreds of articles, books, and studies have been written, numerous tools have been created, and many organizations have already tested a number of approaches. We can learn from all of these successes and failures.

But the only way to begin is to begin. To help start you on this path, we have included a rather extensive, though certainly not all-inclusive. In support of its programme to foster development of agency accountability systems, OPM will also offer assistance to individual agencies in developing strategies for strategic alignment and has created a Governmentwide clearinghouse that will provide information on additional real life, successful approaches that agencies are employing (currently available on the OPM web page). It is in all of our interests to ensure that Government establishes and maintains a highly skilled workforce that can handle the demands of the 21st century. To achieve this goal, we must all work together.

For some reason, people tend to think that the Federal Government has fallen far behind the private sector, and even other public sector entities, when it comes to aligning human resources management with agency mission accomplishment. Although we did not talk directly with private or non-Federal public sector representatives, we conducted a fairly in-depth literature search that tells a somewhat different story.

Private Sector

There are many conflicting views on where the private sector is in regard to HRM alignment. For instance, the Conference Board recently conducted a poll of 155 private sector HR executives, and 63 per cent responded that HR is "never, rarely, or only sometimes" a major player in the companies' strategic process. A Price water house-Coopers poll indicates that although 75 per cent of the responding 70 companies reported that HR's effectiveness is measured by its contribution to business results, only 27 per cent include HR from the beginning of the business planning cycle. Further, 43 per cent rated HR's planning and policy effectiveness as only average while a mere 6 per cent rated it as excellent.

Other private sector surveys and studies over the past few years, however, have found that HR has been integrated into the strategic planning process, HR executives and top company management are strategic planning partners, HR is recognized for the importance of its role in implementing organizational change, and HR is viewed as critical to the success of the business.

Clearly, there are many private sector organizations that exemplify "best-in-class" alignment strategies. They have implemented such alignment approaches as the Balanced Scorecard, Return on Investment, Activity Based Costing, Malcolm Baldrige Award-type criteria, and more. They recognize the importance of their employees to business results, and HR is considered a valued strategic partner. However, even with a number of "best practices" out there, the research agrees that HR alignment, even in the private sector, is still a work in progress.

Non-Federal Public Sector

According to recent research, the non-Federal public sector is in much the same boat as the Federal sector. As the Government Performance Project pointed out in its recent study, State governments run into many of the same HR problems as the Federal Government — rigid rules, lack of strategic management decisions, absence of statewide HR data, lack of workforce planning or the ability to plan for the future, etc. State governments have begun making HR reforms, such as reducing job classifications and streamlining hiring procedures. However, as with the Federal Government, States are focusing more on the efficiency and effectiveness of programmes than how they support the bottom line.

That is not to say that local, State, and even foreign governments have not been able to align themselves with mission accomplishment. A few cases can be most instructive for Federal agencies as they ponder this issue. The City of Hampton, Virginia HR staff has played a large role in increasing the performance of government services through improvements to work environment, organizational structure, work design, employee behaviours and organizational systems.

The state of Washington is developing and enhancing HR information systems in support of mission accomplishment, is using personnel data to identify improvement initiatives, and includes the Director of Personnel in the Governor's Cabinet. The Canadian Treasury Board and HR Council of the Federal Government of Canada are developing approaches to measuring HR efficiency, effectiveness, and mission contribution. There are many other examples of how the public sector is moving toward aligning HR with mission accomplishment. Nonetheless, the research indicates that the non-Federal public sector, too, is only in the beginning stages of this transformation.

2

Business Labour Relations and Tourism

INDUSTRIAL RELATIONS

Good industrial relations, while a recognizable and legitimate objective for an organization, are difficult to define since a good system of industrial relations involves complex relationships between:

a. Workers (and their informal and formal groups, i.e. trade union, organizations and their representatives);
b. Employers (and their managers and formal organizations like trade and professional associations);
c. The government and legislation and government agencies l and 'independent' agencies like the Advisory Conciliation and Arbitration Service.

Oversimplified, work is a matter of managers giving instructions and workers following them - but (and even under slavery we recognize that different 'managing' produces very different results) the variety of 'forms' which have evolved to regulate the conduct of parties (i.e. laws, custom and practice, observances, agreements) makes the giving and receipt of instructions far from simple. Two types of 'rule' have evolved:

- 'Substantive', determining basic pay and conditions of service (what rewards workers should receive);
- 'Procedural,' determining how workers should be treated and methods and procedures.

Determining these rules are many common sense matters like:

- Financial, policy and market constraints on the parties (e.g. some unions do not have the finance to support industrial action, some have policies not to strike, some employers are more vulnerable than others to industrial action, some will not make changes unless worker agreement is made first, and rewards always ultimately reflect what the market will bear);
- The technology of production (the effect of a strike in newspaper production is immediate -it may be months before becoming effective in shipbuilding);

- The distribution of power within the community - that tends to vary over time and with economic conditions workers (or unions) dominating in times of full employment and employers in times of recession.

Broadly in the Western style economies the parties (workers and employers) are free to make their own agreements and rules. This is called 'voluntarism'. But it does not mean there is total noninterference by the government. That is necessary to:

- Protect the weak (hence minimum wage);
- Outlaw discrimination (race or sex);
- Determine minimum standards of safety, health, hygiene and even important conditions of service;
- To try to prevent the abuse of power by either party.

HR Managers Responsibilities

The personnel manager's involvement in the system of industrial relations varies from organization to organization, but normally he or she is required to provide seven identifiable functions, thus:

1. To keep abreast of industrial law (legislation and precedents) and to advise managers about their responsibilities e.g. to observe requirements in respect of employing disabled persons, not to discriminate, not to disclose 'spent' convictions of employees, to observe codes of practice etc. in relation to discipline and redundancy, and similarly to determine organizational policies (in conjunction with other managers) relevant to legal and moral requirements.
2. To conduct (or assist in the conduct) of either local negotiations (within the plant) or similarly to act as the employer's representative in national negotiations. This could be as a critic or advisor in respect of trade etc. association policies or as a member of a trade association negotiating team. Agreements could be in respect of substantive or procedural matters. Even if not directly involved the personnel manager will advise other managers and administrators of the outcome of negotiations.
3. To ensure that agreements reached are interpreted so as to make sense to those who must operate them at the appropriate level within the organization (this can involve a lot of new learning at supervisory level and new pay procedures and new recording requirements in administration and even the teaching of new employment concepts – like stagger systems of work - at management level).
4. To monitor the observance of agreements and to produce policies that ensure that agreements are followed within the organization. An example would be the policy to be followed on the appointment

of a new but experienced recruit in relation to the offered salary where there is a choice of increments to be given for experience, ability or qualification.

5. To correct the situations which go wrong. 'Face' is of some importance in most organizations and operating at a 'remote' staff level personnel managers can correct industrial relations errors made at local level without occasioning any loss of dignity (face) at the working level. 'Human resource management' and the obscurity of its reasoning can be blamed for matters which go wrong at plant level and for unwelcome changes, variations of comfortable 'arrangements' and practices and unpopular interpretation of agreements.
6. To provide the impetus (and often devise the machinery) for the introduction of joint consultation and worker participation in decision-making in the organization. Formal agreement in respect of working conditions and behaviour could never cover every situation likely to arise. Moreover the more demanding the task (in terms of the mental contribution by the worker to its completion) the more highly–educated the workers need to be and the more they will want to be consulted about and involved in the details of work life. Matters like the rules for a flexitime system or for determining the correction of absenteeism and the contents of jobs are three examples of the sort of matters that may be solely decided by management in some organizations but a matter for joint consultation (not negotiation) in others with a more twenty-first-century outlook and philosophy. Human resource management is very involved in promoting and originating ideas in this field.
7. To provide statistics and information about workforce numbers, costs, skills etc. as relevant to negotiations (i.e. the cost of pay rises or compromise proposals, effect on differentials and possible recruitment/retention consequences of this or whether agreement needs to be known instantly); to maintain personnel records of training, experience, achievements, qualifications, awards and possibly pension and other records; to produce data of interest to management in respect of personnel matters like absentee figures and costs, statistics of sickness absence, costs of welfare and other employee services, statements about development in policies by other organizations, ideas for innovations; to advise upon or operate directly, grievance, redundancy, disciplinary and other procedures.

EMPLOYEE EVALUATION

An organization needs constantly to take stock of its workforce and to assess its performance in existing jobs for three reasons:

- To improve organizational performance via improving the

performance of individual contributors (should be an automatic process in the case of good managers, but (about annually) two key questions should be posed:
  - what has been done to improve the performance of a person last year?
  - and what can be done to improve his or her performance in the year to come?).
- To identify potential, i.e. to recognize existing talent and to use that to fill vacancies higher in the organization or to transfer individuals into jobs where better use can be made of their abilities or developing skills.
- To provide an equitable method of linking payment to performance where there are no numerical criteria (often this salary performance review takes place about three months later and is kept quite separate from 1. and 2. but is based on the same assessment).

On-the-spot managers and supervisors, not HR staffs, carry out evaluations. The personnel role is usually that of:

- Advising top management of the principles and objectives of an evaluation system and designing it for particular organizations and environments.
- Developing systems appropriately in consultation with managers, supervisors and staff representatives. Securing the involvement and cooperation of appraisers and those to be appraised.
- Assistance in the setting of objective standards of evaluation / assessment, for example:
  - Defining targets for achievement;
  - Explaining how to quantify and agree objectives;
  - Introducing self-assessment;
  - Eliminating complexity and duplication.
- Publicizing the purposes of the exercise and explaining to staff how the system will be used.
- Organizing and establishing the necessary training of managers and supervisors who will carry out the actual evaluations/ appraisals. Not only training in principles and procedures but also in the human relations skills necessary. (Lack of confidence in their own ability to handle situations of poor performance is the main weakness of assessors.)
- Monitoring the scheme - ensuring it does not fall into disuse, following up on training/job exchange etc. recommendations, reminding managers of their responsibilities.

Full-scale periodic reviews should be a standard feature of schemes since resistance to evaluation / appraisal schemes is common and the temptation to water down or render schemes ineffectual is ever present (managers resent the time taken if nothing else).

Basically an evaluation / appraisal scheme is a formalization of what is done in a more casual manner anyway (e.g. if there is a vacancy, discussion about internal moves and internal attempts to put square pegs into 'squarer holes' are both the results of casual evaluation). Most managers approve merit payment and that too calls for evaluation. Made a standard routine task, it aids the development of talent, warns the inefficient or uncaring and can be an effective form of motivation.

Provision of employee services

Attention to the mental and physical well-being of employees is normal in many organizations as a means of keeping good staff and attracting others.

The forms this welfare can take are many and varied, from loans to the needy to counseling in respect of personal problems.

Among the activities regarded as normal are:

- Schemes for occupational sick pay, extended sick leave and access to the firm's medical adviser;
- Schemes for bereavement or other special leave;
- The rehabilitation of injured/unfit/ disabled employees and temporary or permanent move to lighter work;
- The maintenance of disablement statistics and registers (there are complicated legal requirements in respect of quotas of disabled workers and a need for 'certificates' where quota are not fulfilled and recruitment must take place);
- Provision of financial and other support for sports, social, hobbies, activities of many kinds which are work related;
- Provision of canteens and other catering facilities;
- Possibly assistance with financial and other aid to employees in difficulty (supervision, maybe, of an employee managed benevolent fund or scheme);
- Provision of information handbooks,
- Running of pre-retirement courses and similar fringe activities;
- Care for the welfare aspects of health and safety legislation and provision of first-aid training.

The location of the health and safety function within the organization varies. Commonly a split of responsibilities exists under which 'production' or 'engineering' management cares for the provision of safe systems of work and safe places and machines etc., but HRM is responsible for administration, training and education in awareness and understanding of the law, and for the alerting of all levels to new requirements.

3

Customer Measurement for Business Travel and Tourism

INTRODUCTION

Every company must be able to satisfy and retain customers. That is the key to its business performance. Your job—as an executive in charge of improving quality, customer satisfaction, or loyalty—may be to enable others to act through training and support. Alternatively, if you're in the quality, customer assessment, or development areas of your company, your job may be to do the work directly—to collect, analyse, or use customer data to improve quality, satisfaction, and retention.

Whether you are an enabler or a doer, customer satisfaction and retention are your responsibility. Providing high-quality products and services builds strong relationships with customers and ensures future revenue streams. Even though you may agree about the importance of customers in driving performance, an important question remains. Does your company align its activities to satisfy and retain customers? Too often the answer is either "no" or "not so well." To help understand the problem, consider how a customer focus has evolved in recent decades.

In the 1970s, quality gurus argued that "quality is free." That is, a tireless pursuit of improvement should not only increase efficiency but also increase customer satisfaction in the process, saving enough on costs and bringing in enough new and repeat business to more than cover any expenditures on quality. This was an underlying concept in the success of many Japanese companies. In the 1980s the experts began to focus more directly on increasing customer satisfaction as an explicit goal. Satisfying and keeping customers, it was argued, is simply less expensive than constantly replacing them. More recently, quality and satisfaction have been viewed as not sufficient by themselves. Companies boast of moving "beyond" quality and satisfaction to focus directly on customer loyalty as the key to profitability.

Yet to argue that quality, or satisfaction, or loyalty is what matters misses the point. These factors form a chain of cause and effect, building on each other so that they cannot be treated separately. They represent a system that must be measured and managed as a whole if you want to maximize results. An example from our teaching experiences underscores the nature of the problem and why companies need to take a systems approach to customer measurement and management. Back in 1993 an executive seminar participant from a Fortune 100 company introduced himself as the "customer satisfaction manager" for his organization.

This prompted one of the authors to ask, "What happened to the quality manager?" The participant replied that quality was passé, and that customer satisfaction had become the hot topic in his organization. In fact, being the quality manager had become the "kiss of death" from a career standpoint—a dead-end job! Five years later, a seminar participant from the same company introduced himself as the "customer loyalty manager" for the organization.

Again the natural question arose, "What happened to the customer satisfaction manager?" "Oh, him?" It turned out that the satisfaction manager was now the one with the dead-end job. Many business organizations are beginning to recognize the need to avoid this "Book of the Month Club" mentality and to view customers from a systems perspective.

They want explicit linkages that extend from internal processes to customer perceptions to customer satisfaction to loyalty—and ultimately to bottom-line performance. The framework in this book will give executives hard numbers and not just persuasive theories to show that the connection is real and that improving satisfaction and loyalty really does improve profits. And those on the front lines—the quality engineers and service providers—will get specific guidance on what to improve and how to improve it to get the optimal response from customers. This book will show you how to create an integrated customer measurement and management system that will help you allocate resources and increase profits.

To create such a system, you must first understand your company's entire system for generating profit, from internal quality through to business performance. A systems approach acts on the basis of collected and interpreted customer data—but then you have to use the data to allocate resources and create change in the system or else you merely waste time and money. With an effective customer measurement and management system, you can build organizational value.

To do so, you will continually pursue three key activities that underlie a customer orientation: (1) gather customer information, (2) spread that information throughout the organization, and (3) use the information to maintain, improve, or innovate in products and processes. You need solid information about the concrete product and service attributes or features that customers value, the more abstract consequences and benefits these attributes provide, and ultimately the personal values they serve.

The purpose is to understand what your customers want not only in today's products and services but in tomorrow's as well. When you understand your customers at the various levels that motivate their behaviour, you can see their present needs and predict their future needs as well. To maintain a customer orientation throughout your organization, you need to make sure that customer information gets to everyone who is involved—either directly or indirectly— in improving quality and value and satisfying customers.

This both prepares the entire organization for change and provides benchmarks by which to monitor its performance. Finally, you need to prime the organization to act on the customer information to improve product and service offerings so as to increase satisfaction, loyalty, and profitability. This makes it essential to clarify the links among these three factors and understand how your company delivers a compelling product to its customers. Creating a customer measurement and management system is central to the pursuit of all three of these activities. With such a system in place, you have your customer information in a form that can serve as a basis for both incremental and more revolutionary product and service improvements.

The system also makes it easier to share customer information throughout an organization, enhancing its ability to follow through on that information to make product and process changes. It is essential to view customer measurement from a systems perspective that encompasses multiple areas of measurement and expertise (from engineering and design through market research and strategy to finance and accounting) so that you pick up both concrete and abstract details— both what the customers like and dislike and why they react that way—and develop information that will be genuinely useful.

Now you may well be saying, "But we already do a good job of gathering customer information, spreading it, and acting on the voice of the customer." The question is whether you really adopt the "lens of the customer" in this process or fall into the trap of relying on the "lens of the organization." The lens of the customer shows you your products and services—and the benefits they provide—from your customers' perspective.

You see them as they really are in the marketplace, rather than the different and potentially misleading picture you're likely to get from the lens of your own organization. For example, if you run a convenience store chain you may be inclined to view the chain's stores as providing customers with people (service), products (from soft drinks to gasoline), and operations (such as opening hours), each under the management of a different department or business function. The problem is that customers may not share this perspective. Customers view products and services from the standpoint of the benefits they provide and problems they solve, which may not align well with individual business process areas. In this case, customers are looking for safety, convenience, and cleanliness, which are benefits that are not uniquely provided by specific business process areas. Rather, they cut across the people, products, and operating policies of the stores. Aside from providing a more accurate picture of the drivers of satisfaction and loyalty, adopting the lens of the customer has other advantages. It blurs functional boundaries and provides a common basis and language for communication.

The forging of concrete links from area to area within a company is also a key to effective implementation. When an organization reaches a consensus on the importance of customer benefits that are not defined along functional or business process lines, it finds it much easier to engage in the cross-functional activities required to truly innovate and implement change. We emphasize the word *framework* here. Our aim is to show just what links and models are possible.The actual elements and links in any model vary tremendously from company to company and context to context.

After describing the framework, as suggested, show this point using two very different cases in which companies (Volvo and Sears) have developed models to become more customer focused. The framework includes four general areas: internal quality, external quality and satisfaction, customer loyalty and retention, and financial performance. *Internal quality* encompasses various production and maintenance processes.

In the case of a manufactured product, it includes everything from manufacturing processes to the physical characteristics and attributes that describe the product. In a service and retailing context, it includes the service offer, the physical surroundings, and the satisfaction of employees and the resulting service quality they provide. External quality and satisfaction encompasses what customers see in the purchase and consumption experience: the attributes and benefits that products and services provide and the costs they impose, and the conclusions the customers draw about the company. In the area of customer loyalty and retention, *loyalty* is a customer's intention or predisposition to buy, while *retention* is the behaviour itself (as when a customer returns to a restaurant, comes back to buy the same brand of car, or purchases another financial instrument from the same institution). Although as suggested, use the term *loyalty* at times to encompass both intended loyalty and actual retention, it is important to understand the distinction. When actual retention information is available, it proves extremely valuable in sorting out the drivers of financial performance.

When it is unavailable, as it often is, you can use loyalty measures as a proxy for retention. Quality, satisfaction, and loyalty ultimately affect financial performance, both directly and indirectly. The framework shows this point and highlights the possibility that there may be a tension between direct and indirect effects. Consider first the impact of internal quality. Producing a high-quality product or service at an attractive price indirectly affects financial performance through its effect on external customer perceptions of the purchase-consumption experience. But internal quality may also have a direct effect on costs and revenues.

The "quality is free" argument, improvements in internal quality can increase productivity and lower internal costs and thus directly increase profitability. Recent research suggests, however, that this link is likely to be more positive for products and less positive or even negative for services. Why the difference? Services are produced and delivered at a time and place that is typically dictated by the customer. Thus improving service quality often requires an increase in personnel and operating or contact hours, which raises operating costs.

The external quality, value, and customer satisfaction component of the framework also has both direct and indirect effects on costs and revenues. Indirectly, a positive overall experience predisposes customers to stay loyal towards a product, service, or provider, which generates future sales. Satisfaction thus contributes to financial performance through its effect on loyalty and retention. But satisfaction also has direct effects, independent of loyalty. The cost of maintaining a customer account—or fixing a product—is a direct function of how happy the customer is. Satisfied customers are less likely to demand expensive product repairs or replacements or to invoke service guarantees. Also—even outside the world of TV commercials—people do talk about the products and services they buy, and your company's entry into that stream of word-of-mouth publicity is through perceived quality and satisfaction rather than through loyalty. Satisfaction is *news*—something to talk about—while loyalty is a background state that goes without saying unless something happens to damage it.

The direct effects of loyalty and retention on performance include revenues from repeat purchases, reduction in costs of finding new customers (to replace lost customers), and revenues generated through cross-selling. Another direct effect is the price premium that loyal customers often pay. Because loyal customers are not actively shopping for alternatives, they tend to be insulated from price incentives and offers such as coupons, price cuts, and free merchandise. The recent turnaround at Volvo Car Company provides a good example of how a durable goods manufacturer views the links described in our framework.

In 1991, Volvo was performing poorly in the global automotive market. It ranked as low as twenty-sixth out of thirty-four brands in the J. D. Power Initial Quality Study in the United States, and sales and profitability were suffering. In its comeback effort, Volvo began to develop a customer orientation from a total quality management foundation. Formerly, Volvo had emphasized changing internal quality to improve productivity and reduce costs.

Its management realised, however, that just focusing on internal quality was insufficient. Internal improvements had to matter to the customers before they could create improved external quality, customer satisfaction, and loyalty. Volvo's approach is just one example of the variety of tailored models that are consistent with the framework. Like Volvo, Sears has attempted to radically transform itself into a more customer-focused organization. But since Sears is a retailer that competes primarily on service, its model has evolved quite differently. Internal quality at Sears is primarily about its people and the service they provide. The Sears model draws directly on a service-profit chain that links internal quality (including employee satisfaction and loyalty) to service quality, and the satisfaction generated by service quality to loyalty and financial performance. In developing its model, Sears has discovered both direct effects of satisfaction on financial performance and indirect effects through loyalty, which is consistent with our framework.

A quantitative employee-customer-profit model at Sears has helped the company to establish very specific links that have enabled it to improve financial performance. The model shows, for example, that a 5-point improvement in employee attitudes (on a 0 to 100 scale) drives a 1.3-point improvement in customer satisfaction, which in turn drives a 0.5 per cent improvement in revenue growth. The Volvo and Sears models share a common logic, but each model is uniquely tailored to the organization's own situation. Both models link internal quality through to profitability.

At the same time, each reflects the nature of a specific company, its customers and offerings, and the contexts involved. When you look at your own company, you will see that the same logic will work for you when you develop a similar understanding of your own customers and what you can offer them. The best measurement system can only provide information— it can't make decisions for you. People make decisions, whether it is the convenience store executive who sets corporate priorities, the front-line service manager who translates these priorities into policies and procedures, or the service worker who translates policies and procedures into concrete actions.

At all three levels, decision makers are much more likely to choose to do something that will help the store chain succeed if they understand what matters to customers and how the job at hand can enhance that value. The process of moving from information to decisions draws heavily on *importance-performance analysis.* The most cost-effective areas of product and service performance to improve are those that are important to customers *and* on which, at the same time, the company is performing poorly. Executives and managers must identify these priority areas of high importance and low performance. As an output of this selection process, they can categorize and display the drivers of satisfaction and loyalty using a strategic satisfaction matrix.

The matrix identifies four categories of performance drivers with different market action implications. Again, the aspects to improve first are those where impact or importance is high and performance is weak. This focuses resources and quality improvement efforts likely to have the greatest impact on satisfaction and thus on loyalty and profitability. Those aspects where performance and impact are both high reflect a firm's competitive advantage.

It is essential to maintain if not improve performance on these drivers. When impact and performance are both weak, on the other hand, there is no need to waste resources on improvement. More interesting is the low impact–strong performance category. This may be an area where resources have been wasted in the past because the benefits and attributes are not important to customers. Alternatively, this category may contain drivers of satisfaction that customers see as basic and necessary—so much a part of the product or service that they ignore it as long as it's there when they want it, like electric power or water on tap.

Although such drivers are important in an absolute sense, they have little to no impact on satisfaction because there is little variance in their performance. The danger is that a reduction in performance quality would increase the impact on satisfaction (this danger is often referred to as a "slippery slope"). Another possibility here is to find a new target market segment for the product or service.

For example, if the quality of an electrical system is so constant that it has no impact on satisfaction in one application, the system might be used in applications where minor fluctuations in this quality are more important and therefore likely to have a real impact on satisfaction. There is also a danger that something in this category may become important in the future. For example, few customers considered "environmental friendliness" to be an important factor until recently, but more and more people are beginning to pay attention to this aspect of the goods and services they buy. In a growing variety of fields, companies that predicted the importance of this area and prepared their business accordingly clearly have an advantage over those that did not. The circular nature of the process reflects the continuous nature of a customer orientation.

Customer needs, competitive offerings, and business technologies change constantly, so customer focus is an ideal of constant growth rather than static achievement. The cycle in is thus a continuous process of planning, researching, analysing, deciding, implementing, and learning. This includes identifying the system's purpose or goals within a more balanced set of corporate performance measures (including financial goals, employee satisfaction goals, process improvement goals, knowledge and learning goals, and so forth). The key customer and market segmentation issues upon which the system is based, including the distinction between internal and external customers.

Conducting interviews and focus groups and observing customers provides you with the lens through which customers view products and services. This lens is the basis for your quality-satisfactionloyalty modeling. It discusses ways to develop and administer surveys that assess the attributes and benefits your products and services provide and the overall levels of customer satisfaction and loyalty that result. The goal is to customise the measurement of quality, value, satisfaction, and loyalty for a particular customer segment, company, and context.

Again, the purpose is to identify both the relative importance and performance of key satisfaction and loyalty drivers. It provides guidelines for identifying the area or areas where importance is high and performance is low, which offer the most potential return on quality improvement efforts. We develop a statistical approach to help you estimate your system or model linking quality to loyalty and financial performance. We also provide concrete examples. As emphasized earlier, management must take part in categorizing the output of a customer analysis into a strategic satisfaction matrix. Just where boundaries are set between highversus low-impact drivers and strong versus weak performance depends on a variety of factors, including what you can achieve in the time available, your cost structure, and your overall strategy. Interpreting model outputs also requires appropriate bench for evaluating both performance and importance.

Who should collect your customer data, analyse it, and use it to set priorities and allocate resources? It often seems logical to delegate the satisfaction and loyalty measurement operation to outside research firms and consultants. This is especially true early in the process of becoming a customer-oriented organization, because outside specialists offer specific skills related to collecting and analysing customer data that you do not have. Unfortunately, if you delegate the system, your company does not take ownership of it, and you and your people may fail to learn or acquire the skills necessary to measure and manage customer data on your own.

The consultant's bills, heavy as they are likely to be, are only a small part of the cost of handing off a customer information system. Bear in mind that when customer information is the key to strategy, it should reside within the company. Your best teachers about what is right and wrong with your products and services are your own customers. Direct contact with customers and customer data is a critical part of learning what it takes to satisfy customer needs.

No matter how good the consultants are, they will always function as filters. An important part of establishing a customer orientation as a core competency is creating, over time, internal specialists to measure, model, and manage quality, satisfaction, and loyalty. Early in the process, external experts are apt to be a necessity. They can provide the interviewing, surveying, data warehousing, statistical analysis, and interpretation skills that you may lack or not yet want (or be able) to invest in. Over time, however, continued reliance on external specialists becomes costly and also fails to develop customer measurement and management as a core competency. Internalization of the process allows you to adapt to changing market needs and competitive environments in a cost-effective fashion. More important, your organization accepts ownership of the process and the data—and the decisions that emerge. This is not to say that all parts of the process should be brought in-house in all cases.

You may not want to try to run a survey that involves computer-aided telephone interviews or a Web-based system with highly specialized personnel (such as trained interviewers) and potential economies of scale. Even in the most customer-savvy organization, it may be best to outsource certain parts of the process. At the same time, a truly customer-oriented firm should own rather than rent the ability to observe and to talk to customers, formalize survey instruments, analyse and interpret customer data, and use the output to make resource allocation decisions.

Over the last three decades business organizations have evolved from a focus on quality to a focus on customer satisfaction, and onward to a focus on loyalty as a means of creating value. A customer measurement and management system views each of these areas as an indispensable link in a chain of causes and effects that runs from internal quality through to profitability. The goal of this book is to help you and your organization create an integrated customer measurement and management system for making effective resource allocation decisions and increasing profitability. In the process of building a system, organizations develop internal specialists capable of gathering, analysing, and interpreting customer data.

Truly customer-oriented companies should, over time, add these skills to their core competencies. A systems approach to customer measurement and management also requires that you tailor the system to your unique purpose, customers, and contexts. As an illustration, Volvo's model incorporates the positive effects of improving internal quality on both productivity and customer perceptions of quality, satisfaction, and loyalty. In contrast, a major retailer such as Sears incorporates the central role that satisfied employees play in delivering quality and value to customers. These measurement systems and models are not substitutes for decision making. Rather, they provide the information you need to make resource allocation decisions and manage the process.

The system provides information on how the company and its competitors are performing in different areas and how important the areas are to customers. When combined with cost and strategy considerations, the system allows both enablers and doers to create organizational value through a continuous focus on customers. To maximize the value generated by the system, make sure your company's own staff perform the bulk of the work of collecting and interpreting customer data, so that you get the full benefit of the insights generated by the effort.

Before you dive in and start conducting customer interviews or surveys, you must know how your measurement system will be used. Since a customer orientation builds on internal quality, we'll start with a brief overview of quality management and its role in driving company strategy and customer measures. We'll then discuss two related approaches to translating strategy into action: policy deployment and balanced performance measures.

Then we'll focus on the process of getting started on developing a customer measurement and management system—or improving an existing one—which involves taking a look at the breadth and depth of the proposed system and the role of market segmentation in it. In our customer satisfaction framework, internal quality is the first in the chain of events that drives financial performance.

It's important not to underestimate the role of *total quality management* (or TQM, also known as *company-wide quality management,* CWQM, and as *total quality control,* TQC)—nor to exaggerate it. For longterm survival, businesses have been forced to improve their abilities to change and innovate. But internal quality management is not in itself sufficient to assure success. Internal quality improvements must be linked to improvements in external quality, satisfaction, loyalty, and financial performance. And the links must be established in an environment of constantly evolving customer preferences, markets, competitors, and technologies. The broad principles and methods of quality management apply directly to the development of a customer measurement system.

The concept of quality should unify all of a company's activities. After all, only your customers can ultimately define quality for you! In the end, it doesn't matter how well the production system works, how well marketing functions are performed, or how good the company's strategy is. If no one buys, there will be no revenues.

Quality experts emphasize three basic strategies for successful quality management: use reference models or benchmarks, set priorities for quality improvement, and focus your resources. Do not try to do things completely on your own. Instead, make use of reference models or benchmarks when they're available. Benchmarking is particularly important in developing a customer measurement and management system. Process benchmarking—finding out how things are done— works as well in developing a customer measurement and management system as in any other area of business.

When you can manage it, arrange visits to firms with strong reputations to gauge their practices and learn what they are doing, see how they are doing it, and understand what is possible. Devote some time to reverse engineering their products as well. And don't limit the benchmarking to competitors—in a general area such as customer measurement, you'll find individuals or organizations in many fields who excel in areas that you are interested in improving.

Benchmarking on their processes can help you to learn how to conduct better customer interviews, develop and administer more effective surveys, and analyse customer data in more productive ways—and they're likely to be much more willing to share information with you if you're not trying to sell the same offering to the same customers. For *output* or *performance benchmarking,* you will measure your product or service against direct or indirect competitors on various dimensions such as internal or technical quality, external or perceived quality and value, and overall customer satisfaction, loyalty, and retention. The external benchmarks will help you interpret your findings regarding your own customers and decide just where to devote your resources to get the most mileage from your improvement efforts.

SET PRIORITIES FOR QUALITY IMPROVEMENT

The second basic strategy of quality management is the universal law of priorities. In a quality context, it is often said that 20 per cent of parts, processes, or people account for 80 per cent of quality problems (often called the *Pareto principle*). Each customer and each market will react differently to the various drivers of satisfaction and loyalty, so one of your primary goals in customer measurement is to identify the drivers that are most important to improve.

You need to find out where the impact on customers is high and your current performance is poor. Your goal should be to set priorities and *optimize* rather than *maximize* your quality and satisfaction improvement efforts.

FOCUS YOUR RESOURCES

Once you have chosen the area or areas to change, the third basic strategy of quality management is to concentrate your resources to maximal effect. The goal is to create a company-wide focus on the things that matter most for performance and survival. This is one of the most important yet also most often neglected aspects of quality management. Increasingly, managers face a common problem in that their customer measurement systems point out specific needs for improvement, but their organizations don't respond.

The manager knows what area or areas to attack, but has difficulty getting anyone to do anything about it. This is where the lens of the customer shows its usefulness. Once the concept spreads through an organization the independent actions of each individual and department are much more likely to fit into the overall improvement effort.

TWO WAYS TO TRANSLATE STRATEGY INTO ACTION

Since no amount of information will do you any good if no one will act on it, creating an environment where resources get focused on quality management is in many ways the key element of the process. One basic approach to this problem, called *policy deployment*, has proven very effective where a company has a clear priority regarding what policy to deploy. A variation known as *balanced performance measures* allows a company to determine and deploy a balanced mix of quality improvements.

Policy deployment, or hoshin planning *(hoshin kanri)* as it is sometimes called, is a powerful quality management process that converts a company's strategy into operational change and effectively moves different units within the company in the same direction.

Customer policy deployment, in particular, aims to move the entire organization to focus more on customers in order to increase their satisfaction and loyalty.

Policy deployment includes four major steps:

1. *Mission and Vision:* Clearly state the organization's philosophy, mission, and vision (also called the *president's diagnosis*).

2. *Goals:* Understand exactly where the organization is today and where it wants to be in the short, medium, and long term with regard to specific criteria or goals.
3. *Communication Strategy:* Communicate the mission, vision, and goals throughout the organization.
4. *Priority Setting and Implementation:* Set priorities, align the incentives, and implement quality improvement projects accordingly (using project management).

Making customers a priority became a strategy for Volvo's survival in the intensely competitive global automotive industry.

Back in 1991, the question was how to create a customer orientation in a traditionally engineering-driven company. Volvo quickly realised that policy deployment was a natural means of building on its quality management foundations to move the company from an engineering focus to a customer focus. Here is a summary of how Volvo implemented the four major phases of policy deployment:

- *Volvo's Mission and Vision:* "To be the world's most desired and successful premium car brand."
- *Volvo's Goals:* "To be number 5 in customer satisfaction (according to the J. D. Power IQS study) in 1995 and number 3 in 1997."
- *Volvo's Communication Strategy:* Stop keeping secrets about customer complaints; give employees an open information system and a broad view of the customer value-added process that encompasses the vehicle sales and service experience throughout the life of the vehicle.
- *Volvo's Priority Setting and Implementation:* Use quality teams to focus on the two hundred highest-priority areas (out of two thousand possibilities identified in an initial review), and reward team members based on the degree to which Volvo met its corporate goals as well as on the degree to which the team met its own goals.

Once mission statements work their way through various levels of management, they often end up reading like the Boy Scouts' oath. Companies want to be all things to all people. In contrast, Volvo's vision was specifically to be the most desired successful specialty car brand.

While abstract and forward-looking, the vision nonetheless pointed to a particular segment of the automotive market in which Volvo wanted to excel. Quantitatively, Volvo's goal was defined in terms of placement in a specific independent survey—to be number 5 in its industry by 1995 and number 3 by 1997.

Although any measurement system has its strengths and weaknesses, by defining customer satisfaction using the J. D. Power IQS study, Volvo effectively defined where it was (twenty-sixth out of thirty-four makes) and where it wanted to be at different points in time. Volvo effectively aligned its mission and vision to concrete measures and goals. Volvo's next step was communication. Stellan Flodin, the senior vice president in charge of quality, and Jan-Olof Nilsson, senior vice president of Business Area 900, led the effort to create a communication process and culture of openness across the company. Volvo abandoned its hush-hush approach to quality and customer data in favour of a more open system in which information was made available to anyone who could influence customer satisfaction.

This was critically important at Volvo because its employees perceived their company as doing quite well. Internally, they had been improving products and processes from year to year all along. But externally, relative quality was falling and the company was losing ground to competitors. This decline was a well-kept secret until Volvo decided to change policy and speak freely about its problems.

Many of the problems reported in the IQS studies involved customers' experiences with sales and service, so it was essential that Volvo encompass the entire value-added chain (from production to delivery and dealer service) in its policy deployment process. Over a period of about two years, the company created an environment in which individuals from very different value-adding areas worked together to solve a variety of customer problems. Reported quality problems came to be viewed as opportunities to learn and improve rather than as negative reflections on any particular area, team, or individual.

As noted, Volvo's customer data revealed over two thousand areas in which quality improvements might be made. The final stage of the process, project management, set priorities and put quality teams to work improving approximately two hundred of the most glaring problem areas. On the Volvo 850, for example, customer data revealed that the manual transmission alone generated a surprising number of complaints (about twenty per hundred vehicles). For example, many customers said the manual gear box was too stiff, and people of below average height added that the stick shift was too far away and difficult to reach in some gears. A project team was therefore deployed to improve the quality of the transmission. Additional customer surveys allowed the team to translate customer perceptions into design and part changes that, when introduced, decreased the incidence of complaints by over 50 per cent. A key to making all this happen, however, was that Volvo aligned the project teams' and individuals' goals with overall policy goals.

Team members were compensated based on whether their teams met project goals (such as reducing transmission problems per hundred cars from twenty to ten to five over time) and whether Volvo met its overall corporate goals such as reducing overall problems per hundred cars to reach the number 5 position by 1995 and the number 3 position by 1997. The policy deployment process that Sears is using to create a customer focus is similar to the process at Volvo. The main difference is that, whereas Volvo built on its knowledge of quality management to implement policy deployment from the top down, Sears is using the development of its employee-customerprofit chain to drive the deployment process from the bottom up.

The process has been more implicit than explicit. Retail-service companies have not gone through the same quality management revolution and training as manufacturing companies such as Volvo. But once Sears's employee-customerprofit chain was developed, it became an important tool to drive change in the company's mission, vision, goals, and communication. Everyone from senior managers to store employees had to be taught the logic of the model and its implications, including how the company's competitive environment had changed.

The company held town hall meetings and used learning maps to help employees grasp the logic behind the model so that they, in turn, could apply it at the store level. In the end, the deployment process has helped build a leadership model that incorporates the various aspects of the employee-customer-profit chain. The leadership model is to make Sears a compelling place to work, shop, and invest. Yet the deployment process has progressed more slowly at Sears than at Volvo. The process at Sears has been more data driven, working from the bottom up. Only after the employee-customer-profit chain was developed did Sears executives confront many of the challenges in deploying policy, from a lack of buy-in among top executives to communication problems among their retail employees. And arguably, Volvo has been more successful at implementing its customer orientation and turning the corner on profitability. After some initial success, financial performance at Sears remains weak. These results aren't surprising, and they provide a useful warning to those in service industries.

Product companies tend to have a history of quality management when they begin to implement customer policy deployment, and this gives them a strong head start. Few service companies have gone through the same quality revolution, although there are important exceptions. Disney, Fidelity Investments, and USAA, for example, have long-standing commitments to quality management and its principles.

Disney has used policy deployment in the development of its theme parks for many years. But most service firms simply did not get the wake-up call that hit manufacturing firms in the 1970s and 1980s, when they were confronted with competitors producing higher-quality products in less time and at lower cost. If you manage or work in a service industry such as telecommunication, insurance, or banking, very likely your company is now experiencing or will soon experience the same type of global competition and cost pressures as your counterparts in the manufacturing world. Technology such as the Internet now provides a basis for delivering cost-effective global service.

The warning from product companies is clear. If you hope to continue to prosper, establish a culture that emphasizes quality as your foundation for using customer information to drive organizational change. Balanced performance measures or BPMs share many of the principles of policy deployment. But whereas policy deployment has always been an explicit means of translating strategy into action, BPMs were initially developed as a way of balancing the needs of multiple stakeholders in an organization. Rather than focusing mainly on customers, BPMs recognize that a customer focus must be balanced against the needs of other stakeholders, such as owners, employees, and suppliers. A popular approach to developing BPMs is the balanced scorecard. Companies use the balanced scorecard to assess their performance and strategy in a highly integrated fashion.

The scorecard's four main components are the company's financial perspective, the customer perspective, the internal business process perspective, and the learning and innovation perspective. The *customer perspective* includes those customer measures that are most important for the company to improve, such as targets for customer satisfaction or account penetration. The *financial perspective* includes targets the company sets with respect to both financial (market value) and accounting (revenue and profit) measures.

The *internal perspective* includes internal quality and business process measures, such as the number of hours the company spends talking with customers about current or future projects, or the level of employee satisfaction. The *innovation and learning perspective* include goals and measures for investments in training and new product or service development. For each perspective, goals and measures are developed and drilled down to operational levels for teams and individuals ("personal scorecards"). As balanced performance measurement systems evolved through the 1990s, their relationship to policy deployment has become clear.

For example, in more recent versions of the balanced scorecard, a company's vision and strategy drive a management process that includes strategy feedback and learning, clarifying and translating the vision and strategy, communicating and linking rewards to performance measures, and planning and setting targets. These stages obviously parallel the four main steps in policy deployment described earlier. Yet important differences remain. Whereas a full policy deployment moves an organization in a completely new direction, such as focusing more explicitly on customers, BPMs balance various stakeholders' needs. In this sense, BPMs are a weak form of policy deployment. They more or less presume that the organization is headed in the right direction and align its activities accordingly. A balanced scorecard approach keeps an organization on course through an integrated management and budgeting process. BPMs also lack any guiding framework or model of the drivers of financial performance. The approach focuses generally on synergies among the various perspectives or stakeholder needs.

It is important that you build your measurement system on an evolving understanding of the drivers of financial performance that is tailored to your company and competitive environment, as Volvo and Sears did. Although this book's focus is primarily on the customer perspective, balanced performance measures do serve as a reminder that the measurement and management process described here can be applied to other stakeholders as well. In the Sears model, for example, employee attitudes and beliefs are critically important in driving employee behaviour.

The processes and tools described in this book for developing the lens of the customer can certainly be applied to develop the lens of the employee, supplier, or equity stakeholder as a basis for developing and administering surveys, analysing data, and setting priorities for improvement. When you embark on a strategy of customer-driven quality improvement, questions will arise about how to set up a system to collect the data you need to work with. Many of these questions can be broadly categorized as relating either to *system breadth*— the range of internal and external customers and market segments that you want to measure—or to *system depth*—the level of detail and nature of the information that you gather.

Companies typically serve a range of very different customers both inside and outside the organization. Internal customers may be in the same physical location, as when marketing and finance are customers of information services, or in different locations, as when manufacturing plants are customers of the home office. External customers range from wholesalers and retailers to end users. The customer chain shows three levels of customers: plant customers, retailing customers, and end users. We have kept this example simple to make the relationships easy to see on paper; in practice any given organization or network is likely to have a much larger number of customer levels, as any individual might be considered someone else's customer. And it isn't enough to track exchanges of funds for goods or services, as even external customers don't necessarily pay to assume that role—regulatory agencies are customers for reports, for example, and people downstream (literally or metaphorically) from traditional end users are the ones likely to be customers for ecological and recycling efforts.

To determine just which customers should be your primary measurement and management focus. What links in the customer chain drive your financial performance? Where are the links from quality to satisfaction to loyalty and profitability the strongest? Those are the places where you're likely to get the most mileage out of any investment in improved quality. Even without a detailed measurement system, you probably have some knowledge or understanding of where to start looking.

Think about the nature of the competition and customer choice at each level. The logic of a customer orientation (the idea that quality, satisfaction, and loyalty drive profitability) is based on two critical assumptions. First, the customer is relatively free to choose products and services. This assumption holds for most industries in the developed world today—customers face a dizzying variety of brands of cars, soap, phone service, and most necessities and luxuries, and if one alternative doesn't satisfy there's always another to try. This assumption doesn't always hold true, however—when customers face significant switching costs in moving from one provider to another, or there is only one supplier available, they are essentially hostages.

That is, when it's expensive or difficult to find another supplier, only a very dissatisfied customer will switch to a competitor. Airline customers are often held hostage to the hub-and-spoke system of air travel, where flying on other than the hub airline imposes significant costs in terms of time and convenience. However, no company can count on keeping its customers hostage indefinitely. In the gas and electric supply business, for example, many customers still have few options to choose from—but recent deregulation means that the situation is changing rapidly, and customer satisfaction and loyalty are likely to become drivers of profitability soon. The second important assumption in the logic of a customer orientation is that the important customers are the ones who will generate new business if they're satisfied with their experience—buy replacements for past purchases, buy new offerings, or inspire potential customers to try the company's wares.

Investments to satisfy more transient or one-time customers may not generate future revenues or cost savings. The benefits of increasing satisfaction are thus greatest at the level in the customer chain where your customers have both a choice and a potential to reward you with future revenues at lower costs. Related to the notion of customer choice is the relative *push* versus *pull* of your products and services through the customer chain.

Consider a service provider such as Fidelity, which places investment instruments through a variety of independent retailers. In one region, the end users—the individual investors— may have strong brand attitudes and perceptions that have been created over a long period of time through experience, advertising, and word of mouth. In this case, the most important customer in the chain is probably the end user who goes to a retailer (whether an agency or a Web site) in search of a particular offering.

The choice in this case resides primarily with end users who pull the product through the chain. Although all customers are important at some level, relatively speaking, the satisfaction of the retailer is not as critical in this case as the satisfaction of the end user. To satisfy and retain their own customers, the retailers need to make the Fidelity offerings available to them. Elsewhere, investors may be much more likely to follow the advice of the retailer about which brand to purchase. The retailer may be more established and trusted in the end user's mind than any individual brand. If investors are more likely to defer their choice to a trusted retailer, Fidelity is in a position of pushing the product or service through the chain.

In this case, the most important thing to measure and manage may be the satisfaction of the retailer and its willingness to push the brand on to the end user. The same logic applies regardless of the product or service—if the offering is seen as interchangeable at the end-user level, you have to give the retailer a reason to favour your brand over others.

At each level in the customer chain, the market segmentation scheme is the key element in your strategic market plan to build a customer measurement system. Market segmentation is the process of identifying and targeting unique populations or *segments* of customers and developing tailored marketing strategies to meet the individual segment needs.

To identify and target segments, take the following steps:

1. Group customers into segments based on customer needs, benefits sought, or personal values served.
2. Identify or describe the segments according to their behaviours, lifestyles, or demographics.
3. Evaluate the attractiveness of each segment in terms of, for example, profit potential, risk, capacity utilization, and core competencies required to serve the segment.
4. Determine strategically which segments to target and pursue and, as a result, which segments to measure, analyse, and manage separately.

These steps bring you to a framework for just which customers to measure, analyse, and monitor. Because the drivers of satisfaction and loyalty may be very different from segment to segment, be wary of averaging across segments. Averages can be deceiving. If customer data are aggregated too highly, they provide a profile of an average customer who simply does not exist. If the segments are different enough, they will require separate survey development and analysis. Even when the same survey is applicable to more than one group of customers, be sure to analyse importance and performance levels separately for each group.

SEGMENTATION IN A HOTEL CHAIN

Consider, for example, the needs of business customers and vacation customers at "Wolverine Inns" a fictitious name for a major mid-priced hotel chain we worked with recently. The chain recently segmented its franchisees according to which segment of customers they are most likely to serve, based on the idea that downtown properties cater more to the business customer segment and leisure-area properties cater more to the vacation customer segment. The matrices are used to set priorities for quality improvement.

The company's satisfaction and loyalty survey covers eight general quality areas or customer benefits (reservation process, staff, facilities, grounds, bathroom, room, breakfast, and perceived value) and each area is rated on a variety of attributes. For the moment, just look at the impact and performance aspects of the eight types of benefit. Later as suggested, take up the issue of setting priorities among the attributes that provide each benefit, such as the friendliness, helpfulness, efficiency, and grooming and appearance of the hotel staff. The vertical axes show how each type of property performs on each of the eight benefits using a weighted average of customers' attribute ratings (on a scale where 1 is poor and 5 is excellent).

Both downtown and leisure-area properties, for example, perform very well on the quality of the reservations process. The horizontal axes show the relative importance of each benefit as revealed by its statistical impact on overall satisfaction. For example, the impact score of.75 for quality of the room for the downtown properties shows that as room quality increases by 10 per cent, satisfaction increases by 7.5 per cent (10 per cent ×.75). (This example is based on standardized scale values.) The results reveal vast differences in the drivers of satisfaction across the two property types. Business customers who frequent downtown Wolverine Inn locations look for the hotel to simply provide a clean and comfortable room. They use the hotel for a place to get a good night's sleep and have little interest in its other services. In contrast, a much wider variety of factors drive satisfaction for the vacation customers who frequent the chain's leisure-area properties. The quality of the room is secondary to the quality of service and advice that the staff provides.

The quality of the grounds, bathroom, and breakfast are also more important for the vacation customer. As hotel manager at any given property, you would certainly want to know impact and performance levels for your target customers. Assuming the described results for individual hotels, the downtown manager would see improving the quality of the rooms as the greatest priority, given its high impact and currently moderate performance.

In contrast, the manager of the leisure-area property would see improving the quality of the staff as relatively more important. Neither manager would have much incentive to do anything about perceived value—the customers' view of the price they are paying for the experience—even though it is far and away the lowest performance area in both cases, because the survey results show that neither group of customers cares much about it. Lowering prices would be costly for the hotel and would make it more difficult to sustain improvements in areas that matter to the customers, so it's best to avoid this step unless the hotel has an incentive to change its customer base to one that regards the current price level as a barrier rather than a minor irritant.

After deciding which customer levels to include in the measurement system and what customers or market segments to include, the next step is to ask what level of generality or detail about the lens of the customer the system should contain. Customer satisfaction is a complex matter, made up of the way the customer perceives the concrete attributes of a product, the benefits the customer derives from those attributes, and the personal values that the product supports. All these elements reside with the customer and are beyond the company's direct control, so we refer to them as *external quality factors*. Measurement systems vary in the amount of detail they provide about external factors such as these. For example, macro-level measurement systems such as the American Customer Satisfaction Index (ACSI) only include very general differences in external perceptions of overall quality and value as drivers of satisfaction and loyalty.

Quality is itself measured using customer ratings of the levels of customisation and reliability provided, while value is measured using customer perceptions of the price or prices paid for the quality received. The purpose of measurement systems such as the ACSI is, however, to provide quality, value, satisfaction, and loyalty benchmarks across a very wide range of firms, industry groupings (including products, services, retailers, and government and public agencies), and even countries. Such broad-based comparisons require a measurement system that emphasizes generality and comparability as opposed to depth and detail.

If your goal is to improve or radically reinvent goods and services, you'll need a more detailed and comprehensive information system. It should include information on the range of concrete attributes and abstract benefits that might drive satisfaction and require improvement. The convenience store example and discuss perceived convenience, merchandise quality, and safety as just three of the benefits that directly affect customer satisfaction.

As suggested, discuss how to develop these more detailed or in-depth measurement systems for the purpose of measuring and managing customer data for a particular product or service and market segment. Remember that the information in the measurement system is designed to leverage either incremental (evolutionary) or innovative (revolutionary) activities, or both.

For example, when Volvo discovered that its customers found its manual transmissions difficult to shift (an attribute-level problem), it translated the problem into one of changing certain parts that immediately reduced complaints. In contrast, when product or service designers are pursuing major innovations, they shift upward from the attribute level to more abstract customer benefits and personal values as input to the design process. Developing a fuel cell or electric vehicle, for example, requires matching the benefits and consequences that the new technology provides (such as zero emissions and moderate performance) with the benefits and values that are important to target customers (such as a willingness to trade off vehicle performance for environmental impact). Product or service design is then a process of developing a whole new configuration of product and service attributes to better serve customer needs.

We are often asked when to engage in revolutionary innovation rather than more evolutionary continuous improvement. The key, of course, is to avoid focusing on one to the exclusion of the other, but rather to balance both activities. Masaaki Imai, who was instrumental in developing the *kaizen* or continuous improvement process, emphasizes the importance of maintaining a balance among three activities: maintaining the quality of existing products, services, or processes; achieving kaizen or continuous improvement; and achieving innovation.

The temptation, Imai argues, is to focus only on innovation as a means of making rapid changes and leapfrogging the competition. This ignores the long-term benefits that continuous improvement brings to a company. When all three activities are balanced, the result is a formidable competitive advantage. Disney is a great example of an organization that consistently manages to balance all three activities. The regular development of new characters for use in movies, television shows, and theme parks is a constant source of innovation.

At the same time, Disney works to maintain or keep improving every stage of its customers' experience. The combination has created a legendary service organization that is built on a quality foundation *and* reinvents itself on a regular basis. Measuring quality, customer satisfaction, and loyalty should be an ongoing, repetitive process. It is difficult, however, to make general recommendations about just how frequently to measure. The frequency varies from company to company and depends on the audience, the stability or volatility of the product or service, and the nature of the market. For instance, if you have relatively few customers it may not be desirable to survey them too often. Needless to say, your customers should never feel that the process is burdensome.

And once you do a survey and set some priorities, be sure to implement the changes before you launch another survey. Otherwise, your customers will ask the obvious question: "Why should I bother filling out this survey when you didn't pay any attention to the last one?" A product's life cycle also affects the frequency of measurement. You need frequent contact with customers early on, when the market is evolving and changes to the product or service can have a great impact on a company's success. Consider the battle between Ericsson and Nokia in the cellular phone market. The early adopters of cellular phones were business people.

They simply wanted a reliable phone, which gave Ericsson the edge. But Ericsson did not keep up with the evolution of customer needs in the market and emergence of new market segments that demanded more features and design improvements. This allowed Nokia to achieve a greater advantage as the market evolved. Later in a product's life cycle, customers are much harder to attract, more valuable to keep, and more costly to lose, so again you want close and frequent customer contacts. And, of course, it is always important to listen carefully to customers when the threat of competition has increased.

The general point is that contact with customers should become more frequent during certain critical stages of the product life cycle and market dynamics. Keeping these contingencies in mind, we recommend a customer satisfaction survey at least yearly.

More frequent surveys are likely to have little effect on your improvement efforts when the product and the market are stable. If competition is really active and is moving quickly in a market, it may be necessary to carry out more frequent studies—perhaps even on a quarterly basis. But make sure you have enough resources to process and implement the findings, or the efforts are wasted. It is often a good compromise to measure every six months in times of change. Finally, remember that there's a difference between customer measures and surveys as the basis of a measurement and management system and more informal surveys or methods designed to take a quick pulse or to identify problems as they occur.

The latter methods typically focus on the most recent episode or transaction with a customer (such as the latest stay at the hotel or visit to the bookstore), and are often loosely structured (an informal interview by the manager or an open-ended "opinion" card). Their value towards allocating resources and deciding strategy is limited. At the same time, they may be a valuable source of information for service managers or front-line service personnel to catch and resolve certain classes of problems as they occur.

Providing external quality and customer satisfaction depends directly on the quality of your company's internal processes, operating policies, strategies, and plans. Whether your company provides products or services (or both), quality management provides a solid foundation for developing and deploying strategy and measuring quality through the lens of the customer. You will see the three basic strategies of quality management. As suggested, describe the use of reference models or benchmarks to interpret and analyse customer data. As suggested, show you how to optimize rather than maximize customer satisfaction and loyalty by setting priorities for quality improvement.

Finally, as suggested, describe ways to maximize use of available resources to implement the change. Policy deployment and its variants, including balanced performance measures, are important tools for creating a more universal and consistent focus. These approaches provide companies with a means of translating their customer strategies into action. Just where to begin building the system requires decisions regarding which customers to include, or system breadth, and how much detail to provide, or system depth. You want to include the kinds of customers that drive business performance. To do this, you will need to ask "which of our internal or external customers are both a source of future profits and have a choice about where they take their business?" To drive profitability, produce and deliver high-quality products and services to satisfy and retain these customers.

When including customers in the measurement system, remember that customers do not all value the same things and behave in the same way. Build your customer measurement systems on an understanding of how your customer base at any given level (such as retail or end-user) is segmented. Segmentation is a process of identifying individuals or populations of customers with unique needs and wants. By paying attention to segment differences you will avoid the pitfall of setting priorities based on "average" customers who don't exist. In your planning process, also consider just how much detail you will need to measure and how you will use your measurement system.

At a general level, macro-level customer measurement systems provide for broad-based comparisons and benchmarking but give only general guidance about what companies should improve (such as product or service quality or value). In this book, the focus is on measurement systems that are more specific to the company or segment; they provide detailed information regarding concrete product or service attributes as well as information about more abstract consequences and benefits.

By continually improving the concrete attributes of existing offerings and finding completely new ways to provide customer benefits, you can leverage your customer data to create a truly exemplary level of performance and competitive advantage. To link internal quality to profitability, you have to find out how customers see the products and services they purchase and consume. Your first step will be to develop a model of how customers view your firm's products, services, and activities—the "lens of the customer" that will guide the rest of your efforts. As discussed earlier, people inside an organization too often develop customer surveys from their own perspective, or how they believe customers view their products and services. The result is a survey or measurement instrument that embodies the lens of the organization rather than the lens of the customer. You'll often see airline surveys organized in this fashion, for example, full of questions broken out by organizational activity (check-in, preflight service, food and beverage, flight crews, and cabin environment).

A survey that aligns question areas with organizational responsibility in this fashion does have the advantage of producing recommendations that are fairly straightforward to implement. If the survey results and prioritysetting process indicate that flight crews are most in need of improvement, then the responsibility for making improvements within the organization is clear. Unfortunately, this type of survey may warp or entirely miss issues that cross organizational boundaries, as when flight crews get blamed for being short-tempered about carry-on baggage that should never have been allowed into the cabin in the first place.

Customers tend to form opinions regarding such benefits as service, convenience, and safety that cut across the functional areas of an organization. It is essential, therefore, that the measurement system be based squarely on the lens of the customer. In addition, having a survey instrument that better captures the customers' perception of the company makes the data easier to analyse. We are able to explain more variation in key customer evaluations and behaviours, such as satisfaction and loyalty, when the questionnaire is based on the customers' view.

For an airline, such a questionnaire might address a whole range of activities from seat reservations through boarding to baggage claim under the heading of convenience, and everything from the gate lobby staff to the seat cushions under the heading of comfort. The concrete attributes of a product or service and the abstract benefits it generates occupy different levels in the customers' lens.

This distinction is very useful but may take some getting used to. The rectangular objects at the left-hand side represent the concrete aspects or dimensions on which customers can readily report performance via survey measures (such as whether a sales staff keeps its appointments and returns telephone calls and e-mail messages). The circular objects to the right of the attributes represent the relatively abstract or *latent* variables that capture the benefits or consequences that the attributes provide or, at an even more abstract level, the personal values that they serve. For simplicity, as suggested, refer to all the abstract drivers of satisfaction and loyalty as *benefits.*

As in a traditional marketing perspective, the customer satisfaction model embodies the view that products and services compete primarily on the benefits they provide or the needs they fulfill. The concrete attributes of the product or service are only the means to these more abstract ends. Letters, e-mail messages, and faxes all, for example, provide the benefit of communication. You can thus view benefits as the primary drivers of satisfaction in the lens. Notice, however, that benefits may be measured using different numbers of concrete attributes.

Satisfaction in the model is defined as a customer's overall evaluation of the purchase and consumption experience with a product, service, or provider. This definition is quite different from transaction-specific definitions of satisfaction that capture a customer's immediate reaction to a particular episode or experience. Why discard the immediate response in favour of a more cumulative or overall definition of satisfaction? Although it seems more remote, the latter turns out to be more directly tied to customers' repurchase intentions and behaviour.

Customers' repurchase decisions are affected by their entire purchase and consumption history with a company or brand, not just the last trip to the restaurant or last shipment from a supplier. Although we list loyalty, broadly defined, as the desired outcome of satisfaction, there are other constructs we could have shown there as well. Customer satisfaction may also lead to an enhanced reputation and greater brand equity for the company, which will in turn attract additional customers who are disposed to develop loyalty of their own. The also see overall satisfaction and loyalty in circles, treating them as abstract constructs that can be measured in concrete terms. Overall satisfaction is reflected in different concrete satisfaction measures, which might include a satisfaction scale, how the product or service performs overall versus customer expectations, performance versus an ideal product or service in the category, and performance versus "best in class" competitors.

Similarly, loyalty may be measured using a variety of behavioural intentions (ratings of the likelihood that customers will return, will purchase other products and services from the company, or will speak positively of their experience to others) or actual behaviours (such as whether customers do return, how often they return and how much they purchase when they do, and whether they bring or refer additional customers). Note the dotted arrow that runs from an attribute-benefit cluster directly to customer loyalty.

This captures the possibility that customers' intentions or decisions to repurchase are affected directly by certain benefits. In a recent study of satisfaction with hair care providers, for example, we found that the quality of the haircut, the relationship with the stylist, and the atmosphere of the salon all affect loyalty via overall satisfaction. However, the timeliness and ease of scheduling an appointment have direct effects on loyalty in addition to their effects on satisfaction. Price can also affect loyalty directly— customers are likely to weigh price or value much more when evaluating loyalty than when evaluating satisfaction.

"I love his work, but I can't afford to go back every month" You can't develop the lens of the customer by sitting around and reflecting on how customers view the world. Instead, you need in-depth, qualitative research to show you the issues from the customers' own perspective. Keep in mind that the goal of conducting qualitative research (such as interviews and focus groups) is not to immediately set priorities for quality improvement— it is to identify a comprehensive range of issues (benefits and attributes) that potentially drive satisfaction, loyalty, and profitability. The customer sample that you use at this stage of the research should represent a good cross-section or range of customers from the population or target market of interest, but it need not be truly random as you're not looking for statistical validity at this point. The lens or model that results from this qualitative research provides the foundation for more systematic survey research, which in turn becomes the primary basis for setting priorities when you get to that stage of the process.

Marketing books offer a wide choice of qualitative methods that you can use to identify product and service attributes and the customer benefits they provide—one-on-one interviews, group interviews or focus groups, protocol methods (having customers "think out loud" while using or evaluating a product or service), and a variety of observation techniques. Here, we focus on one qualitative technique that is particularly well suited to the development of a customer model or lens: the *critical incident technique* (CIT). The CIT can be used to identify satisfaction drivers for a range of internal and external customers.

It typically involves an interview in which individuals or groups of customers are asked to provide a list of the things that they like and dislike about the product, service, or company in question. Bob Hayes, an expert on the CIT approach, "A critical incident is a specific example of the service or product that describes either *positive* or *negative* performance. A positive example is a characteristic of the service or product that the customer would like to see every time he or she receives that service or product. A negative example is a characteristic of the service or product that would make the customer question the quality of the company." The critical incidents themselves should be as specific as possible in describing a single feature of the customer's purchase and consumption experience.

Hayes argues that a good critical incident should cover a single behaviour or characteristic, and should either describe the service provider in behavioural terms or describe the service or product using specific adjectives. One retailer noted positively that "the range (variety) of products is good"—pointing to a particular characteristic of the tires (the available range) using a specific adjective (good). Another retailer noted negatively that "regional representatives arrive too seldom"—pointing to a specific behaviour of the local salesperson (waiting too long between visits). If the critical incidents are too general, the interviewer needs to ask additional questions to clarify what the customer really has in mind. For each specific incident, it is also useful to ask the customer for comments on the significance and consequences of the incident.

Such questions will elicit valuable information for the next stage of the process, categorizing the incidents into attributes and benefit groupings. When encouraged to elaborate, for example, the retailer who praised the product range pointed out that carrying a range of tire products allowed him to offer "a tire for almost every customer that walks into my store." The one who said the regional representative arrived too seldom said that "he should come every month ...just to see how things are going." Overall, the CIT process involves a number of steps that are helpful to describe using an activity-based flowchart.

Step 1 is to compile and assess whatever relevant secondary research or knowledge pertaining to the lens of the customer already exists within the company. (One should avoid, of course, any biases from the lens of the organization.) Perhaps similar studies have been conducted in slightly different research contexts that shed light on how customers view the product or service. Step 2 is to make initial visits to different customers early in the process. We have found this important for two reasons. First, the visits will provide firsthand observations of the

QUALITY-SATISFACTION

You'll usually need several sources of data to establish all the links from quality through to profits. Consider the experience at Sears and Volvo. Sears uses one survey to measure internal quality in the form of employee perceptions and attitudes and a second survey to measure external quality and satisfaction from the customers' perspective. Information from both sources is then combined with financial performance information for individual stores to trace the links in the employee-customer-profit chain. Volvo tracks internal quality with engineering-based measures of vehicle performance, and uses customer surveys to track external quality.

Now we focus on ways to develop and administer the survey that measures customer perceptions of quality, satisfaction, and loyalty. The lens of the customer will serve as a blueprint for your survey, identifying the attributes to include and the order they should appear. To make the survey results useful, however, you will also need to specify and include measures of satisfaction and loyalty so as to be able to combine the individual customer responses into a meaningful pattern of causes and effects.

Step 1: The Preliminaries

As in any other activity, if you don't know what you want to get out of customer measurement, it's going to be hard to tell if you've found it. So before you develop the survey itself, you need to figure out what information is required—which is a function of what you're planning to do with it—as well as how to segment your customer base, what survey method or methods to use, and how to sample the population.

What Information Is Required?

Start by restating in simple terms what you want your customer survey to tell you, and what you plan to do about it. This might be as generic as "We want to know what our customers want so we can give them more of it—and what they don't want, so we can avoid including it, " or it might be tailored to your particular business.

Then look back at the lens of the customer and list the attributes and benefits it identifies as having the potential to drive customer satisfaction and loyalty. Then list some direct questions about customer satisfaction and loyalty. From a statistical standpoint, these are the primary dependent variables that the model is to explain based on customer perceptions of attribute and benefit performance.

Make sure that the things you're asking about are at least partially under your control, so the results will be meaningful and useful. There is no point in finding out that your customers are uniformly unhappy that every day they get a day older, unless you're in the business of providing some way to preserve youth and prolong life. So consider just how the results will affect areas and individuals in your organization and what actions you may need to take based on the results.

How to Segment Survey Respondents?

The next step is to figure out which market segments to include in the survey—and just how to classify respondents into those segments. The choice of segments should be based on their importance in your strategic market plans. Beyond the choice of key segments (such as "daily" and "weekly" convenience store customers), another important question related to segmentation and sampling is whether to include current, past, or potential customers in the research. Companies are often content to focus only on current customers.

Unfortunately, if current customers are systematically different from those you've lost or those you would like to pursue in the future, your results from a currentcustomer survey could be misleading or incomplete. Market segment classifications may be based on information collected prior to the survey. Existing research may already have determined which customers are classified into which segments.

If survey respondents can be identified and classified into segments beforehand, then it is perhaps unnecessary to have segment-related information in the survey itself. Otherwise it will be critical to include information in the survey that allows you to sort or select customers by segment. The sorting or selection criteria may be direct or indirect.

The Indirect Approach

Using the indirect approach, you might include descriptive items in the survey such as demographic variables (age, sex, income level, education level, ethnic background), geographic variables (city, country, or geographic area), and experience-related variables (frequency of purchase or consumption of the product or service, confidence in evaluating the product or service, and so on).

These measures would then be analysed *after* the surveys are administered to develop distinct clusters or groups of customers that differ on the variables of interest (such as male versus female or frequent versus infrequent convenience store customers). This approach is indirect in the sense that the descriptive measures are only proxies for identifying more needs-based segments. A disadvantage of this approach is that it can lead to the inclusion of so many descriptive variables that the survey becomes long and cumbersome.

An advantage of the approach is that it provides a database that can be used to develop and identify new segments. This allows you to *cut,* or sort the data, in various anticipated and unanticipated ways. Descriptive variables are typically collected near the end of the survey. If a customer feels sensitive about answering particular questions (such as age, income, or education level), encountering such questions up front may bias the responses to the whole questionnaire or lead the customer to give up on it entirely.

The Direct Approach

Using the direct approach, you provide an existing segmentation within which customers place themselves in a needs-based segment. Often companies have some existing knowledge of the major segments or populations in their customer base. If simple descriptions of each of the different segments can be included in the survey, customers can indicate directly which segment they most identify with. For the convenience store survey, for example, independent research conducted prior to the survey helped us define five major segment profiles. We then used the profiles to develop descriptive statements for each segment:

- *Segment 1:* I tend to visit a convenience store several times a day for snacks as well as meals.
- *Segment 2:* I am a parent who occasionally goes to a convenience store mainly to buy fill-in items, emergency items, or things for the kids.

- *Segment 3:* I visit a convenience store daily to buy one or two items such as a soda, coffee, cigarettes, or candy.
- *Segment 4:* I go to a convenience store once or twice a week to buy a snack, soda, or coffee.
- *Segment 5:* I shop at a convenience store less than once a week, mainly to buy snacks and party items or items for a trip.

In the resulting convenience store survey, we asked survey respondents to indicate which of these statements best described their behaviour. The primary advantage of this approach is that it is based directly on an existing segmentation scheme. This greatly simplifies the analysis of the survey data. The responses are simply sorted according to their segment identification and analysed.

The disadvantage of using existing segment profiles is that it assumes that the profiles provide an accurate description of the underlying segments. If the nature of the segments changes between the segmentation study and the quality-satisfaction-loyalty survey, the results of the latter will be skewed in unpredictable ways. We recommend using a hybrid of the direct and indirect segmentation approaches when possible. Using existing segment profiles simplifies subsequent analysis and bases the analysis squarely on a segmentation scheme. But it is helpful to include some additional descriptive questions. The convenience store questionnaire, for example, augments the segment-level questions with a small number of demographic questions used in U.S. census questionnaires.

The hybrid approach allows for some exploratory analysis using the demographic variables to sort or cluster respondents into new segments. The demographics also provide descriptive details of the segment profiles, such as whether "daily" convenience store customers tend to be male, female, older, younger, and so on. Prior to developing the survey, you also need to decide just how to communicate with customers and administer the survey. The choice of survey methods has important implications for the nature of the questions and scales involved. There are various approaches, the more common being one-on-one interview surveys, telephone surveys, Web-based surveys, and written surveys. Each method has its strengths and weaknesses.

The choice of methods should depend on the context. One-on-one interviews are well suited to business-to-business applications, where the population of customers is relatively well defined (such as those customers who purchase a certain type of chemical or part). Conducting personal interviews is a good way to increase response rates; it shows customers that you are deeply interested in their opinions. This is important if your organization has a reasonably small number of key customers that you want to take special care of. A disadvantage of one-on-one interviews is that they can become difficult to manage when the sample of respondents is large.

Problems also arise when the individual conducting a survey interview has a vested interest in the results of the survey, as when the salespeople's bonus system is tied to the data that they collect from customers. Anyone who has purchased or leased a new automobile in the last few years might remember the pleas from salespeople to "give me 10s on the survey—my bonus depends on it!" It is crucial to maintain independence and objectivity in these cases through the use of a third party within the company (such as a manager or a salesperson who does not serve that customer) or an independent data collection agency to conduct the actual interviews.

Telephone surveys, particularly those using a computeraided telephone interview or CATI system, are particularly well suited to end-user products and services where representative samples of consumers are needed from a large population. The advantages of telephone interviews include their relatively low cost per completed interview and the control the interviewer has over who is responding to the survey (compared, for example, to written or mail surveys). A human interviewer can clarify any misunderstandings or problems that a respondent may have in answering a survey question. And when they encounter respondents who are simply not able or willing to respond to the survey, trained interviewers can quickly say thank you and terminate the interview. The disadvantage of the telephone interview approach is that interviewers may generate unpredictable effects of their own.

They must be carefully trained, as the way questions are stated is likely to have an impact on how customers respond. Through the use of randomization techniques (such as random-digit dialing), telephone interviewing typically yields more representative samples of customers in a population than you get with other methods. Using this approach, time zones and area codes can be systematically sampled. The American Customer Satisfaction Index survey, a large national survey, uses this approach to obtain valid cross-sections of U.S. consumers.

The survey samples are checked against census data using demographic profiles to ensure that they are properly balanced with respect to age, sex, income and education levels, and ethnic background. Internet-based surveys are growing in importance as the population of Web users becomes more representative of specific customer groups. Web surveys offer significant advantages in that data can be collected, transferred, and updated continuously online. And unlike CATI survey participants, Web respondents have a written version of the survey available on the computer screen to help keep the questions and scales clearly in mind—and they all see exactly the same questions, which eliminates the danger of interviewer bias.

Web surveys have already become the preferred method of data collection in those industries where Web samples are representative of the customer base (as for certain financial services and online retail operations). Yet many customer populations continue to contain large percentages of individuals from lower income and education categories that do not have direct access to the Web (such as convenience store and mass merchandise retailer customers). This situation is likely to change in the near future. Infrastructure changes, such as the diffusion of broadband cable, will broaden the population of Web users in the years to come. Even now, creative solutions can be used to give more customers Web access for the purpose of conducting a survey. For example, a kiosk system can be placed in a location that all customers could access (such as a convenience store or an employee lounge). A crosssection of customers could be encouraged to use the kiosk using personal communication or incentives (such as store coupons).

Easy-to-read touch-screen displays can be used to collect, transfer, and even analyse the data on-line. Another alternative is to use printed versions of the survey that can be handed out or mailed to customers and later scanned and processed on-line. Written surveys, particularly mail surveys, remain a popular approach to data collection. An advantage of written surveys is their relative low cost *per targeted respondent,* or survey sent. Written surveys can be mailed or distributed efficiently to a relatively large number of customers.

The problem is that response rates tend to be low for this approach. Because of the low yield, direct mail often proves more expensive than telephone or Webbased surveys and the respondents are not as representative of the customer population. The quality of the survey data also suffers in that, compared to phone or interview surveys, written surveys offer less control over the interview itself. Written surveys may be passed along for others (subordinates or other family members) to fill out and there is no easy way to clear up misunderstandings or ensure that the respondent is responding carefully to the questions.

One solution to the weaknesses inherent in any one method of data collection is to combine elements of more than one approach. For example, one-on-one or small group interviews can be used to explain the purpose of the survey and motivate participation. To ensure anonymity, written surveys could then be left with the respondents to fill out and return after the interview. Another successful approach in retail contexts is to use store intercepts in combination with written, telephone, or Web surveys. The store intercepts are used to explain the survey and motivate participants to participate in it, while the follow-up survey (in writing, by phone, or by Web page) allows respondents to participate at their convenience.

Sampling is the process of selecting respondents or customers from a population for inclusion in the survey. Naturally, then, sampling starts with the customer population or populations of interest. Your market segmentation scheme and the specific segments that you have decided to include in the research largely define your customer population.

The wide variety of techniques for sampling from customer populations fall into three General categories:

1. Census samples
2. Judgment samples
3. Statistical samples

Census samples involve gathering information from every possible member of a population, such as all of an organi-zation's customers—or all customers in a given segment. Census samples are perfectly representative because the sample and the population are one and the same. Census samples are feasible primarily when the population size is relatively small (such as potential purchasers of jumbo jet engines or highly specialized industrial tools). If you define your population as all customers who have recently recorded transactions, your own records can supply a census sample of current customers.

When the population of customers is too large for a census sample, judgment or statistical samples are called for. Judgment samples involve—as you would expect—using your judgment to decide who should and should not be included. One common method of judgment sampling is to take a list customers and pick people well dispersed with respect to age, sex, income, education, and so on.

The drawback is that the inclusion of respondents in the sample is at the discretion of the researcher. This makes it difficult to generalize any results to the population at large. At the same time, this approach is useful when the goal is simply to identify potentially important issues, as when conducting qualitative research. For example, that the primary goal of using the CIT (critical incident technique) method is to find out what attributes and benefits to include in a more systematic survey. Statistical sampling involves using statistical probability to determine a sample.

Hayes tells us that the primary differences between judgment and statistical sampling are that statistical sampling involves the use of random selection to include cases or respondents in the sample, the ability to statistically determine an appropriate sample size, and the ability to determine how representative the sample is of the population. Thus statistical sampling allows for greater generalization of the study results to the population as a whole.

Examples of statistical sampling methods include random-digit dialing of customers (as through CATI systems) and systematic sampling from a customer list (start at a random point and then pick customers at set intervals, say, every tenth or hundredth name, until you have the number you need for your sample). Respondents in the ACSI survey, for example, are selected using random-digit dialing. Naturally, the choice of a sampling method or methods is a function of both the size and accessibility of the customer population or populations of interest and the purpose of the research.

Once you've cleared away the preliminary survey questions, the next issue that you face in developing the survey is just how to measure benefit and attribute performance and importance. With respect to performance, the survey results should provide reliable and sensitive measures of customer benefits, customer satisfaction, and loyalty. When measuring importance, you must choose between direct customer measures of importance (using, for example, scales or other rating tasks) and derived importance or impact measures based on statistical analysis. There are two important factors to consider when you measure perceived customer benefits, customer satisfaction, and loyalty. First is the abstract nature of the constructs involved. Customers do not obtain satisfaction directly from the concrete attributes and features that describe product and service offerings. Rather, satisfaction and loyalty are a function of the benefits and consequences that the attributes provide. These benefits (such as convenience, safety, and service quality), being abstract or latent constructs, cannot be observed or measured directly using single survey items and scales.

The same is true for such overall evaluations as customer satisfaction and loyalty. Abstract or latent variables are reflected in a variety of concrete measures. Benefits are reflected in the attribute ratings that make up the benefit, satisfaction is reflected in a variety of overall performance ratings, and loyalty in a variety of behavioural intentions. The best way to empirically measure these latent variables is to use multiple concrete *proxies,* or survey measures.

For example, qualitative research shows that a convenience store customer's perception of convenience is reflected in ratings of store location, hours of operation, speed and efficiency of employees, and the availability of parking. A latent variable can be measured using a weighted average or *index* of these survey measures. The convenience index of a convenience store thus becomes a weighted average of a customer's ratings of store location, hours of operation, speed and efficiency of employees, and the availability of parking. Overall satisfaction becomes a weighted average of a customer's ratings on such measures as satisfaction, overall performance versus expectations, and overall performance versus a "best in class" competitor.

The second factor to consider when measuring perceived customer benefits, customer satisfaction, and loyalty is the distribution of the data as it relates to your need for *sensitive measures*—measures that can differentiate among fairly small differences in the underlying conditions. This is an ongoing problem in customer surveys because perceptions of quality and satisfaction almost never fall on a normal distribution. That is, there are typically no bell-shaped curves in the data. In a competitive economy, only those competitors with relatively high quality and satisfaction ratings tend to survive. As we know this results in quality and satisfaction data that is strongly *skewed* (where most of the responses are bunched near the high end of the quality and satisfaction scale and the tail of the distribution trails off towards the low end of the scale). The measurement challenge is to be able to distinguish among customers that are crowded together at the high end of the scale.

To show the problem, consider what happens if you use a very insensitive measure of satisfaction. When asked yes-or-no questions (say, Are you satisfied?), the overwhelming majority of customers answer yes. In a recent study of airline passengers we found 95 per cent of customers responding yes when asked to evaluate their satisfaction on a yes-no scale. Unfortunately, yes-or-no questions give you no way to distinguish among customers that range from moderately to very satisfied.

The sensitivity of the scale improves when you move to a 5-point scale (where 1 = poor performance or very dissatisfied and 5 = excellent performance or very satisfied). Research on quality and satisfaction scales suggests that using a 10-point scale is better still. Going beyond 10-point scales, however, is not beneficial as respondents have trouble using all the scale points. Most sensitive of all is the use of multiple 10-point scale questions to form an index.

Consider that any given survey measure is composed of two sources of variation, that which is supposed to be measured (what statisticians call the "true score") and that which is not meant to be measured (the "error"). The *true score* is what the various items in an index have in common, while the *error* is more a function of the biases or problems inherent in individual survey questions.

By averaging the measures into a single index, you can increase the amount of true score and reduce the overall error variance (relative to an individual survey measure or question) as error from the individual questions is canceled out. As a result, in statistical analysis and modeling, when you use indices in place of single item measures, you explain more of the variation in satisfaction and loyalty, and the relationships involving quality, satisfaction, and loyalty are stronger. In state-of-the-art quality and satisfaction modeling, the use of indexing to measure abstract or latent variables has become the norm. Consider a simple example of the value that indices bring to an analysis. When you assess the financial health of your company, you know that any one marketing, accounting, or finance measure (customer retention, return on investment, return on capital employed, stock price) is an imperfect reflection of overall state of the company.

Taken together, however, the measures provide a more accurate picture of financial health than is possible using any single measure. The next step is to decide whether to use direct or derived measures of attribute and benefit importance. Many satisfaction measurement systems rely heavily on the "gap" model, in which the measure of what needs improvement in quality or satisfaction is the difference between customers' direct ratings of attribute importance and direct ratings of performance (performance minus importance).

There are three kinds of direct measures commonly used in marketing research:

- *Direct scale ratings:* Respondents rate the importance of a product or service's attributes on a scale ranging, for example, from "not at all important" to "very important."
- *Point allocation methods:* Respondents distribute importance "points" (say 100 points) among a given set of attributes where the

proportion of points allocated to an attribute indicates its importance.

- *Paired comparison ratings:* Respondents rate the relative importance of attribute pairs.

Paired comparison ratings can place tremendous burdens on respondents because of the number of attribute pairs involved. They have also been heavily criticized for producing arbitrary measures of importance.Direct scale ratings are considered more accurate (less biased) than point allocations and easier for respondents to provide than either point allocations or paired comparison ratings. These factors make direct scale ratings the more popular choice, so the remainder of this discussion will focus on this method of assessing customer responses. The primary advantage of direct importance scale ratings and the gap model is their ease of implementation. They require minimal analysis (plotting averages and taking difference scores) and can be easily understood at various levels in an organization, from front-line service personnel to CEOs.

Yet there are several problems associated with using direct measures. The method assumes that customers understand what you mean by "important" and also that they know just what attributes are important to them—and are willing to tell you about it. In the end, we find that asking customers directly to rate the impact that an attribute has on their satisfaction and loyalty is an extremely difficult task. Direct importance measures often result in socially acceptable or status quo answers and poor discrimination.

Using direct scale ratings, for example, respondents have a difficult time differentiating among those attributes that are most important to them. We have rarely found significant differences in importance among the top-rated fifteen to twenty attributes in a survey. Research also shows that the importance measures or weights that people report and those that they use when making a decision often differ dramatically. The insight that direct ratings provide drops off as the number of attributes increases.

We show both the strengths and weaknesses of the gap model using a study in which we examined the drivers of satisfaction for a pharmacy. Approximately a hundred customers evaluated twenty-nine attributes of a retail pharmacy.The mean values of rated attribute importance are ordered from least to most important and plotted question by question (where 1 = not at all important and 10 = very important).

The corresponding attribute performance measures are also plotted (where 1 = poor performance and 10 = excellent performance). The key attributes to improve are those where the "gap" (performance minus importance) is lowest. On the positive side, gap models are relatively easy to implement, analyse, and explain. The analysis simply involves plotting the two dimensions, importance and performance, and examining their differences. This often makes gap models a good option for companies that are just beginning to develop a customer orientation. The models identify the "low-hanging fruit"—the obvious gaps that need to be closed—and get the company into the habit of monitoring customers.

The prioritysetting logic is also the same as for the strategic satisfaction matrix. Attributes on which both importance and performance are rated high are core competencies, while attributes with high importance and low performance need improvement. However, a major problem with the approach is that customers rate most everything as important. The conclusion is that the company needs to improve most of the items with low performance ratings, and it's hard to tell which ones would make the most difference to results.

Basically, importance scales are effective at highlighting the *least* important attributes but ineffective at highlighting the *most* important attributes. The direct importance ratings are simply not diagnostic. It is primarily the *performance* measures that drive the priority-setting process. Another problem with direct importance measures and the gap model is that the survey has a tendency to grow. Because the approach requires at least two ratings for each attribute, the survey becomes nearly twice as long as a survey where importance measures are derived by other (statistical) means. One question is required to rate an attribute's performance and another to rate its importance.

Direct importance ratings may be the only option when the customer population (or the sample size) is too small or ease of implementation is an overriding concern. Where feasible, however, it is much more economical to take the statistical approach and add good dependent variables, such as satisfaction and loyalty, for use in a regression analysis. Importance measures do not need to be measured directly. They can be derived statistically from attribute performance ratings and ratings of overall satisfaction. Because statistical estimations are more objective and less biased, they are often superior to direct customer ratings. Statistical analysis provides estimates of importance as the impact that one variable has on another. Customers indicate how they perceive a product or service to perform on a number of attributes as well as their overall satisfaction and loyalty. Variation in performance and satisfaction across customers allows the researcher to estimate (using regression or regression-based statistical techniques) the impact that different aspects of quality and value have on satisfaction and loyalty.

Statistically determined importance ratings can avoid many of the problems that you encounter with direct importance ratings. But the quality of the statistical estimates can vary significantly. *The important question is whether or not the estimation builds on the lens of the customer!* The lens should be viewed as a blueprint for both survey development *and* analysis. A major problem facing regression-based estimates of impact or importance centres on the correlation among the drivers of satisfaction.

If attribute ratings are too highly correlated, that is, if changes in one rating tend to follow changes in another without regard to outside factors—what statisticians refer to as lacking sufficient *independence*—the statistical estimates of impact may be poor. The lens of the customer, which is based on thorough analysis of qualitative research, shows just which attributes go together in the customer's mind. By combining multiple attribute ratings together into benefit indices, the lens provides a means of reducing correlation among the satisfaction drivers; it increases their independence.

The result is a set of benefit and attribute importance weights that are superior to those that can be collected directly from customers. Once you go through the background analysis outlined thus far, you'll be in a position to develop a survey instrument you can use with confidence.

The process described here follows the flowchart which we have found useful in developing and administering our own quality-satisfactionloyalty surveys. The primary purpose of the opening statement is to persuade your targeted respondents to take part in the survey. There are three main messages that can be communicated in an opening statement to help maximize the response rate:

- Emphasize the importance of the topic or problem area to respondents.
- Emphasize that the primary purpose of the research is to better understand the problem.
- Emphasize that the organization or entity conducting the research will use the results to improve the situation.

In the convenience store survey, the emphasis in the opening statements is on the latter two points. The statements point out that the survey is meant to understand what quality areas are important to convenience store customers and that the results will be used to guide quality improvement efforts. The opening statements may also include screener questions needed to identify customers.

The convenience store survey screens respondents to include those individuals who have visited a convenience store within the last three months. The screener in the survey also provides an explanation that convenience stores do not include grocery store chains, drug or discount stores, or mass merchandisers. If asked, the interviewer explicitly defines a convenience store as "typically a small franchised market that is open long hours."

These explanations and definitions were added as a result of pretesting and revising the survey. Once respondents have been screened and agree to participate, their first task is to evaluate attribute performance levels. In some cases the ratings may only apply to the product, service, or retailer of interest (say, stores in the Seven-Eleven chain). In other cases the ratings may apply to multiple competitors (say, Seven-Eleven, Quik Stop, and other widely known chains).

Before providing the information, the survey must instruct respondents on how to perform the task. This includes who or what is being rated and how to use the scales. The types of scales and their explanation depend partly on the method used to collect the data. If, for example, it is important to explain multiple anchors on the scale (such as what a 1, 2, 3, 4, or 5 actually means in the context of the survey), it is easier to do this in a written or Web-based survey where respondents can refer to the written anchors. It is more difficult to do so in a telephone survey. Because the respondent has no written list to refer to, the emphasis is typically on keeping only the two endpoints in mind.

In the convenience store survey, for example, it is explained that a rating of 1 means poor performance and a rating of 10 means excellent performance. Keep in mind that the choice of scales and the need to label scale points depends on the researcher's approach to measurement.

Given the abstract nature of the constructs and the need for sensitive measures, we strongly advocate using indices to measure customer benefits, customer satisfaction, and loyalty. The use of indices gets you away from very concrete, individual scales where each point on the scale is ascribed some meaning. Indices resemble temperature scales—they just show that the reported value is higher or lower than some benchmark.

The meaning you attach to the index levels is based on how a product or service performs against competitors and over time. By deemphasizing concrete scale points in favour of more sensitive indices, you have less need to ascribe meaning to anything more than the end points. We recommend using 10-point scales, where 1 is poor and 10 is excellent, to evaluate performance across data collection methods.

The next parts of the survey present all of the attributes the lens of the customer research recommended for evaluation. The lens of the customer provides a blueprint as to how the attributes are organized— how they go together in a customer's mind.

The survey should leverage this lens and present the attributes in clusters defined by the benefit categories (quality of the service, product offerings, store layout, and so on). Particular to the convenience store survey is the inclusion of two questions at the beginning of this part to assess customer perceptions of store reputation. Satisfaction is the customer's overall evaluation of his or her experiences with a product or service provider. In your subsequent analysis, it will be a major dependent variable that you will explain using your measures of attribute and benefit performance. Satisfaction is a latent variable that will be manifested in a variety of more concrete performance ratings.

As we have said, it is critical to combine multiple measures of satisfaction in a satisfaction index. In addition to a simple rating of satisfaction, other measures include evaluations of overall product or service performance against different benchmarks.

You might ask customers to evaluate performance versus their expectations, versus an ideal product or service provider in the category, or versus a "best in class" competitor. Notice that we do not advocate using any one of these as a proxy for satisfaction.

Rather, satisfaction as a latent or abstract construct is what all of the various evaluations have in common. The measures simply represent different benchmarks that customers use to evaluate performance and from which an index can be constructed. The convenience store survey has respondents evaluate performance using three different questions. The first asks them to express overall satisfaction, the second asks for an evaluation of performance versus expectations, and the third seeks an evaluation of performance versus an ideal product or service in the category.

These questions were modeled directly on those used in the ACSI survey, which have been shown to provide a very reliable and sensitive measure of satisfaction. An added benefit of using the ACSI questions is that it allowed us to benchmark the survey results for convenience stores against other industries and firms included in the ACSI survey. Whereas satisfaction measures apply more or less universally across industries and contexts, loyalty measures do not.

The desired outcomes of satisfaction are highly specific to the nature of the business, product, and service involved. Volvo, for example, has specified a range of desired customer outcomes, from the repeat purchase of a Volvo vehicle to the purchase of Volvo financing, Volvo insurance, the purchase and use of a Volvo gas card, and the spread of positive word-ofmouth advertising. If your customers are retailers who turn around and sell your product to end users, loyalty may take the form of the *push*—the sales effort they make on your behalf. If your product is a once-in-a-lifetime purchase (a piece of jewelry or a collector's item), loyalty may involve the customer's willingness to buy other products or services from you (cross-selling) and to tell other potential customers about your offerings.

In an industrial context, the level of satisfaction may have little effect on whether a customer buys at least some of your products and services. At the same time, it may have a great effect on just how *much* they buy (account penetration). Another desired outcome may include the trust that customers place in you and their resulting commitment to maintaining a relationship.

Our point is simply that, whereas satisfaction measures are more or less universal, loyalty measures must be customised. In the convenience store survey, the desired outcomes for the store chains and franchisees are rather straightforward.

They include enhancing the customers' likelihood of visiting the store again in the future and their likelihood of recommending the store to others. The measures used in the Råtorp Tire Company survey were quite different. As in the convenience store survey, they included the likelihood that the customer (in this case a retailer) would continue to purchase, but they also included whether the proportion of products ordered from the manufacturer would likely increase or decrease in the future (account penetration) and the degree to which the retailer would recommend the manufacturer's products to its customers (push).

Descriptive questions (including market segment profiles and demographic questions) are typically added near the end of the survey. As noted earlier, the main reason for this placement is that the questions, being more personal in nature, are apt to lead a respondent to terminate the survey if asked early on. Once the interviewer has developed some rapport with the respondent and the interview has the momentum provided by answering the performance, satisfaction, and loyalty questions, descriptive information is often easier to get. The primary purpose of the descriptive questions is to group customers by characteristics such as age and income level for later analysis, so as to track their representativeness and discover possible new segments. The convenience store survey contains both a direct question regarding segmentation and a group of indirect demographic questions that can be used to segment or describe customers.

As noted earlier, the primary benefit of having respondents selfselect into preexisting segments is the ease of subsequent analysis. The drawback is that it presumes that the segments do not change or evolve significantly over time. A golden rule of survey research is to conduct one or more tests before you put any survey into the field. The primary purpose of preliminary testing is to identify and resolve whatever problems respondents might have in answering the questions. Pretesting tells you whether the survey is able to collect the desired information, and where you need to reword questions to make them simpler and easier to understand. If the pretest is weak and major revisions are required, the revised survey should be tested again before being put into the field. Pretesting is not just the domain of those who administer the survey; it can raise questions of strategic relevance to top management as well.

Another rule we like to follow is to involve both those directly involved in the survey process and those who will use the information to make resource allocation decisions. In pretesting the convenience store survey, for example, we learned several lessons. One was that many people were unclear as to just what a convenience store was in the first place. Does it include gas stations that sell some other merchandise?

Grocery store chains that sell gasoline? This led to the inclusion of more specific screening questions and definitions that the interviewer could use as needed. Pretesting also raised questions about what benchmarks the customer should use to evaluate the competitiveness of a convenience store's prices. Should the benchmarks be limited to other convenience stores, or should they include other stores that sell similar merchandise (such as grocery stores for bread, milk, and soft drinks). Based on top management input, it was decided to let customers compare prices to other stores at which they may buy similar merchandise.

The reason was that executives at the various chains were very interested in the gap between perceived and actual price differences between convenience stores and other types of stores. Whereas convenience stores are often perceived as having relatively high prices, actual price differences are often small or nonexistent. Just how the survey is arranged and conducted is largely a function of the method of contact. Telephone surveys often involve random-digit dialing or random selection from a customer list.

The interviewer makes a pitch for participation and, if the time is not convenient, can arrange for a better time to call back. Before collecting survey data in a one-on-one interview, the respondent is usually called and an explicit appointment is made. Store intercepts are also a valuable tool for selling the survey—persuading people to take part in later administration either by phone, Web, or mail. Web surveys may use an e-mail message to introduce and gain interest in the survey and then instruct the respondent on how to access the survey.

Customers may also self-select to participate in surveys that are available on a company's Web site. Just who administers the survey is a function of both the sheer number of respondents and the need for objectivity. We suggest that people within the sponsoring company administer the survey themselves as long as the number of respondents is not too large and administrators can remain objective. A truly customer-oriented company should not routinely leave the job of collecting customer data to outsiders. But for a large-sample survey, it will be more cost-effective to use a professional data collection firm. If the interviewer's compensation is a function of customer responses (the number of "10s" on the survey), the objectivity of the responses and resulting data will be compromised. If a more objective interviewer cannot be found within the company, it would again be best to use a third party to collect the data. The development of a quality-satisfaction-loyalty survey builds directly on the lens of the customer. Survey development should not be a process in which people from different parts of a company sit around and decide what they would like to see on the survey.

Rather, the lens of the customer provides a blueprint for deciding which attributes to include and the benefit categories to use for organizing them. Even before developing a survey it is important to understand what populations or market segments to survey, what data collection method or methods to use, and how to sample from the target populations. In leveraging the lens of the customer, the construction of a quality-satisfaction-loyalty survey should follow certain guidelines. Benefits, satisfaction, and loyalty are abstract constructs that cannot be measured directly using any one concrete survey item.

They are best measured using an index of multiple measures or proxies. Indices also provide for more sensitive measures than single survey items, so they can explain more of the variation in satisfaction and loyalty and are better at identifying important satisfaction drivers. The importance that customers place on attributes and benefits has traditionally been determined by two different approaches: direct measures of importance and those derived from statistical analysis. Among the different direct measures, direct scales (ratings from "not important" to "very important") are often preferred. They are straightforward to collect and as good as or better than other direct approaches (such as point allocation or paired comparisons).

Yet, when done properly, statistically derived measures of importance are better than direct measures at objectively capturing the impact attributes and benefits have on satisfaction and loyalty. It is important for statistical analyses to leverage the lens of the customer when grouping variables for analysis. Otherwise, even the most rigorous statistical estimates may be a poor reflection of reality. With the lens of the customer in mind and the data collection methods chosen, you can complete the survey instrument in a systematic way. First, assess attribute performance by benefit category. After that, obtain overall evaluations of satisfaction. Then select loyalty measures and customise them to fit the product, service, or context.

To some, loyalty is simply a matter of whether a customer comes back to buy the same product or use the same service. To others, loyalty is a matter of how much more customers will buy (account penetration) or what else they will buy (cross-selling). After adding descriptive questions to help identify market segments, pretest the survey to identify any unforeseen problems. Arranging and conducting the survey yields the data that serves as input to the next phase of the process. W hen it comes to analysing your customer survey data, you have a lot of options.

We recommend a variation on *principal-components regression (PCR)* that is relatively simple to use and provides as much detailed information as you need to make quality improvement decisions. It combines two statistical methods: principal-components analysis and regression analysis. *Principal-components analysis* is a data reduction tool that shows what any group of survey measures have in common, so you can develop the benefit, satisfaction, and loyalty indices. *Regression analysis* relates these indices to each other and lets you determine the benefit, satisfaction, and loyalty impact scores.

We present a flowchart to show the necessary steps used to apply PCR to the lens of the customer. To support our recommendation. We begin by describing just what information you can and should be obtaining from your analysis. After describing our data analysis method, illustrating the links with examples from Volvo and a major hotel chain. These financial links, which highlight the payoff from investments suggested by customer measurement, will help you inspire people to make real quality improvements based on the information the survey process develops. When you analyse satisfaction and loyalty data, you're really looking for answers to two relatively simple questions.

Where does your company need to improve quality or value to increase satisfaction and loyalty? And once satisfaction and loyalty are improved, what are the payoffs? The basic assumptions are that improved quality leads to increased satisfaction, which in turn makes customers more loyal, and that you get more profit from loyal customers than from those who don't care where they get the product or service you're selling. Now, how do you quantify the links?

The prerequisite is that your measurement system should provide sensitive *and* reliable measures. Your goal is to provide managers with truly diagnostic information—with levers they can push to improve quality and satisfaction. You don't want results that suggest that everything (or nothing) is important, or results that show differences (as among competitors) or changes (over time) that are not valid and meaningful. In other words, you want a system that produces results you can trust. Finally, you want to be able to predict what happens when satisfaction increases.

How likely are customers to come back and how much more revenue or profit will they generate? To make your measurement system a reality, you will need to analyse your survey data to produce multiple levels of information in the system. The circles labeled "satisfaction" and "loyalty" are the key to understanding your customers' overall consumption experience. Best measured using indices made up of multiple concrete measures, these abstract constructs are important in benchmarking performance versus competitors and tracking performance over time.

These benefit-level indices are the heart of the lens of the customer. They provide an overall view of how you are performing in quality areas as defined by your customers. But because these indices are abstract, they cannot be acted upon directly. Action requires moving down to the level of the underlying concrete attributes. Attribute values are obtained directly from the quality-satisfaction-loyalty survey ratings.

For the benefits and attributes, 1 is poor performance and 10 is excellent performance. But setting priorities requires you to measure impact as well, that is, the extent to which a change in an attribute will lead to a change in satisfaction, loyalty, and other desired customer outcomes. As there are attribute and benefit levels of performance, so there are also attribute and benefit levels of impact. The benefit-level impacts, indicate how much impact each benefit has on customer satisfaction. It is helpful to focus initially on these benefit-level impacts to gain an understanding of the consumption experience. Looking at the attribute or question level impacts will help you relate your improvement efforts to the everyday activities of the company that have the highest payoff.

Attribute impacts are more the focus of continuous improvement efforts, while benefit impacts are the focus of innovation efforts—attempts to find completely new ways to deliver the benefits that customers value. A benefit-level impact of 0.5 shows that a 1-unit change in that benefit index is associated with a 0.5-unit increase in the satisfaction index. Once you have impact information at every level of the model, you can quantify the change that improving an attribute or benefit would make in loyalty (and subsequent profitability, once this data is added to the model). The impact of changing an input to the model (an attribute) on the output of the model (loyalty or profitability) is simply the product of all impacts in the chain of causes and effects.

(Where there is more than one path or chain of cause-and-effect relationships, it would be the sum of the different impact chains.) If you are familiar with traditional PCR, you will see that our approach to principal-components regression has some unique features. Traditional PCR factor-analyses all the attribute ratings simultaneously to produce a set of independent components or factors. It ignores benefit clusters of the type we recommend you develop using qualitative research to create the lens of the customer.

The problem is that the approach is too data driven; the factor analysis dictates the lens. In contrast, our approach uses the benefit groupings or clusters in the lens as a theory or model to structure the PCR analysis. This approach provides the technical sophistication and diagnostic information that your analysis requires. The main alternative to using our version of PCR is *partial least squares* (PLS). Both our PCR approach and PLS use the lens of the customer as a guide to structure the analysis. PCR is a two-step approach in which the benefit, satisfaction, and loyalty indices are first estimated using a series of principal-components analyses.

The researcher then uses these indices or latent variables in a series of regression models to estimate a causal chain of events (as from quality through to financial performance). PLS performs both of these steps for the researcher. It estimates an entire causal chain or model using an iterative estimation procedure that integrates aspects of principal-components analysis and multiple regression. Researchers in the areas of quality, marketing, and consumer research regard PLS as the state of the art in customer satisfaction modeling.

The disadvantage of PLS is that it requires special software and training, and the software is neither user-friendly nor easy to find. If you have mastered PLS, by all means use it. At a conceptual level, our flowchart and procedure for evaluating the quality of your analysis still applies. Otherwise, we recommend that you use PCR, which is straightforward to do using easily available and user-friendly software packages. Comparing the two approaches we find a 0.99 correlation in estimated benefit-level impacts and a 0.98 correlation in estimated attribute-level impacts. In other words, the results are virtually identical.

The following parts describe how to analyse a customer satisfaction model using our PCR method. The sole purpose of analysis is to make sense out of the data you collect. This part includes a step-by-step guide to analysing data sets that you can use if you're in charge of performing or managing the data analysis. Even if you're remote from the actual research and your responsibility is to create an environment where customer data will be developed and used, the guide will still be useful as it will demystify the process and, as a consequence, make you more constructively critical when evaluating the output of an analysis. The first major accomplishment will be to create the latent variables for benefits, satisfaction, and loyalty. Then the process will go on to derive the actual values for the impact of one level of the model on the next, and to establish benchmark values for the benefit, satisfaction, and loyalty indices. The combination of impacts and indices will provide the cause-effect chain. Once you've built the lens of the customer for your products or services and seen the valuable information it can help you produce, it's tempting to sit back and ask, "Well, now what do the numbers say we should do?"

But it's not that simple. The critical next phase of the process is to use the information to set priorities for improvement. And don't underestimate the importance of obtaining top management input to your action plans at this point. This may require some persistence. Too often managers view measurement systems, including the quality-satisfaction-loyalty model we present here, as a means of avoiding tough decisions—but "the numbers" don't pay the bills, and they don't make decisions, either.

Managers who are in charge of implementing their company's strategies and hold the authority to budget and who allocate resources to improve quality and satisfaction cannot absent themselves from the process. The numbers simply help managers base their decisions on facts. We first discuss management's role in using the output of the measurement system to set priorities for improvement. We then discuss how to implement the priorities. We bridge the gap between the customer benefits and product or service attributes that need improvement and the internal changes they require.

Setting priorities requires both impact and performance information for the various drivers of satisfaction and loyalty. But to set priorities, you must make some critical decisions regarding just what constitutes high versus low impact and high versus low performance. These decisions require you to consider a number of factors beyond the information in your impact-performance chart, including your strategy and competencies as well as relevant benchmarks, costs, and market dynamics. The basic logic is to categorize the various benefit and attribute drivers of satisfaction into one of the four cells of the matrix, each of which is associated with its own market action implications. Generally, the essential areas to improve are those where impact or importance is high and performance is low. Customers are essentially telling us that we are falling short in these important areas. Improvements to these areas will effectively focus resources where they have the greatest impact on satisfaction and subsequent loyalty and profitability.

This is also the cell in which you are most competitively vulnerable. If competitors do an excellent job in these areas, they will lure your customers away. Those areas that are important to customers and in which your performance is strong represent your core competencies and competitive advantages. It is essential to maintain if not improve performance on these drivers. The implications for the opposite cell, where impact is low and performance is weak, are also clear. Generally, there's no reason to waste resources on improving these areas. The customers, performance here just doesn't matter.

The implications for the remaining cell, in which impact is low yet performance is high, are less straightforward. This may be an area where resources have been wasted in the past because the benefits and attributes are not important to customers. In one recent application, for example, we found that customers at an IKEA furniture store in the United States rated traditional Swedish amenities—a child-care facility and a Swedish bake-shop—very positively. Nonetheless, these amenities had little to no impact on satisfaction and loyalty. From a cost-benefit standpoint, we concluded that having the amenities was not costeffective for the U.S.-based store. Alternatively, benefits and attributes in the low impact-high performance category may contain drivers of satisfaction that customers consider to be basic and necessary.

Customers may find these benefits and attributes everywhere they look and take them for granted. Although important in an absolute sense, these features offer no differentiation because there is little to no variance in their performance across customers and competitors. Airline safety is a classic example here—as long as the planes aren't falling out of the sky, passengers tend to regard one airline as much the same as another. That doesn't mean that any airline can afford to ease off on safety! The same sort of consideration can apply in less dramatic circumstances as well. In the IKEA project, we found that "ease of assembly" was also rated highly and had little impact.

Our conclusion here, however, was to make certain that we assure continued high performance on this benefit. Withdrawing resources and reducing performance would only serve to put us on a "slippery slope" and decrease satisfaction. The area would quickly return to the high impact–low performance category. Another possibility in the high performance–low impact quadrant is to find a new target market segment for the product or service. It may well be possible to find new customers who would especially value these benefit areas (such as customers who would value the child-care and bakery facilities in the IKEA store).

But data analysis does not determine where to draw the cell boundaries. Managers must draw the lines and decide just where the improvement should occur. Again, the impact-performance charts are a primary input to this decision process, but there are several other factors that you need to consider. Your strategic market plan leads you to focus on particular segments of customers to leverage core competencies.

But what if your customer data analysis suggests that you improve in areas that are inconsistent with your basic strengths? Management must decide whether or not the areas that need improvement are those in which core competencies and a competitive advantage can be achieved. If not, you may be pursuing customers you can't please with your strengths, at the risk of alienating customers who currently value your offerings. Perhaps you should reconsider your entire strategic market plan instead. At the same time, the information may be very valuable in deciding on network partners who can help provide customers with the benefits they need. Think back to the convenience store survey, which revealed that safety is the primary driver of satisfaction for customers. In practical terms, safety is not something that a convenience store can completely control, so the implication may be to network and collaborate with those who can have more effect. In some cities, for example, convenience stores provide an area where local law enforcement officers can take a break, make phone calls, and do paperwork.

This win-win solution saves the officers time and creates a greater atmosphere of safety than the stores could provide on their own. It is also critically important to benchmark both impact and performance when using this information to set priorities. In the Råtorp Tire Company case, impact-performance charts are supplied for three main competitors in the market. As the reader quickly finds out, making decisions for Råtorp requires a careful consideration of impact and performance levels for the competitors as well. In an absolute sense, impact may be high and performance low in a given area, suggesting the need to make improvements.

But what if your closest competitor shows even lower performance and higher impact? It may be a mistake to improve that area if there are others that also call for attention. Relatively, it may be a competitive strength, at least in the short run. At the same time, do not ignore the absolute levels of impact and performance. Over the long haul, the absolute levels of performance and impact highlight your vulnerabilities, as well as those of your competitors, and suggest where new competitors may enter or improve to take customers away.

When you tie your model and analysis to increased profit per customer, you then have some idea that the costs typically incurred to improve quality are covered. But in most cases, managers must consider the relative costs of making improvements when deciding which areas to improve. Remember that the goal is to optimize rather than maximize satisfaction and loyalty. If two areas show equally low performance and high impact, managers should ask, "Which is more cost-effective to improve?"

One source of cost information is management itself. Another is through the use of tools such as QFD that translate product improvements into internal change and explicitly consider cost information. Finally, consider where your market is headed over time. Just what factors will become more or less important? For personal computers, will processing speed become less of a differential advantage going forward? For convenience stores, will prepared foods become a greater source of differentiation and impact? Both social and technological forecasting are important bases for predicting these market dynamics, but are beyond the scope of our discussion.

The exercise provides the output of a survey and data analysis for Råtorp and its two main competitors. We strongly encourage you to work through the data in the case and set priorities for Råtorp. Based on the data, consider what you expect the competition to do as well. The case will force you to consider several factors, including what Råtorp's strategy should be, how the benchmarks influence interpretation of the results, how the competition is likely to evolve over time (such as the role filled by import brands), and what the improve-ments might cost.

The case emphasizes that the task of moving from information to decisions is far from trivial. It requires significant reflection and input from managers in a position to set and implement a strategic market plan. Once you have targeted which benefits and attributes to improve, you have to figure out just how to improve them. In effect, you need to build a bridge from your model of customer perceptions and behaviours to your internal metrics, parts, processes, and people. When you do this, you'll soon find that—as with any bridge—the traffic on this one flows both ways.

The framework integrates aspects of two leading approaches to improving quality and satisfaction: *quality function deployment* (QFD) and customer satisfaction modeling. Together, the two approaches show qualitatively different steps in the overall process of translating satisfaction into its means of accomplishment. Our satisfaction models translate overall satisfaction down into the customer benefits that drive satisfaction and into the product and service attributes that provide the benefits. These are the uppermost stages of the framework.

The lower stages, taken from QFD, translate these attributes further down into their means of accomplishment or production. It is important to consider what we mean by *translation* in the framework. Consistent with the arrows is a process of moving from the most abstract information of interest to the most concrete.

Customer satisfaction is customers' overall evaluation of their purchase and consumption experience. Moving downstream in the framework from satisfaction to production is, therefore, a process of translating abstract, subjective evaluations into concrete, objective means of accomplishment. In contrast, the process of moving up in the framework from concrete processes and attributes to abstract benefits and overall satisfaction is more of an inductive or *change monitoring* process.

After determining what changes to make, it is important to track the changes back upstream in the process. Did, for example, the changes we made internally have a subsequent effect on customer perceptions and satisfaction? To what degree did our improvements to production processes improve process operations, parts deployment, engineering or design characteristics, and ultimately attribute and benefit performance? The combination of translation and change monitoring forms a two-way traffic that is essential to close the loop on the quality improvement process.

A central point of the framework is that QFD picks up where satisfaction modeling leaves off. The product and service attributes that are the output of the priority-setting process represent the input to QFD. The four houses or phases of QFD thus represent phases four through seven of an overall translation process. The translation is, however, different for pure products than for pure services. For products, targeted attributes must be translated into engineering or design characteristics, parts characteristics, process operations, and finally production requirements. Because services are co-produced by customers and employees at a time and place of the customer's choosing, service production is a different beast. In service applications of QFD, targeted attributes for improvement must be translated into service qualities (for example, hotel arrival), service functions (airport shuttle service), service process designs (number of shuttles, routes, and personnel), and operating policies and procedures (daily schedules and contingency plans). An important implication of the framework is that for a given product or service, there are at least seven conceptually distinct stages in the overall translation and change monitoring process.

It highlights the difficulties and challenges that we face even after a satisfaction model is analysed and priorities are set. Our goal here is not to exhaustively discuss the implementation phases, but rather to introduce you to QFD as one tool that has helped thousands of companies around the world to link their customer data to product and service improvements. A thorough treatment of how tools such as QFD are used to implement product-driven product and process changes is beyond the scope of this book.

It is, in fact, the subject of our next book in the UMBS Management Series. The work is usually documented in a series of matrices. Its primary benefits are reduced design costs and development time. Other benefits include improving communication and cohesion within a product development or improvement team and solidifying design decisions early in the development cycle. Generally there are two variants of the QFD methodology.

The first is the four-phase system captured and presented in more detail later. In this approach, QFD starts with an input list of customer-desired attributes. These attributes are often ordered hierarchically to handle the large number required to describe a product (such as an automobile door system). At a higher level of abstraction are the benefit categories similar to those used in our satisfaction model (such as that a door system "operates well").

At a lower level of abstraction are the more concrete attributes (such as that a door system is "easy to close from the outside"). The QFD translation process begins in Phase 1, the "House of Quality, " where attributes are translated into engineering characteristics. In subsequent phases—often called *houses*— engineering targets are translated into parts characteristics;

targeted parts characteristics are translated into key process operations; and key process operations are translated into production requirements or work instructions. As mentioned, this system is altered when applied to services.

The second variant of QFD recognizes that the four-phase system that only fulfills a portion of the planning that is needed for a new product. Separate matrix systems are required to incorporate product quality deployment, technology deployment, cost deployment, and reliability deployment throughout the planning, design, trial, manufacturing, and service phases of product development and launch.

4

Business Tourism Action Plan

Business planning is often conducted when:

- Starting a new venture (organization, product or service)
- Expanding a current organization, product or service
- Buying a current organization, product or service
- Working to improve the management of a current organization, product or service

There are a wide variety of formats for a business plan. The particular format and amount of content included in a plan depends on the complexity of the organization, product or service and on the demands of those who will use the business plan to make a decision, eg, an investor, funder, management, Board of Directors, etc.

Overall, the contents of a business plan typically aim to:

1. Describe the venture (new or current organization, product or service), often including its primary features, advantages and benefits
2. What the organization wants to do with it (buy it, expand it, etc.)
3. Justification that the plans are credible (eg, results of research that indicate the need for what the organization wants to do)
4. Marketing plans, including research results about how the venture will be marketed (eg, who the customers will be, any specific groups (or targets) of customers, why they need the venture (benefits they seek from the venture), how they will use the venture, what they will be willing to pay, how the venture will be advertised and promoted, etc.)
5. Staffing plans, including what expertise will be needed to build (sometimes included in business plans) and provide the venture on an ongoing basis
6. Management plans, including how the expertise will be organized, coordinated and led
7. Financial plans, including costs to build the venture (sometimes included in business plans), costs to operate the venture, expected revenue, budgets for each of the first several years into the future,

when the venture might break-even (begin making more money overall than it has cost), etc.

Business planning is usually conducted when starting a new organization or a new major venture, for example, new product, service or programme. Essentially, a business plan is a combination of a marketing plan, strategic plan, operational/management plan and a financial plan. Far more important than the plan document, is the planning process itself.

Business planning usually includes a thorough examination of the idea for a new product/service, if there's really a market for it, who the competitors are, how the idea is uniquely positioned to be competitive and noticeable, how the idea will be produced to a product/service, how much it will cost, how it will be promoted, what overall goals must be accomplished, how the development and ongoing operations will be managed and what resources are needed (including money). As noted above, a business plan is a combination of a marketing plan, financial plan, strategic plan and a operational/management plan. Here are a variety of perspectives.

To start, you need to plan your strategy very well. Your restaurant has to focus on some key elements that'll set it apart from the thousands of other eateries out there. These could be location, cuisine, decoration or even—good luck with this one—price.

Maybe it's located where there's a lot of traffic, or across the hall from a gym, or near a bookstore, or outside a theater. Maybe there are no fish tacos in your town, or no good Italian restaurants. Maybe there are no cafes near the river with outside seating. You have to know why you're different. In short, don't try to please everybody generally; find your niche market, and please those people very well.

By differentiating your restaurant, you make marketing it much easier. Marketing is critical to restaurant success, but marketing can be expensive. And in most cases, the most effective restaurant marketing depends on repeat business and word-of-mouth. Think about how you choose a restaurant yourself—do you look through your Entertainment book or other coupon source? Do you research with a Zagat guide or online reviews? Or do you ask for recommendations from friends? Ask yourself how people will describe your restaurant and why they'll recommend it. If you can't put that short conversation into easy words, you're in trouble.

Also, if you have a choice, don't start a low-priced restaurant. Low-priced restaurants are much harder to market than mid- to high-priced restaurants. Fast-food franchises are everywhere, and they have a huge corner on that market. People believe in cheap food when they see strong branding and lots of customers. You don't want to be the dive on the corner that can't attract business.

Unless you're already partnered with an investor, you should assume you won't be. In general, restaurants aren't targets for professional investors because they're so risky. The few exceptions include celebrities who back restaurants that capitalize on their names, and well-known chefs and successful restaurant owners opening new venues.

Not having access to startup financing doesn't mean you shouldn't start the business. It means you should carefully decide whether you're going to start slowly, minding expenses, or borrow enough money to start big. Your borrowing options include commercial bank loans, which require assets you can stake as collateral, and SBA loans, which require less collateral than bank loans but still require you to put up 30 percent of the starting costs to qualify for the guaranteed loan. When in doubt about loans go straight to your favourite bank and ask for advice.

Be sure to count your startup costs well. You don't want to get into a bind where you've spent half of what you thought you needed and you've run out of money. You'll probably have to rent a location and spend a few months fixing it up, and you may need employees some employees to help out during the fix-up period, too. Unless you're moving into an existing restaurant, you'll need to buy kitchen equipment, tables and chairs, cash registers, phone systems and décor to establish ambience. And then you need to budget for what's called "working capital" for the startup period when your spending exceeds your sales. Some say you need at least six months of expenses ready to go; others recommend having 12 months covered.

Your sales forecast is also important. We like to build a sales forecast based on unit sales, meaning meals and drinks, not just gross sales amounts. That helps us break the sales forecast into components I can count. How many tables do you have? How many meals will you serve on Friday night when the place is almost full? What does an average meal cost? How many drinks come with the meals? Then calculate unit sales, average revenue per unit and average cost per unit.

Then comes your expense forecast. With meals and drinks already priced out, your remaining operating expenses are mainly people, rent and other fixed costs. Estimate those per month, and match them to your sales forecast.

When all the costs are tallied, you'll get a good picture of the cash flow and how much money you'll need to keep the restaurant operational. During the early months of startup, your cash flow probably won't cover all your expenses, so you'll want your plan to include how you'll cover the difference.

Finally, as you get started, remember that business plans continually go out of date, and good business plans are never done. You should take an hour or so every month to review the difference between what you planned and what actually happened, and update your plan accordingly.

A business plan is often the entry-level requirement to getting government money, investor capital or bank loans. Although, you may have a complete picture of the business in your head, investors and bankers need to see if you really have an understanding of the business and have thought it through.

Preparing a plan is a long and daunting task but in the end the business owner often sees things from a new perspective and has mitigated any risks.

The business plan is not just for banks and investors but also supplies you with a blueprint of succeeding in business. The plan provides you with the direction of your company and is a guidepost for your employees too.

The primary job of a business owner is to manage and run a business. The term manage implies the task of planning and execution. Are you considering bringing in an outside expert to help with your business plan? The idea is appealing to some because planning is daunting and there are experts out there—if you can afford them. However, it's not nearly as simple as you'd like.

Critical fact: your business plan isn't a stand-alone document; it's you, your business and your promise. You have to know every date, every deadline, every last word, and every number in your plan. Investors invest in people, not plans. They buy the jockey more than the horse. Expert help can't change this fundamental principle. It must be your plan, yours down to your bones, and it must not be the consultant's plan.

If you work within the framework that the business plan is yours, then there are some things that outside help can do for your plan and your planning process. If you have the money to spend, and you find the right person or resource, here the benefits of hiring outside help:

- A professional plan review. Does your plan cover the most obvious points? Does it have any obvious logical holes? Is it easy to read and is it easy to find the most important information? Ask an expert to review it.
- Help with the financials. You don't have to be an MBA or accountant to plan your business, but some of the underlying math and financial principles can be daunting. The ideal is doing it yourself with an expert looking on and coaching.
- General planning coaching. An outside expert can facilitate your thinking and planning by guiding discussion towards key issues, drawing out definitions, highlighting and focusing on important points.
- Industry-specific coaching. Don't reinvent wheels when you can leverage off of an expert's experience.
- Contacts and introductions. Be careful with this one, however, because you're swimming in shark-infested waters here (and I'm referring to the consultants as sharks, not just the investors). There are good consultants who deliver on promises, but there are far more bad consultants who make promises. A consultant can get you an investor no matter how good the plan, because the investor wants (or doesn't want) you, not your plan.

Please be sure to avoid the common problems with outside planning consulting. Some of these come up far too often:

- Misunderstanding the deliverables. Don't pay for vague promises. Business-plan review, coaching and help with the financials are credible deliverables, but getting your plan financed isn't credible because that depends on you, not your plan.

- Wanting a turnkey business plan. That just won't work. If a consultant wants to go away without you and come back with a plan, you go away first.
- Not checking references. Always ask for references of previous clients and talk to those people.
- Paying in advance. Some consultants need to ask a fair payment up front, but not the whole thing.

The worst element of outside consulting is the consultants who let you think that paying their fees will get you investment, when in fact they're just going to give you advice. This happens too frequently and it's the clients' fault too, not just the consultants.

You should immediately mistrust somebody who promises open doors and contacts as part of the job. The promise isn't credible unless the consultants very carefully filter their prospective clients and take only those whose background, track record, team and business proposition are likely to succeed. Otherwise, they're making false promises because the investors invest in the people, not the plan.

Writing a business plan is one of the least favourite activities of the majority of small business owners. The traditional rule of credit is if you want to grow and operate your business you will need a business plan to find capital. This is quickly changing as more and more business owners learn about business plan-free financing.

Change has swept through industries, society and careers. Over the last few years, change and its companion, information technology, is altering the face of small business lending.

The relationship-based banking in the small loans and credit market is becoming irrelevant. The decision of loan approval is determined by a computerized credit scoring programme unless a business requires a loan or credit product over $100,000.

Market planning

A product is nothing without a market. Regardless of how novel a product or service is, there must be a way to turn the need it satisfies into revenues. Each hotel, club, restaurant and casino has different needs for handling common issues such as modeling volume driven relationships, multiple templates for different planning needs (e.g. owned vs. franchised locations), and deployment to disparate and multiple locations. Your operation needs the flexibility to meet these divisional challenges while maintaining consistency across your business. Business Objects Planning for Hospitality delivers on both counts:

- Reduce operating expenses, improve staffing levels, and optimize revenues - all while shortening cycle time

- Track the key business drivers for your diverse operations, food and beverage, room occupancy and operations

Though time-consuming, multi-layered, and complex budgeting is a critical component of planning and controlling your day-to-day hospitality and leisure operations. To ensure more timely and accurate budgets, hotels, restaurants, casinos, and food service operators need to streamline and formalize the budgeting process-and produce detailed, yet flexible budgets that are fully aligned with strategic goals.

Business Objects solutions create budgets, sales forecasts, and payroll plans that automatically incorporate data from your long-range plans, source systems, and end users so you can move into action faster.

Whether you are running a single hotel, restaurant, or casino-or a worldwide chain of properties-you need access to timely and accurate information to make the right decisions. Incomplete or out of- date data can hamstring employees, hamper decision making, and compromise enterprise performance. With a comprehensive reporting solution, hospitality and leisure organizations like yours can ensure that the right information gets to the right people at the right time enabling management teams to make smart decisions that improve performance.

STRATEGIC PLANNING IN HOTEL MANAGEMENT

Strategic planning involves defining objectives and developing strategies to reach those objectives. It may employ methods like SWOT analysis to help clarify objectives and strategies. Strategic planning uses "the big picture" to pursue large scale, long term objectives. This is in contradistinction to "tactical" planning, which has to focuss on short term, smaller objectives. "Long range" planning typically projects current activities and programs onto a model of the external world, thereby predicting likely results. "Strategic" planning tries to "create" more desirable future results by (a) influencing the outside world or (b) adapting current programs and actions so as to have more favourable outcomes in the external environment.

Within business, strategic planning may provide overall direction strategic management to a company or give specific direction in such areas as:

- Financial strategies
- Human resource/organizational development strategies
- Information technology deployments
- Marketing strategy

We want to do Strategic Planning to:

- Have the capability to obtain the desired objective
- Fit well both with the external environment and with an organization's resources and core competencies - it should appear feasible and appropriate

- Have the capability of providing an organization with a sustainable competitive advantage - ideally through uniqueness and sustainability
- Prove dynamic, flexible, and able to adapt to changing situations
- Suffice on its own - specifically providing favorable outcomes without the need for cross-subsidization

Most strategic planning methodologies depend on a three-step process (sometimes called the STP process):

- Situation - evaluate the current situation and how it came about
- Target - define goals and/or objectives (sometimes called ideal state)
- Path - map a possible route to the goals/objectives

An alternative approach is called Draw-See-Think

- Draw - what is the ideal image or the desired end state?
- See - what is today's situation? What is the gap from ideal and why?
- Think - what specific actions must be taken to close the gap between today's situation and the ideal state?
- Plan - what resources are required to execute the activities?

In general terms, strategic planning can proceed incrementally or revolutionarily.

Strategic planning as a set of logical and creative steps

1. Clarification of objective (end-state) to be pursued. The following terms have been used in the literature: desired end states, plans, policies, goals, objectives, strategies, tactics and actions. Definitions vary, overlap and fail to achieve clarity. The following concept has been found useful. The items listed above may be organized in a hierarchy of means and ends and numbered as follows: Top Rank Objective (TRO), Second Rank Objective, Third Rank Objective, etc. From any rank, the objective in a lower rank answers to the question "How?" and the objective in a higher rank answers to the question "Why?" The exception is the Top Rank Objective (TRO): there is no answer to the "Why?" question. That is how the TRO is defined. An example may help to clarify the concept presented above.
2. Information gathering and analysis. This includes an external assessment (such as environmental scanning), and an internal resource assessment. Morphological analysis may be applied to both internal resource assessments and external assessments. SWOT (Strengths, Weaknesses, Opportunities, Threats) Analysis may be used to assess those aspects of the organization and the environment that are important to achieving the objective of the strategic plan.
3. Evaluation of the feasibility of the objective in view of the SWOTs.
4. Strategy-development. This is a creative step that answers these four questions: How can we use the Strengths, stop the Weaknesses, exploit the Opportunities and defend against the Threats in pursuit of the selected objetive.

5. Developing Action Programs for the more attractive strategies, covering: Name of the strategy, Benefits to be expected from implementing this programme, Actions: What will be done? Responsible persons: Who will be in charge of the programme? Timing: When will the programme start? When will it be completed? Location(s): Where will the programme be implemented? Resources: What will be needed: people, money, information, other resources? Control System: How will progress be measured and reported? Rewards for performance, if any. Contingency plans: What will be done if results fall short?

Strategy as Revolution

- Identify the unquestioned beliefs in the organization and challenge them - look for opportunities to re-write the rules of the environment
- Look for major discontinuities in technology, and embrace such changes wholeheartedly - do not waste time making small incremental adjustments - stand by to create a completely new business model at any time
  - More a mind-set than a formal technique
  - Not rule or ritual-oriented, not reductionist, not reactive, not autocratic

Theorists frequently make the distinction between strategy and tactics. Strategy involves planning how to get where one wants to go. Tactics can potentially comprise the implementation of such over-arching plans.

They deal with specific actions by particular people or by particular groups. Some theorists see it as a mistake to separate strategy and tactics. Constantinos Markides describes strategy formation and implementation (tactics) as an on-going, never-ending, integrated process requiring continuous re-assessment and reformation. He sees strategic planning as both planned and emergent - dynamic and interactive. J. Moncrieff also stresses strategy dynamics - he recognizes strategy as partially deliberate and partially unplanned.

The unplanned element comes from two sources:

1. Emergent strategies - resulting from the emergence of opportunities and threats in the environment
2. Strategies in action - ad hoc actions by many people from all parts of an organization

Strategic plans typically look 5 or more years into the future. They differ in this respect from tactical plans (sometimes referred to as functional plans), which look 2 to 4 years into the future; and from operational plans [such as budgets] which have an annual scope.

Finally, strategic planning is not what you think you want to do but a thing that you have to do.

Situational Analysis

When developing Corporate strategies, analysis of the company and environment as it is at the moment and how it will be in the future, is very necessary, this is called the analysis phase of strategic planning. The analysis has to be executed at an internal level as well as an external level to identify all opportunities and threats of the new strategy.

One aspect of internal analysis that has been underestimated through the last decades in developing corporate strategies is the field of corporate cultures. Consultants, when developing corporate strategies, are mostly focused on tangible internal and external factors when analyzing the company and did not really take the cultural, often intangible and invisible, aspects into account.

Identifying Cultures

When creating new corporate strategies, or adjusting existing ones, as said in the introduction, the business consultant most generally starts by analyzing the following aspects of an organization:

1. Visionary aspects such as goals and objectives.
2. Situational aspects such as financial information, company structure and systems and the business which the company is operating in.
3. External aspects concerning the environment, market findings, competitors and rules and legislations that apply to the region the company is in.
4. Technical aspects that concern the amount of risk involved in the new strategy, the time span the strategy has to be enrolled in and resources and inputs required.

The one aspect that is not often thought of is the cultural aspect of a company. With culture we mean:

"Culture is a series of values, standard interpretations, insights and ways of thinking that is shared by members of an organization and is passed on to new members of this organization."

This is hardly plausible when thinking of the resistance and problems a group of employees can cause if they oppose to-be-employed or already-employed strategies. The relation between culture and strategy has been described thoroughly by Kono :

"The product-market strategy defines the work which employees have to do. If the work requires a high level of competence and new skills, this revitalizes the culture. The strategy also affects the financial performance and the level of salaries and incentives which are available to employees. On the other hand, the effective implementation of new strategies depends on the creativity of the employees and their willingness to change."

Kono precisely describes the relation that the company culture and the company strategy have with each other, they are interdependent. So it is key to analyze the company culture as well as possible, to be able to adjust the 'to be developed' strategy the best way possible to avoid conflicts and maximize compatibility.

Perspectives

To analyze the culture of a company, one has to use some kind of perspective to look at the artifacts (visible or not) that are active within the company and describe its culture. Basically two important schools with their perspectives can be distinguished:

- Ethnographical versus clinical analysis
- Functionalistic versus Interpretionistic analysis

This approach towards analyzing corporate cultures has been developed by Schein and makes the distinction between the following two ways of looking at artifacts within a company:

- Ethnographical – Focused on concrete data to understand the culture, which is mostly used for scientific research. Researchers who use this ethnographical way of analysis start with some predefined assumptions and try to find proof for these assumptions when investigating the organization.
- Clinical – Focused on cultural processes that are active within the organization and how these processes can be adjusted or modified to achieve a certain goal. Hereby looking at indicators such as artifacts, values and assumptions.

Functionalistic Versus Interpretionistic Approach

- The functionalistic approach towards analyzing culture is concerned with merely the same aspects as the clinical approach and is aimed at analyzing current cultural signals that can possibly be extracted to be used in other organizations
- The interpretionistic approach is more interested in the processes that form the coherence between employees in the same company. The interpretionistic approach thus is more aimed at communicational processes between employees in contrary to the more 'describing' way of the functionalistic approach.

Visible Artifacts

Visible artifacts include the following and can be experienced and analysed fairly easy because of the extrovert character they have. Visible artifacts include:

- Rituals and ceremonies
- Organization Stories
- Symbols
- Business Language

The business language of a company is the use of language employees speak, common used words and textual expressions that characterize the companies culture.

Invisible Artifacts

Next to visible artifacts, a company's culture also thrives on processes and events that are not that easily seen by outside consultants or even in-house employees.

These include:

- Value (personal and cultural)
- Assumptions
- Perspectives
- Attitudes
- Feelings

When looking at these invisible artifacts, one can state that these are of great value when creating a new corporate strategy, the attitudes and feelings that employees have towards for example radical changes can make or break your corporate strategy. The company's strategy also depends on the external / internal focus and needs from the environment of the company.

Culture Types

When setting the external versus internal strategic focus against the environmental needs (flexibility versus stability) The following figure emerges: to be very externally oriented when it comes to the strategic focus. Companies that hold this culture are flexible and able to respond to outside needs and changes fast and adequately. Employees are stimulated to be innovative. Examples of these companies today are mainly in the services-sector such as online marketplaces like eBay or online communities such as Hyves in the Netherlands.

- Mission Culture: The mission culture is externally oriented like the adjustment based entrepreneurial culture, but is not subject to quick environmental and external changes. Companies that have the mission culture are focused on reaching targets that have been set earlier in order to be competitive. A company such as Iriver (Korea), which is a company that produces mp3 players, is a good example. Iriver is very externally focused, and copies existing mp3 player models like the Apple iPod, but is also very focused on internal targets to guarantee low prices.
- Clan Culture: The clan culture is focused at flexibility when it comes to external needs, but this is reached through excellence of the employees, which makes the strategic focus internally focused. Examples of companies who fit the clan culture are Baan and IBM who are mainly considering the wellbeing of their employees as top priority and have the intention not to fire a single employee from the company perspective.
- Bureaucratic Culture: The bureaucratic culture is internally focused and operates in a market that is not demanding high flexibility.

Examples are some government institutions or insurance companies. When a company's culture is analyzed, by using one of the perspectives used before, artifacts will make clear in what part of the quadrant (or very possibly also a combination of more than one) a company is in according to their culture. This information can be valuable to adjust the corporate strategy too but it can also be valuable to identify the current culture and change it according to for example changing needs from the external environment.

Changing Cultures and Strategy

When a corporate strategy is developed, or an existing strategy is altered, the previous sections prove that the culture aspect of an organization is important because it can oppose new strategies when culture and strategy do not fit together.

When a culture does not match the strategy that is going to be deployed (which for some reason cannot be altered to the culture because of a changing external environment for example), some tactics to change this culture are available.

Approaches

1. The All-Out attack: The all out approach of implementing a new culture consists of removing all the cultural and strategic plans that are active at the moment and turn it all around. This is mainly done when a big conglomerate acquires another company and wants to enroll their own culture and strategic goals.
2. The inside venture approach: This tactic is based on the power of internal rewards and innovation. A company encourages employees to be innovative and come up with new ideas, and reward their employees with their own project team when the idea is feasible enough. This leads to a better external focus (employees are more focused on customer needs) and results in a company that is very flexible to the environmental needs.
3. Strategic alliance or Alliances: Include efforts such as joint ventures with other companies.
4. Organizational and Personnel management approach: When changing a corporate culture, expanding of the organizational (which formulates and regulates the strategies) and personnel departments is advisory.

Resistance

When situations change, especially not for the better, people generally resist this. When changing a culture, resistance will most probably also occur, resistance which most of the time is the result of the organizational climate, the shared meaning of employees about the way things go around in the company. Afterall, humans are creatures of habit and generally resist organisational change.

The existence of subcultures can also be a great cause of resistance and opposition against new plans. Subcultures, as the name says, are cultures with other assumptions and beliefs when compared to the general companywide culture. Subcultures can be horizontal (within the same hierarchical layer) or vertical (from manager to work floor employees) which in general can even cause more problems when changes are at hand.

Measurements

- A status ladder system: A skill based method of paying your employees, derived from Japan, which pays employees according to the knowledge and capabilities they have instead of the jobs they perform.
- Salary Reduction
- Job Transfers
- Early retirements
- Less recruiting

These measurements are mainly meant to keep employees at the company, even though the new corporate strategy will change things inside the company.

The External Environment

The element of the environment that has the most immediate impact, and one which dominated management activities in the 1980s and 1990s - competitive strategy. Following the widely accepted frameworks developed by Michael Porter, this initially concentrates on the competitive features of different industry types, and in particular the entry barriers to them. The main part, however, revolves around competitive responses and strategies, especially between leaders and followers.

However, Pfeffer and Salancik made the following comment:

"The key to organizational survival is the ability to acquire and maintain resources. This problem would be simplified if organizations were in complete control of all the components necessary for their operation. However, no organization is completely self-contained. Organizations are embedded in an environment composed of other organizations. They depend on those organizations for the many resources they themselves require. Organizations are linked to environments by federations, associations, customer-supplier relationships, competitive relationships and a socio-legal apparatus defining and controlling the nature and limits of those relationships."

Most organizations, however, seem (at least formally) to ignore this dimension of their business. If they are well managed, they devote immense efforts to optimizing the internal factors which are within their control; but they barely notice what is happening outside, and make little attempt to formally manage that side of their activities, except for some marketing responses. A major element of that outside environment is made up from the factors which are now grouped under the global heading of 'marketing'. Beyond this, however, there is a whole range of social and political factors which may have even greater impact. Not least is the impact of government regulation, which may make or break whole sectors of industry.

Theoretical Frameworks

As is frequently the case in marketing, a number of alternative frameworks for studying the wider environment are offered, the most conventional of which describes it in terms of an ' - onion :

This is a useful approach, since it distinguishes between three different degrees of interaction:

- Organization (or internal environment) -This includes those activities, contained totally - within - the organization itself, which make up the daily life of most organizations.
- Marketing environment -This is the area of the external environment which has the most immediate impact on organizations, and is generally recognized by them (and is the subject of much of this book).
- External environment -This is often not recognized as a force impinging on organizations; and yet, as we have seen, it may well contain the - major - factors which determine the performance of that organization.

These external factors are most often grouped as the - STEP - factors (Social, Technological, Economic and Political). They can have dramatic effects on organizations. The (political) results of legislation, for example, determine the boundaries of the actions of most organizations, and yet they are often 'taken as read', and are a relatively unnoticed element of organizational performance.

Cultural traditions are not easily overturned, but over the years they can change quite significantly - without the organizations involved noticing. From the 1970s to the Millennium, for example, the role of woman in society - and, in particular, woman's role at work - changed dramatically; and this was of considerable significance to those supplying services to women. No longer could they assume that the average woman was the stereotypical housewife. The women's magazine industry, as one example, was changed out of all recognition.

Over the past two decades there have been major changes in a number of areas of the overall sociocultural environment. The 'Information Revolution' in particular had a measurable impact on the patterns of employment; with economists pointing to a degree of 'structural unemployment' caused by its progress. It is arguable, indeed, that the social effects of this particular 'revolution' will dominate many of the changes in society over the coming two decades.

Related to this particular 'technological' driver, there have been a number of predictions made about how society will change. One of the earlier ones, and also one of the most influential, was that by Daniel Bell, concerning the development of the - post-industrial society -

As early as the 1970s he specified five dimensions, or components, of this:

1. Economic sector: the change from a goods-producing to a service economy
2. Occupational distribution: the pre-eminence of the professional and technical class
3. Axial principle: the centrality of theoretical knowledge as the source of innovation and of policy formulation for the society
4. Future orientation: the control of technology and technological assessment
5. Decision making: the creation of a new 'intellectual technology'.

As with many such 'forecasts', the pace of change has been slower than Daniel Bell expected. However, Bell recognized that his 'forecast' was based as much on hope and desire as on rational projection. In the context of his fifth element, for instance, he added:

"The goal of the new intellectual technology is neither more or less to realize a social alchemist's dream, the dream of `ordering' the mass of society... That this dream - as utopian, in its way, as the dreams of a perfect `commonwealth' - has faltered is laid, on the part of its believers, to the known human resistance.

From the point of view of the marketer, perhaps the most important predicted change is that from a materialist society to a post-materialist one. It is only fair to report that 'post-materialism' is taking longer to arrive than its most ardent supporters would wish.

Some changes are, however, totally predictable. The most obvious, and possibly the most important, are those resulting from demography. The 'baby boom' of the 1960s, and the subsequent dramatic decline in birth rates, have produced very different cohorts of population; with accompanying (totally predictable) changes in earnings and consumption.

The impact of changing technology is also a major factor in the development of the external environment. The 'Information Revolution' already mentioned is just one example of changes driven by technology.

The direct impact of new technology on organizations may be obvious. Even then, 'marketing myopia' -where they are so involved in short-term problems that they cannot see wider perspectives which will determine the future - may blind them to the obvious. Less apparent, though, are the social or 'structural' changes generated by such new technology. The 'Information Revolution' is having its wider impact, for one example, by allowing much smaller organizations to achieve 'economies of scale'. In the larger organizations it is having a different effect by encouraging horizontal communications (via electronic mail) to take over from the traditional vertical (hierarchical) organization; and in the process is creating new structures which are close to those of Japanese companies.

Peter Senker identified four main 'drivers' in the field of technology:

1. Information technology
2. New materials
3. Environmental issues
4. Biotechnology

Some of the 'theory' of marketing is also shared with other academic disciplines - or at least appears to be! Thus, although the 'market' is clearly at the heart of marketing, it has also become central to economic theory; and, indeed, to the basic philosophies of 'capitalism'. The way in which each of these two disciplines approaches the concept of the market could not, however, be more different.

The population in general, and the business community in particular, have uncritically accepted the basic tentets of economics as the given fundamentals of business life. Put simply, it is widely believed that economic theory accurately describes what happens in the wider business world. The reality (at least as described by marketing theory - and, even more clearly, by marketing practice) is often very different.

In the earliest days there was very little practical difference between economics and any theory of business management; or of 'marketing' as then practised, in a society which had few surpluses to exchange. Adam Smith wrote his justifiably renowned - Wealth of Nations - as a treatise to be studied as much by businessmen as by government.

Even in the Victorian period, 'neoclassical' economics, as developed by Alfred Marshall for example, was still spending much of its time trying to describe practical business processes, albeit in more scientific terms. The 'laws of supply and demand', which now lie at the heart of modern micro-economics, represented a practical attempt to describe how prices were set at a time when almost all major markets were commodity markets, and the one variable which the seller could control was price.

At that time the political debate, led by Karl Marx, revolved around the ownership of the capital involved (and hence, most importantly, ownership of the profit), together with the associated division of wealth and income. 'Capitalism' was about just that - about who owned the capital. It too, in its own perverse way, was firmly based on conventional economic theory. Even so, business economics, or the related 'micro-economics', remained closely linked to actual business activities through the first half of the twentieth century.

Economists, however, increasingly focused on the need to create a body of theory which would justify their claim that economics was a legitimate academic discipline. At this time 'macro-economics', that element which described the factors pertaining to the economy as a whole (and was clearly the responsibility of government rather than business), was split off as a separate subject - particularly after the pioneering work of Lord Keynes became generally accepted - to become the part of economics which received the most publicity.

The debate about whether the government should control demand or supply was won, in the 1970s, by the latter view (now espoused by many governments).

Over the same period, the political basis of capitalism has also shifted. As described above, the key factor had been seen to be the ownership of capital; the prime need was for 'profit' to stimulate the 'entrepreneur' to innovate, and improve business efficiency. Indeed, it had previously been widely believed that the strength of the capitalist West derived from that profit motive, which by itself led to enterprises almost automatically being better managed; for the good of all involved.

Unfortunately, by the 1970s, after the development of the global money markets, and after Kenneth Galbraith's very influential teachings, it had become clear that, at least in terms of routine operations, ownership of capital had largely become divorced from the management of most large organizations.

The political theme then became that of the 'market'. The great benefit of 'capitalism', it thus emerged, was that the 'market' was the best (and only 'natural') mechanism for allocating resources; for deciding how demand could be met. 'The discipline of the market' or the 'virtue of market-led economies', then became the central theme of 'capitalist' governments; and is now espoused almost as enthusiastically by the governments of the former communist bloc.

Modern micro-economics experiences no theoretical problem in describing the activities of the ' - perfect firm - '. This 'ideal' organization is involved in perfect competition, where price is the one dominant factor (and this, above all, is the element manipulated in the many economic equations which are used to describe that firm). All decisions are taken rationally, based upon maximization of monetary outcomes (profit), where all the relationships are exactly known; and can be plotted upon definitive graphs.

In the 1990s the 'transaction cost' approach explored the relationships between economic theory and business management, by looking at the difference in `transaction costs' between the alternatives considered, as the reason for the logical choice made. This field of theory has, in particular, concentrated upon business structure - including the `make' or `buy in' decision. Here it argued, with some success, that the firm's decision as to whether to `make' a component itself or buy it from a supplier is (or at least should be) taken on `cost' grounds (though the definition of `cost' was complex than normal). Transaction costs however further got complicated and therefore a number of ERP solutions cropped up to reslove them to a great extent.

Whatever the approach, micro-economics finds considerable difficulty in dealing with ' - imperfect competition -', since no generally agreed model for representing this state of affairs has yet emerged. Worst of all, particularly in the current climate of uncertainty, it cannot easily handle the 'fuzzy' relationships which do not fit neatly into the exact equations. Finally, as Kenneth Galbraith and others so succinctly observed, management decision-making is often anything but rational; and is frequently not designed to achieve the simple monetary outcomes which are the staple diet of economics - and instead reflect rather more complex motivations.

Marketing, which has grown as a business function over this period (while economics has waned, in terms of its comparable use as a business management tool), thrives on precisely these elements, which are the stuff of real business life. Thus, the aim of every brand manager is to make competition ever - more - imperfect (aiming for the 'ideal' brand which holds a monopoly over its customers, who will stridently demand Carlsberg beer and reject any alternatives). In this environment the 'intangible' (and often seemingly irrational) needs and wants of the customer predominate. The tools of marketing are frequently the 'creative' tools which address the 'fuzzy' areas; of formulating the most attractive product or service, and of developing the most effective promotions. Having to compete on price, as the micro-economists would ideally wish for, is usually seen as defeat by such marketers.

Thus, there are many disadvantages to adopting the pure economic view-point. On the other hand, there still remain some clear advantages to investigating such an economic perspective. In particular, economics has benefited from almost a century of concentrated academic activity; developing a rigorous, logical, framework. It is the rigidity of thinking imposed by this framework which has often now detached it from real life. But the very strength of this body of academic theory means that economics can offer a useful reference framework with which to compare many marketing decisions.

The boundaries within which organizations can operate are frequently set by legislation; from the ingredients they can legally put into their products to the buildings that their employees are allowed to work in. Pressure groups campaign directly to change legislation, but also work indirectly to change the public's buying habits.

Organizations themselves may well join pressure groups, to force government to protect their entrenched positions, and are often very successful.

It might be thought that only the larger organizations are the direct targets of pressure groups or have the resources to be involved in pressure groups themselves; but it is just as important that the smaller organizations understand the political machinations which are taking place around them, and which have a major, albeit relatively unseen, impact.

Most aspects of marketing transactions will be covered by one or other form of legislation; not least that of contract law. The marketing manager or sales manager, then, must be well aware of those aspects that most directly affect them; and this will vary from industry to industry, and from country to country. The chemicals industry, for instance, is driven by legislation on safety, whereas financial services providers in the UK look to the Financial Services Act. Most managers, however, should at least understand exactly what their own contract means; and, even more importantly, what the implications are when others insist that their own contractual terms are followed instead.

The laws which affect your business need to be handled expertly, by specialists, for two main reasons:

- Specificity - there is a vast array of laws, only some of which affect individual industries or organizations in specific countries
- Currency - more importantly, laws change, often quite rapidly

The pressure group which has had the most direct impact on organizations in recent years has been that of the consumer movement; to which has now been added the environmental lobby and the green movement. The motivation of these movements has been sincere, no matter how annoying they may have been to the producers that they have targeted. They have aimed to benefit the consumer - high ideals, which are in stark contrast with those of some of the rather more self-interested industrial pressure groups.

These movements are often closer to the average consumer than the supplier. What they urge often makes very good marketing sense; and their views are often a sound guide to what future legislation may bring.

A concept which has recently emerged is that there are a number of different groups which can claim an interest or 'stake' (Gareth Morgan actually referred to them as 'multiple stakeholders') in the organization. Using a now more usual terminology, Lusch and Lusch define the 'public' of an organization as 'any group which has an actual or potential interest or impact on an organization's ability to achieve its objectives'.

Traditionally, especially in the view of economists, only the owners (the 'stockholders') have been legitimately entitled to an interest in what the organization does. More recently it has been recognized that employees' interests should also be taken into account.

The power of the financial stakeholders should not, however, be under-estimated. It is often seen in its most active form (at least by the defenders) when acquisitions or mergers take place (not infrequently on an 'unfriendly' basis).

The rationale for mergers and acquisitions is not always financial. It is, indeed, often for reasons related to marketing; in the diplomatic terms which accompany such manoeuvres, 'to obtain some synergy from complementary marketing assets', or in more forthright terms, 'to try and increase monopolistic control over customers'.

Strategic planning is a very important business activity. It is practiced widely. In spite of that, it is not done well. All strategic planning and decision processes must start with agreed upon objectives (desired end states). In practice and in the literature, this is a murky area.

The following terms have been used in Strategic Planning: desired end states, plans, policies, goals, objectives, strategies, tactics and actions. Definitions vary, overlap and fail to achieve clarity.

Differences between a current situation and a future aspirational state can appear as a deficiency or as a gap. Objectives and goal management serve to eliminate this gap. Some writers distinguish between goals (inexactly formulated aims that lack specificity) and objectives (aims formulated exactly and quantitatively as to time-frames and magnitude of effect). For example, a gambler might have the ambiguous goal: "I want to get lucky tonight". Converting this into an objective, it might become: "I want to make $100 at the blackjack table by 8 o'clock tonight." Not all authors make this distinction, preferring to use the two terms interchangeably.

In the financial arena, or when talking statistically, one often refers to goals as "targets". People typically have several goals at the same time. "Goal congruency" refers to how well the goals combine with each other. Does goal A appear compatible with goal B? Do they fit together to form a unified strategy? "Goal hierarchy" consists of the nesting of one or more goals within other goal(s).

One approach recommends having short-term goals, medium-term goals, and long-term goals. In this model, one can expect to attain short-term goals fairly easily: they stand just slightly above one's reach. At the other extreme, long-term goals appear very difficult, almost impossible to attain. Strategic management jargon sometimes refers to "Big Hairy Audacious Goals" (BHAGs) in this context.) Using one goal as a stepping-stone to the next involves goal sequencing. A person or group starts by attaining the easy short-term goals, then steps up to the medium-term, then to the long-term goals. Goal sequencing can create a "goal stairway".In an organizational setting, the organization may co-ordinate goals so that they do not conflict with each other. The goals of one part of the organization should mesh compatibly with those of other parts of the organization.

Individuals within organizations will typically have personal goals. Although individuals often have goals that oppose organizational goals (such as having as high a salary as possible), if personal goals diverge too incompatibly from organizational goals they may result in limited progress towards the mere organizational goals.

Organizations sometimes summarize goals and objectives into a mission statement and / or a vision statement:

- A Definition of Vision in a dictionary: 'An Image of the future we seek to create'.

A vision statement describes in graphic terms where the goal-setters want to see themselves in the future. It may describe how they see events unfolding over 10 or 20 years if everything goes exactly as hoped.

- A definition of Mission in a dictionary: purpose, reason for being; also, an inner calling to pursue an activity or perform a service.

Many people mistake vision statement for mission statement. The Vision describes a future identity and the Mission describes how it will be achieved. A Mission statement may define the purpose or broader goal for being in existence or in the business. It serves as an ongoing guide without time frame. The mission can remain the same for decades if crafted well. Vision is more specific in terms of objective and future state. Vision is related to some form of achievement if successful.

For example, "We help transport goods and people efficiently and cost effectively without damaging environment" is a mission statement. Ford's brief but powerful slogan "Quality is Job 1" could count as a mission statement. "We will be one amongst the top three transporters of goods and people in North America by 2010" is a vision statement. It is very concrete and unambiguous goal.

Mission and Values go hand in hand. To make the mission statement effective, it needs to be aligned with the prevailing culture of its stakeholders, organization, market and political sphere. A lofty mission statement means nothing if it is not in congruence with the values practiced by the organization. A statement of values provides guiding principles when ethical issues related to realizing the Vision, and undertaking the Mission, arise.

A mission statement can resemble a vision statement in a few companies, but that can be a grave mistake. It can confuse people. The vision statement can galvanize the people to achieve defined objectives, even if they are stretch objectives, provided the vision is SMART (Specific, Measurable, Achievable, Realistic and Timebound). A mission statement provides a path to realize the vision in line with its values. These statements have a direct bearing on the bottomline and success of the organization.

Features of an effective vision statement may include:

- Clarity and lack of ambiguity
- Paint a vivid and clear picture, not ambiguous
- Describing a bright future (hope)
- Memorable and engaging expression
- Realistic aspirations, achievable
- Alignment with organizational values and culture, Rational
- Time bound if it talks of achieving any goal or objective

In order to become really effective, an organizational vision statement must (the theory states) become assimilated into the organization's culture. Leaders have the responsibility of communicating the vision regularly, creating narratives that illustrate the vision, acting as role-models by embodying the vision, creating short-term objectives compatible with the vision, and encouraging others to craft their own personal vision compatible with the organization's overall vision.

In general, strategic plans can fail for two types of reasons: inappropriate strategy and poor implementation.

Inappropriate strategies may arise due to:

- Failure to define end states (objectives) correctly
- Incomplete SWOT analysis with respect to the desired end state(s)
- Lack of creativity in identifying possible strategies

- Strategies incapable of obtaining the desired objective
- Poor fit between the external environment and organizational resources - infeasibility

Poor implementation of a strategy may happen due to:

- Over-estimation of resources and abilities
- Under-estimation of time, personnel, or financial requirements
- Failure to coordinate
- Ineffective attempts to gain the support of others or resistance
- Failure to follow the plan
- Loss of senior management focus and continued sponsorship

CONDUCTING STRATEGIC PLANNING

Many managers spend most of their time "fighting fires" in the workplace. — their time is spent realizing and reacting to problems. For these managers — and probably for many of us — it can be very difficult to stand back and take a hard look at what we want to accomplish and how we want to accomplish it.

We're too buy doing what we think is making progress. However, one of the major differences between new and experienced managers is the skill to see the broad perspective, to take the long view on what we want to do and how we're going to do it. One of the best ways to develop this skill is through ongoing experience in strategic planning.

The following guidelines may help you to get the most out of your strategic planning experience.

1. The real benefit of the strategic planning process is the process, not the plan document.
2. There is no "perfect" plan. There's doing your best at strategic thinking and implementation, and learning from what you're doing to enhance what you're doing the next time around.
3. The strategic planning process is usually not an experience. It's like the management process itself — it's a series of small moves that together keep the organization doing things right as it heads in the right direction.
4. In planning, things usually aren't as bad as you fear nor as good as you'd like.
5. Start simple, but start!

You may want to consider using a facilitator from outside of your organization if:

1. Your organization has not conducted strategic planning before.
2. For a variety of reasons, previous strategic planning was not deemed to be successful.
3. There appears to be a wide range of ideas and/or concerns among organization members about strategic planning and current organizational issues to be addressed in the plan.

4. There is no one in the organization whom members feel has sufficient facilitation skills.
5. No one in the organization feels committed to facilitating strategic planning for the organization.
6. Leaders believe that an inside facilitator will either inhibit participation from others or will not have the opportunity to fully participate in planning themselves.
7. Leaders want an objective voice, i.e., someone who is not likely to have strong predispositions about the organization's strategic issues and ideas.

Strategic planning should be conducted by a planning team.

Consider the following guidelines when developing the team.

1. The chief executive and board chair should be included in the planning group, and should drive development and implementation of the plan.
2. Establish clear guidelines for membership, for example, those directly involved in planning, those who will provide key information to the process, those who will review the plan document, those who will authorize the document, etc.
3. A primary responsibility of a board of directors is strategic planning to effectively lead the organization. Therefore, insist that the board be strongly involved in planning, often including assigning a planning committee (often, the same as the executive committee).
4. Ask if the board membership is representative of the organization's clientele and community, and if they are not, the organization may want to involve more representation in planning. If the board chair or chief executive balks at including more of the board members in planning, then the chief executive and/or board chair needs to seriously consider how serious the organization is about strategic planning!
5. Always include in the group, at least one person who ultimately has authority to make strategic decisions, for example, to select which goals will be achieved and how.
6. Ensure that as many stakeholders as possible are involved in the planning process.
7. Involve at least those who are responsible for composing and implementing the plan.
8. Involve someone to administrate the process, including arranging meetings, helping to record key information, helping with flipcharts, monitoring status of prework, etc.
9. Consider having the above administrator record the major steps in the planning process to help the organization conduct its own planning when the plan is next updated.
10. Different types of members may be needed more at different times in the planning process, for example, strong board involvement in

determining the organization's strategic direction (mission, vision, and values), and then more staff involvement in determining the organization's strategic analysis to determine its current issues and goals, and then primarily the staff to determine the strategies needed to address the issues and meet the goals.

11. In general, where there's any doubt about whether a certain someone should be involved in planning, it's best to involve them. It's worse to exclude someone useful then it is to have one or two extra people in planning — this is true in particular with organizations where board members often do not have extensive expertise about the organization and its products or services.
12. Therefore, an organization may be better off to involve board and staff planners as much as possible in all phases of planning. Mixing the board and staff during planning helps board members understand the day-to-day issues of the organization, and helps the staff to understand the top-level issues of the organization.

Planning Meetings

1. New planners usually want to know how many meetings will be needed and what is needed for each meeting, i.e., they want a procedure for strategic planning. The number of meetings depends on whether the organization has done planning before, how many strategic issues and goals the organization faces, whether the culture of the organization prefers short or long meetings, and how much time the organization is willing to commit to strategic planning.
2. Attempt to complete strategic planning in at most two to three months, or momentum will be lost and the planning effort may fall apart.

Scheduling of Meetings

1. Have each meeting at most two to three weeks apart when planning. It's too easy to lose momentum otherwise.
2. The most important factor in accomplishing complete attendance to planning meetings is evidence of strong support from executives. Therefore, ensure that executives a) issue clear direction that they strongly support and value the strategic planning process, and b) are visibly involved in the planning process.

One example of a brief planning process is the following which includes four planning meetings and develops a top-level strategic plan which is later translated into a yearly operating plan by the staff:

1. Planning starts with a half-day or all-day board retreat and includes introductions by the board chair and/or chief executive, their explanations of the organization's benefits from strategic planning and the organization's commitment to the planning process, the

facilitator's overview of the planning process, and the board chairs and/or chief executive's explanation of who will be involved in the planning process. In the retreat, the organization may then begin the next step in planning, whether this be visiting their mission, vision, values, etc. or identifying current issues and goals to which strategies will need to be developed. (Goals are often reworded issues.) Planners are asked to think about strategies before the next meeting.

2. The next meeting focuses on finalizing strategies to deal with each issue. Before the next meeting, a subcommittee is charged to draft the planning document, which includes updated mission, vision, and values, and also finalized strategic issues, goals, strategies. This document is distributed before the next meeting.
3. In the next meeting, planners exchange feedback about the content and format of the planning document. Feedback is incorporated in the document and it is distributed before the next meeting.
4. The next meeting does not require entire attention to the plan, e.g., the document is authorized by the board during a regular board meeting.
5. Note that in the above example, various subcommittees might be charged to gather additional information and distribute it before the next planning meeting.
6. Note, too, that the staff may take this document and establish a yearly operating plan which details what strategies will be implemented over the next year, who will do them, and by when.
7. No matter how serious organizations are about strategic planning, they usually have strong concerns about being able to find time to attend frequent meetings. This concern can be addressed by ensuring meetings are well managed, having short meetings as needed rather than having fewer but longer meetings, and having realistic expectations from the planning project.

A frequent complaint about the strategic planning process is that it produces a document that ends up collecting dust on a shelf — the organization ignores the precious information depicted in the document.

The following guidelines will help ensure that the plan is implemented.

(Note that reference to boards of directors is in regard to organizations that are corporations.)

1. When conducting the planning process, involve the people who will be responsible for implementing the plan. Use a cross-functional team (representatives from each of the major organization's products or service) to ensure the plan is realistic and collaborative.
2. Ensure the plan is realistic. Continue asking planning participants "Is this realistic? Can you really do this?"
3. Organize the overall strategic plan into smaller action plans, often including an action plan (or work plan) for each committee on the board.

4. In the overall planning document, specify who is doing what and by when (action plans are often referenced in the implementation section of the overall strategic plan). Some organizations may elect to include the action plans in a separate document from the strategic plan, which would include only the mission, vision, values, key issues and goals, and strategies. This approach carries some risk that the board will lose focus on the action plans.
5. In an implementation section in the plan, specify and clarify the plan's implementation roles and responsibilities. Be sure to detail particularly the first 90 days of the implementation of the plan. Build in regular reviews of status of the implementation of the plan.
6. Translate the strategic plan's actions into job descriptions and personnel performance reviews.
7. Communicate the role of follow-ups to the plan. If people know the action plans will be regularly reviewed, implementers tend to do their jobs before they're checked on.
8. Be sure to document and distribute the plan, including inviting review input from all.
9. Be sure that one internal person has ultimate responsibility that the plan is enacted in a timely fashion.
10. The chief executive's support of the plan is a major driver to the plan's implementation. Integrate the plan's goals and objectives into the chief executive's performance reviews.
11. Place huge emphasis on feedback to the board's executive committee from the planning participants.
    Consider all or some of the following to ensure the plan is implemented.
12. Have designated rotating "checkers" to verify, e.g., every quarter, if each implementer completed their assigned tasks.
13. Have pairs of people be responsible for tasks. Have each partner commit to helping the other to finish the other's tasks on time.

A frequent complaint about strategic plans is that they are merely "to-do" lists of what to accomplish over the next few years. Or, others complain that strategic planning never seems to come in handy when the organization is faced with having to make a difficult, major decision. Or, other complains that strategic planning really doesn't help the organization face the future. These complaints arise because organizations fail to conduct a thorough strategic analysis as part of their strategic planning process. Instead, planners decide to plan only from what they know now. This makes the planning process much less strategic and a lot more guesswork. Strategic analysis is the heart of the strategic planning process and should not be ignored.

Phases in Planning

Whether the system is an organization, department, business, project, etc., the basic planning process typically includes similar nature of activities carried out in similar sequence. The phases are carried out carefully or — in some cases — intuitively, for example, when planning a very small, straightforward effort. The complexity of the various phases (and their duplication throughout the system) depend on the scope of the system. For example, in a large corporation, the following phases would be carried out in the corporate offices, in each division, in each department, in each group, etc.

During planning, planners have in mind (consciously or unconsciously) some overall purpose or result that the plan is to achieve. For example, during strategic planning, it's critical to reference the mission, or overall purpose, of the organization.

For example, during strategic planning, planners often conduct a "SWOT analysis". (SWOT is an acronym for considering the organization's strengths and weaknesses, and the opportunities and threats faced by the organization.) During this analysis, planners also can use a variety of assessments, or methods to "measure" the health of systems.

Based on the analysis and alignment to the overall mission of the system, planners establish a set of goals that build on strengths to take advantage of opportunities, while building up weaknesses and warding off threats. The particular strategies (or methods to reach the goals) chosen depend on matters of affordability, practicality and efficiency. Objectives are selected to be timely and indicative of progress toward goals. Responsibilities are assigned, including for implementation of the plan, and for achieving various goals and objectives. Ideally, deadlines are set for meeting each responsibility.

The above information is organized and written in a document which is distributed around the system.

This critical step is often ignored — which can eventually undermine the success of many of your future planning efforts. The purpose of a plan is to address a current problem or pursue a development goal. It seems simplistic to assert that you should acknowledge if the problem was solved or the goal met. However, this step in the planning process is often ignored in lieu of moving on the next problem to solve or goal to pursue. Skipping this step can cultivate apathy and skepticism — even cynicism — in your organization. Don't skip this step.

A common failure in many kinds of planning is that the plan is never really implemented. Instead, all focus is on writing a plan document. Too often, the plan sits collecting dust on a shelf. Therefore, most of the following guidelines help to ensure that the planning process is carried out completely and is implemented completely — or, deviations from the intended plan are recognized and managed accordingly.

Going back to the reference to systems, it's critical that all parts of the system continue to exchange feedback in order to function effectively. This is true no matter what type of system. When planning, get input from everyone who will responsible to carry out parts of the plan, along with representative from groups who will be effected by the plan. Of course, people also should be involved in they will be responsible to review and authorize the plan.

New managers, in particular, often forget that others don't know what these managers know. Even if managers do communicate their intentions and plans verbally, chances are great that others won't completely hear or understand what the manager wants done. Also, as plans change, it's extremely difficult to remember who is supposed to be doing what and according to which version of the plan. Key stakeholders (employees, management, board members, funders, investor, customers, clients, etc.) may request copies of various types of plans. Therefore, it's critical to write plans down and communicate them widely.

For example, it's difficult to know what someone should be doing if they are to pursue the goal to "work harder". It's easier to recognize "Write a paper". It's difficult to know what the scope of "Writing a paper" really is. It's easier to appreciate that effort if the goal is "Write a 30-page paper". If I'm to take responsibility for pursuit of a goal, the goal should be acceptable to me. For example, I'm not likely to follow the directions of someone telling me to write a 30-page paper when I also have to five other papers to write. However, if you involve me in setting the goal so I can change my other commitments or modify the goal, I'm much more likely to accept pursuit of the goal as well.

Even if I do accept responsibility to pursue a goal that is specific and measurable, the goal won't be useful to me or others if, for example, the goal is to "Write a 30-page paper in the next 10 seconds". It may mean more to others if I commit to a realistic goal to "Write a 30-page paper in one week". However, it'll mean more to others (particularly if they are planning to help me or guide me to reach the goal) if I specify that I will write one page a day for 30 days, rather than including the possibility that I will write all 30 pages in last day of the 30-day period.

The goal should stretch the performer's capabilities. For example, I might be more interested in writing a 30-page paper if the topic of the paper or the way that I write it will extend my capabilities. I'm more inclined to write the paper if the paper will contribute to an effort in such a way that I might be rewarded for my effort.

Plans should specify who is responsible for achieving each result, including goals and objectives. Dates should be set for completion of each result, as well. Responsible parties should regularly review status of the plan. Be sure to have someone of authority "sign off" on the plan, including putting their signature on the plan to indicate they agree with and support its contents. Include responsibilities in policies, procedures, job descriptions, performance review processes, etc.

During the planning process, regularly collect feedback from participants. Do they agree with the planning process? If not, what don't they like and how could it be done better? In large, ongoing planning processes (such as strategic planning, business planning, project planning, etc.), it's critical to collect this kind of feedback regularly.

During regular reviews of implementation of the plan, assess if goals are being achieved or not. If not, were goals realistic? Do responsible parties have the resources necessary to achieve the goals and objectives? Should goals be changed? Should more priority be placed on achieving the goals? What needs to be done?

Finally, take 10 minutes to write down how the planning process could have been done better. File it away and read it the next time you conduct the planning process.

Far too often, primary emphasis is placed on the plan document. This is extremely unfortunate because the real treasure of planning is the planning process itself. During planning, panners learn a great deal from ongoing analysis, reflection, discussion, debates and dialogue around issues and goals in the system. Perhaps there is no better example of misplaced priorities in planning than in business ethics. Far too often, people put emphasis on written codes of ethics and codes of conduct. While these documents certainly are important, at least as important is conducting ongoing communications around these documents. The ongoing communications are what sensitize people to understanding and following the values and behaviors suggested in the codes.

A prominent example of this type of potential problem is when planners don't prefer the "top down" or "bottom up", "linear" type of planning (for example, going from general to specific along the process of an environmental scan, SWOT analysis, mission/vision/values, issues and goals, strategies, objectives, timelines, etc.) There are other ways to conduct planning.

Systems thinking

Systems thinking is an approach to analysis that is based on the belief that the component parts of a system will act differently when isolated from its environment or other parts of the system, and argues against Descartes's reductionist view. It includes viewing systems in a holistic manner, rather than through purely reductionist techniques. Systems thinking is about gaining insights into the whole by understanding the linkages and interactions between the elements that comprise the whole "system", consistent with systems philosophy. Systems Thinking recognizes that all human activity systems are open systems; therefore, they are affected by the environment in which they exist. Systems Thinking recognizes that in complex systems, events are separated by distance and time; therefore, small catalytic events can cause large changes in the system. Systems thinking acknowledges that a change in one area of a system can adversely affect another area of the system; thus, it promotes organizational communication at all levels in order to avoid the silo effect.

Systems thinkers consider that:

- A "system" is a dynamic and complex whole, interacting as a structured functional unit
- Information flows between the different elements that compose the system
- A system is a community situated within an environment
- Information flows from and to the surrounding environment via semi-permeable membranes or boundaries
- Systems are often composed of entities seeking equilibrium, but can exhibit oscillating, chaotic, or exponential growth/decay behaviour

Systems thinkers are particularly interested in studying systems because changing a system frequently leads to counterintuitive system responses. For example feedback loops may operate to either keep the organization in check or unbalance it.

Traditional decision making tends to involve linear cause and effect relationships. By taking a systems approach, we can see the whole complex of bidirectional interrelationships. Instead of analysing a problem in terms of an input and an output, for example, we look at the whole system of inputs, processes, outputs, feedback, and controls. This larger picture will typically provide more useful results than traditional methods.

System thinking also helps us integrate the temporal dimension of any decision. Instead of looking at discrete "snapshots" at points in time, a systems methodology will allow us to see change as a continuous process.

Systems Thinking is a world view based on the perspective of the systems sciences, which seeks to understand interconnectedness, complexity and wholeness of components of systems in specific relationship to each other. Systems thinking is not only constructivist, rather systems thinking embraces the values of reductionist science by understanding the parts, and the constructivist perspectives which seek to understand wholes, and more so, the understanding of the complex relationships that enable 'parts' to become 'wholes'.

A system is any set (group) of interdependent or temporally interacting parts. Parts are generally systems themselves and are composed of other parts, just as systems are generally parts or holons of other systems.

Systems thinking techniques may be used to study any kind of system — natural, scientific, human, or conceptual.

Systems thinking often involves considering a "system" in different ways:

Rather than trying to improve the braking system on a car by looking in great detail at the composition of the brake pads (reductionist), the boundary of the braking system may be extended to include not only the components of the car, but the driver, the road and the weather, and considering the interactions between them.

Looking at something as a series of conceptual systems according to multiple viewpoints. A supermarket could be considered as a "profit making system" from the perspective of management, an "employment system" from the perspective of the staff, and a "shopping system" — or perhaps an "entertainment system" — from the perspective of the customers. As a result of such thinking, new insights may be gained into how the supermarket works, why it has problems, or how changes made to one such system may impact on the others.

Systems thinking uses a variety of techniques that may be divided into:

- Hard systems - involving simulations, often using computers and the techniques of operations research. Useful for problems that can justifiably be quantified. However it cannot easily take into account unquantifiable variables (opinions, culture, politics, etc), and may treat people as being passive, rather than having complex motivations.
- Soft systems - Used to tackle systems that cannot easily be quantified, especially those involving people holding multiple and conflicting frames of reference. Useful for understanding motivations, viewpoints, and interactions and addressing qualitative as well as quantitative dimensions of problem situations. Soft systems are a field that utilizes foundation methodological work developed by Peter Checkland, Brian Wilson and their colleagues at Lancaster University. Morphological analysis is a complementary method for structuring and analysing non-quantifiable problem complexes.
- Evolutionary systems - the development of Evolutionary Systems Design by Bela H. Banathy integrates critical systems inquiry and soft systems methodologies to create a meta-methodology applicable to the design of complex social systems. These systems, similar to dynamic systems are understood as open, complex systems, but further accounts for their potential capacity to evolve over time. Banathy uniquely integrated the multidisciplinary perspectives of systems research (including chaos, complexity, cybernetics), cultural anthropology, evolutionary theory, and others.

BUSINESS CONTINUITY PLANNING

Business Continuity Planning (BCP) is an interdisciplinary peer mentoring methodology used to create and validate an exercised logistical plan for how an organization will recover and restore partially or completely interrupted critical function(s) within a predetermined time after a disaster or extended disruption.

BCP may be a part of an organizational learning effort that helps reduce operational risk associated with lax information management controls. This process may be integrated with improving information security and corporate reputation risk management practices.

British Standards Institute is planning to release a new independent standard for BCP — BS 25999. The draft of standard had been put up for public comments and the final standard is expected in early 2007. This standard would reduce the reliance on Information Security oriented standards which dealt with BCP marginally.

A completed BCP cycle results in a formal printed manual available for reference before, during, and after disruptions have occurred. Its purpose is to reduce adverse stakeholder impacts determined by both the disruption's scope and duration. Measureable Business Impact Analysis (BIA) "zones" include civil, economic, natural, technical, secondary and subsequent.

Business Continuity Planning is not a new concept; plans for disasters, like Noah's Ark, are evidenced from the beginning of human history. Prior to January 1, 2000, governments anticipated computer failures, called the Y2k problem, in important public utility infrastructures like banking, power, telecommunication, health and financial industries. Since 1983, regulatory agencies like the American Bankers Association and Banking Administration Institute (BAI) required their supporting members to exercise operational continuity practices (later supported by more formal BCP manuals) that protect the public interests. Newer regulations were often based on formalized standards defined under ISO/IEC 17799 or BS 7799.

Both regulatory and global business focus on BCP arguably waned after the problem-free Y2K rollover. This lax attitude unequivocally ended September 11th 2001, when simultaneous terrorist attacks devastated downtown New York City and changed the 'worst case scenario' paradigm for business continuity planning.

BCP methodology is scalable for an organization of any size and complexity. Even though the methodology has roots in regulated industries, any type of organization may create a BCP manual, and arguably every organization should have one in order to ensure the organization's longevity. Evidence that firms do not invest enough time and resources into BCP preparations are evident in disaster survival statistics. Fires permanently close 44% of the business affected. In the 1993 World Trade Center bombing, 150 businesses out of 350 affected failed to survive the event. Conversely, the firms affected by the Sept 11 attacks with well-developed and tested BCP manuals were back in business within days.

A BCP manual for a small organization may be simply a printed manual stored safely away from the primary work location, containing the names, addresses, and phone numbers for crisis management staff, general staff members, clients, and vendors along with the location of the offsite data backup storage media, copies of insurance contracts, and other critical materials necessary for organizational survival. At its most complex, a BCP manual may outline a secondary work site, technical requirements and readiness, regulatory reporting requirements, work recovery measures, the means to reestablish physical records, the means to establish a new supply chain, or the means to establish new production centers. Firms should ensure that their BCP manual is realistic and easy to use during a crisis. As such,

BCP sits along side crisis management and disaster recovery planning and is a part of an organization's overall risk management.

The development of a BCP manual has five main phases:

1. Analysis
2. Solution design
3. Implementation
4. Testing and organization acceptance
5. Maintenance

Much of the BCP material on the internet is sponsored by consultancies who offer fee-based services for BCP solution development, however basic tutorials are freely available on the internet for properly motivated organizations.

The analysis phase in the development of a BCP manual consists of an impact analysis, threat analysis, and impact scenarios with the resulting BCP plan requirement documentation. An impact analysis results in the differentiation between critical and non-critical organization functions. A function may be considered critical if the implications for stakeholders of damage to the organization resulting are regarded as unacceptable. Perceptions of the acceptability of disruption may be modified by the cost of establishing and maintaining appropriate business or technical recovery solutions. A function may also be considered critical if dictated by law. Next, the impact analysis results in the recovery requirements for each critical function. Recovery requirements consist of the following information:

- The time frame in which the critical function must be resumed after the disaster
- The business requirements for recovery of the critical function, and/ or
- The technical requirements for recovery of the critical function

The organizations also banned face-to-face contact between opposing team members during business and non-business hours. With such a split, organizations increased their resiliency against the threat of government-ordered quarantine measures if one person in a team contracted or was exposed to the disease. Damage from flooding also has a unique characteristic. If an office environment is flooded with non-salinated and contamination-free water (e.g.m, in the event of a pipe burst), equipment can be thoroughly dried and may still be functional.

After defining potential threats, documenting the impact scenarios that form the basis of the business recovery plan is recommended. In general, planning for the most wide-reaching disaster or disturbance is preferable to planning for a smaller scale problem, as almost all smaller scale problems are partial elements of larger disasters. A typical impact scenario like 'Building Loss' will most likely encompass all critical business functions, and the worst potential outcome from any potential threat. A business continuity plan may also document additional impact scenarios if an organization has more than one building. Other more specific impact scenarios - for example a scenario for the temporary or permanent loss of a specific floor in a building - may also be documented.

After the completion of the analysis phase, the business and technical plan requirements are documented in order to commence the implementation phase. For an office-based, IT intensive business, the plan requirements may cover the following elements which may be classed as ICE (In Case of Emergency) Data:

- The numbers and types of desks, whether dedicated or shared, required outside of the primary business location in the secondary location
- The individuals involved in the recovery effort along with their contact and technical details
- The applications and application data required from the secondary location desks for critical business functions
- The manual workaround solutions
- The maximum outage allowed for the applications
- The peripheral requirements like printers, copier, fax machine, calculators, paper, pens etc.

Other business environments, such as production, distribution, warehousing etc will need to cover these elements, but are likely to have additional issues to manage following a disruptive event.

The goal of the solution design phase is to identify the most cost effective disaster recovery solution that meets two main requirements from the impact analysis stage. For IT applications, this is commonly expressed as:

1. The minimum application and application data requirements
2. The time frame in which the minimum application and application data must be available

Disaster recovery plans may also be required outside the IT applications domain, for example in preservation of information in hard copy format, or restoration of embedded technology in process plant. This BCP phase overlaps with Disaster recovery planning methodology. The solution phase determines:

- The crisis management command structure
- The location of a secondary work site (where necessary)
- Telecommunication architecture between primary and secondary work sites
- Data replication methodology between primary and secondary work sites
- The application and software required at the secondary work site, and
- The type of physical data requirements at the secondary work site.

The implementation phase, quite simply, is the execution of the design elements identified in the solution design phase. Work package testing may take place during the implementation of the solution, however; work package testing does not take the place of organizational testing.

The purpose of testing is to achieve organizational acceptance that the business continuity solution satisfies the organization's recovery requirements. Plans may fail to meet expectations due to insufficient or inaccurate recovery requirements, solution design flaws, or solution implementation errors. Testing may include:

- Crisis command team call-out testing
- Technical swing test from primary to secondary work locations
- Technical swing test from secondary to primary work locations
- Application test
- Business process test

At minimum, testing is generally conducted on a biannual or annual schedule. Problems identified in the initial testing phase may be rolled up into the maintenance phase and retested during the next test cycle.

Maintenance of a BCP manual is broken down into three periodic activities. The first activity is the confirmation of information in the manual. The second activity is the testing and verification of technical solutions established for recovery operations. The third activity is the testing and verification of documented organization recovery procedures. A biannual or annual maintenance cycle is typical.

All organizations change over time, therefore a BCP manual must change to stay relevant to the organization. Once data accuracy is verified, normally a call tree test is conducted to evaluate the notification plan's efficiency as well as the accuracy of the contact data. Some types of changes that should be identified and updated in the manual include:

- Staffing changes
- Staffing persona
- Changes to important clients and their contact details
- Changes to important vendors/suppliers and their contact details
- Departmental changes like new, closed or fundamentally changed departments.

Risk Management

Risk Management is the process of measuring, or assessing, risk and developing strategies to manage it. Strategies include transferring the risk to another party, avoiding the risk, reducing the negative effect of the risk, and accepting some or all of the consequences of a particular risk. Traditional risk management focuses on risks stemming from physical or legal causes (e.g. natural disasters or fires, accidents, death, and lawsuits). Financial risk management, on the other hand, focuses on risks that can be managed using traded financial instruments.

In ideal risk management, a prioritization process is followed whereby the risks with the greatest loss and the greatest probability of occurring are handled first, and risks with lower probability of occurrence and lower loss are handled later. In practice the process can be very difficult, and balancing between risks with a high probability of occurrence but lower loss vs. a risk with high loss but lower probability of occurrence can often be mishandled.

Intangible risk management identifies a new type of risk - a risk that has a 100% probability of occurring but is ignored by the organization due to a lack of identification ability. For example, knowledge risk occurs when deficient knowledge is applied. Relationship risk occurs when collaboration ineffectiveness occurs. Process-engagement risk occurs when operational ineffectiveness occurs. These risks directly reduce the productivity of knowledge workers, decrease cost effectiveness, profitability, service, quality, reputation, brand value, and earnings quality. Intangible risk management allows risk management to create immediate value from the identification and reduction of risks that reduce productivity.

Risk management also faces difficulties allocating resources. This is the idea of opportunity cost. Resources spent on risk management could have been spent on more profitable activities. Again, ideal risk management minimizes spending while maximizing the reduction of the negative effects of risks.

Establishing the context includes planning the remainder of the process and mapping out the scope of the exercise, the identity and objectives of stakeholders, the basis upon which risks will be evaluated and defining a framework for the process, and agenda for identification and analysis of risk involved in the process.

After establishing the context, the next step in the process of managing risk is to identify potential risks. Risks are about events that, when triggered, cause problems. Hence, risk identification can start with the source of problems, or with the problem itself.

- Source analysis- Risk sources may be internal or external to the system that is the target of risk management. Examples of risk sources are: stakeholders of a project, employees of a company or the weather over an airport.
- Problem analysis -Risks are related to identified threats. For example: the threat of losing money, the threat of abuse of privacy information or the threat of accidents and casualties. The threats may exist with various entities, most important with shareholder, customers and legislative bodies such as the government.

When either source or problem is known, the events that a source may trigger or the events that can lead to a problem can be investigated. For example: stakeholders withdrawing during a project may endanger funding of the project; privacy information may be stolen by employees even within a closed network; lightning striking a Boeing 747 during takeoff may make all people onboard immediate casualties.

The chosen method of identifying risks may depend on culture, industry practice and compliance. The identification methods are formed by templates or the development of templates for identifying source, problem or event. Common risk identification methods are:

- Objectives-based Risk Identification- Organizations and project teams have objectives. Any event that may endanger achieving an objective partly or completely is identified as risk. Objective-based risk identification is at the basis of COSO's Enterprise Risk Management - Integrated Framework
- Scenario-based Risk Identification In scenario analysis different scenarios are created. The scenarios may be the alternative ways to achieve an objective, or an analysis of the interaction of forces in, for example, a market or battle. Any event that triggers an undesired scenario alternative is identified as risk.
- Taxonomy-based Risk Identification The taxonomy in taxonomy-based risk identification is a breakdown of possible risk sources. Based on the taxonomy and knowledge of best practices, a questionnaire is compiled. The answers to the questions reveal risks.

Once risks have been identified, they must then be assessed as to their potential severity of loss and to the probability of occurrence. These quantities can be either simple to measure, in the case of the value of a lost building, or impossible to know for sure in the case of the probability of an unlikely event occurring. Therefore, in the assessment process it is critical to make the best educated guesses possible in order to properly prioritize the implementation of the Risk Management Plan.

The fundamental difficulty in risk assessment is determining the rate of occurrence since statistical information is not available on all kinds of past incidents. Furthermore, evaluating the severity of the consequences (impact) is often quite difficult for immaterial assets. Asset valuation is another question that needs to be addressed. Thus, best educated opinions and available statistics are the primary sources of information. Nevertheless, risk assessment should produce such information for the management of the organization that the primary risks are easy to understand and that the risk management decisions may be prioritized. Thus, there have been several theories and attempts to quantify risks. Numerous different risk formulae exist, but perhaps the most widely accepted formula for risk quantification is: Rate of occurrence multiplied by the impact of the event equals risk.

Later research has shown that the financial benefits of risk management are less dependent on the formula used but are more dependent on the frequency and how risk assessment is performed.

In business it is imperative to be able to present the findings of risk assessments in financial terms. Robert Courtney Jr. proposed a formula for presenting risks in financial terms. The Courtney formula was accepted as the official risk analysis method for the US governmental agencies. The formula proposes calculation of ALE (Annualised Loss Expectancy) and compares the expected loss value to the security control implementation costs.

Once risks have been identified and assessed, all techniques to manage the risk fall into one or more of these four major categories:

- Tolerate (aka Retention)
- Treat (aka Mitigation)
- Terminate (aka Elimination)
- Transfer (aka Buying Insurance)

Ideal use of these strategies may not be possible. Some of them may involve trade-offs that are not acceptable to the organization or person making the risk management decisions.

Risk Avoidance

Includes not performing an activity that could carry risk. An example would be not buying a property or business in order to not take on the liability that comes with it. Another would be not flying in order to not take the risk that the airplane were to be hijacked. Avoidance may seem the answer to all risks, but avoiding risks also means losing out on the potential gain that accepting (retaining) the risk may have allowed. Not entering a business to avoid the risk of loss also avoids the possibility of earning profits.

Risk Reduction

Involves methods that reduce the severity of the loss. Examples include sprinklers designed to put out a fire to reduce the risk of loss by fire. This method may cause a greater loss by water damage and therefore may not be suitable. Halon fire suppression systems may mitigate that risk, but the cost may be prohibitive as a strategy.

Modern software development methodologies reduce risk by developing and delivering software incrementally. Early methodologies suffered from the fact that they only delivered software in the final phase of development; any problems encountered in earlier phases meant costly rework and often jeopardized the whole project. By developing in increments, software projects can limit effort wasted to a single increment. A current trend in software development, spearheaded by the Extreme Programming community, is to reduce the size of increments to the smallest size possible, sometimes as little as one week is allocated to an increment.

Risk Retention

Involves accepting the loss when it occurs. True self insurance falls in this category. Risk retention is a viable strategy for small risks where the cost of insuring against the risk would be greater over time than the total losses sustained. All risks that are not avoided or transferred are retained by default. This includes risks that are so large or catastrophic that they either cannot be insured against or the premiums would be infeasible.

War is an example since most property and risks are not insured against war, so the loss attributed by war is retained by the insured. Also any amounts of potential loss (risk) over the amount insured is retained risk. This may also be acceptable if the chance of a very large loss is small or if the cost to insure for greater coverage amounts is so great it would hinder the goals of the organization too much.

Risk Transfer

Means causing another party to accept the risk, typically by contract or by hedging. Insurance is one type of risk transfer that uses contracts. Other times it may involve contract language that transfers a risk to another party without the payment of an insurance premium. Liability among construction or other contractors is very often transferred this way. On the other hand, taking offsetting positions in derivatives is typically how firms use hedging to financially manage risk.

Some ways of managing risk fall into multiple categories. Risk retention pools are technically retaining the risk for the group, but spreading it over the whole group involves transfer among individual members of the group. This is different from traditional insurance, in that no premium is exchanged between members of the group up front, but instead losses are assessed to all members of the group.

Creating the plan

Decide on the combination of methods to be used for each risk. Each risk management decision should be recorded and approved by the appropriate level of management. For example, a risk concerning the image of the organization should have top management decision behind it whereas IT management would have the authority to decide on computer virus risks.

The Risk Management Plan should propose applicable and effective security controls for managing the risks. For example, an observed high risk of computer viruses could be mitigated by acquiring and implementing anti virus software. A good Risk Management Plan should contain a schedule for control implementation and responsible persons for those actions. The risk management concept is old but is still not very effectively measured

Implementation

Follow all of the planned methods for mitigating the effect of the risks. Purchase insurance policies for the risks that have been decided to be transferred to an insurer, avoid all risks that can be avoided without sacrificing the entity's goals, reduce others, and retain the rest.

Initial Risk Management Plans will never be perfect. Practice, experience, and actual loss results will necessitate changes in the plan and contribute information to allow possible different decisions to be made in dealing with the risks being faced.

Risk analysis results and management plans should be updated periodically. There are two primary reasons for this:

1. To evaluate whether the previously selected security controls are still applicable and effective, and

2. To evaluate the possible risk level changes in the business environment. For example, information risks are a good example of rapidly changing business environment.

If risks are improperly assessed and prioritized, time can be wasted in dealing with risk of losses that are not likely to occur. Spending too much time assessing and managing unlikely risks can divert resources that could be used more profitably. Unlikely events do occur but if the risk is unlikely enough to occur it may be better to simply retain the risk and deal with the result if the loss does in fact occur.

Prioritizing too highly the Risk management processes could keep an organization from ever completing a project or even getting started. This is especially true if other work is suspended until the risk management process is considered complete.

It is also important to keep in mind the distinction between risk and uncertainty. Risk can be measured by Impacts x Probability.

As applied to corporate finance, risk management is a technique for measuring, monitoring and controlling the financial or operational risk on a firm's balance sheet.

The Basel II framework breaks risks into market risk (price risk), credit risk and operational risk and also specifies methods for calculating capital requirements for each of these components.

In Enterprise Risk Management, a risk is defined as a possible event or circumstance that can have negative influences on the Enterprise in question. Its impact can be on the very existence, the resources (human and capital), the products and services, or the customers of the Enterprise, as well as external impacts on Society, Markets or the Environment.

In addition, every probable risk can have a pre-formulated plan to deal with its possible consequences (to ensure contingency if the risk becomes a liability).

From the information above and the average cost per employee over time, or Cost Accrual Ratio, a project manager can estimate

- The cost associated with the risk if it arises, estimated by multiplying employee costs per unit time by the estimated time lost (cost impact, C where C = Cost Accrual Ratio S)
- The probable increase in time associated with a risk (schedule variance due to risk, Rs where Rs = PS):
  - Sorting on this value puts the highest risks to the schedule first. This is intended to cause the greatest risks to the project to be attempted first so that risk is minimized as quickly as possible.
  - This is slightly misleading as schedule variances with a large P and small S and vice versa are not equivalent. (The risk of the RMS Titanic sinking vs. the passengers' meals being served at slightly the wrong time).

- The probable increase in cost associated with a risk (cost variance due to risk, Rc where Rc = P*C = P*CAR*S = P*S*CAR)
  - Sorting on this value puts the highest risks to the budget first.

Risk in a project or process can be due either to Special Cause Variation or Common Cause Variation and requires appropriate treatment. That is to re-iterate the concern about extremal cases not being equivalent in the list immediately above.

Risk Management Activities as Applied to Project Management

In project management, risk management includes the following activities:

- Planning how risk management will be held in the particular project. Plan should include risk management tasks, responsibilities, activities and budget.
- Assigning a risk officer - a team member other than a project manager who is responsible for foreseeing potential project problems. Typical characteristic of risk officer is a healthy skepticism.
- Maintaining live project risk database. Each risk should have the following attributes: opening date, title, short description, probability and importance. Optionally a risk may have an assigned person responsible for its resolution and a date by which the risk must be resolved.
- Creating anonymous risk reporting channel. Each team member should have possibility to report risk that he foresees in the project.
- Preparing mitigation plans for risks that are chosen to be mitigated. The purpose of the mitigation plan is to describe how this particular risk will be handled – what, when, by who and how will be done to avoid it or minimize consequences if it becomes a liability.
- Summarizing planned and faced risks, effectiveness of mitigation activities and effort spend for the risk management

Risk management is simply a practice of systematically selecting cost effective approaches for minimising the effect of threat realization to the organization. All risks can never be fully avoided or mitigated simply because of financial and practical limitations. Therefore all organizations have to accept some level of residual risks.

Whereas risk management tends to be pre-emptive, Business Continuity Planning (BCP) was invented to deal with the consequences of realised residual risks. The necessity to have BCP in place arises because even very unlikely events will occur if given enough time. Risk management and BCP are often mistakenly seen as rivals or overlapping practices. In fact these processes are so tightly tied together that such separation seems artificial. For example, the risk management process creates important inputs for the BCP (assets, impact assessments, cost estimates etc). Risk management also proposes applicable controls for the observed risks. Therefore, risk management covers several areas that are vital for the BCP process. However, the BCP process goes beyond risk management's pre-emptive approach and moves on from the assumption that the disaster will realise at some point.

Financial Risk Management

Financial risk management is the practice of creating value in a firm by using financial instruments to manage exposure to risk. Similar to general risk management, financial risk management requires identifying the sources of risk, measuring risk, and plans to address them. As a specialization of risk management, financial risk management focuses on when and how to hedge using financial instruments to manage costly exposures to risk.

In the banking sector worldwide, Basel Accord are generally adopted by internationally active banks to tracking, reporting and exposing operational, credit and market risks.

Finance theory (i.e. financial economics) prescribes that a firm should take on a project when it increases shareholder value. Finance theory also shows that firm managers cannot create value for shareholders, also called its investors, by taking on project that shareholders could do for themselves at the same cost. When applied to financial risk management, this implies that firm managers should not hedge risks that investors can hedge for themselves at the same cost.

This notion is captured by the hedging irrelevance proposition: In a perfect market, the firm cannot create value by hedging a risk when the price of bearing that risk within the firm is the same as the price of bearing it outside of the firm. In practice, financial markets are not likely to be perfect markets. This suggests that firm managers likely have many opportunities to create value for shareholders using financial risk management. The trick is to determine which risks are cheaper for the firm to manage than the shareholders. A general rule of thumb, however, is that market risks that result in unique risks for the firm are the best candidates for financial risk management.

IMPORTANT MANAGEMENT AREAS IN PLANNING

The purpose of a Management Plan is to identify values, threats (real and potential) to those values, and uses that are consistent with maintaining ecological character while sustaining the livelihoods of local communities.

The 5 key steps in the Management Planning process are:

1. Identifying priority values
2. Identifying threats to the priority values
3. Identifying the sources of those threats
4. Developing management strategies and recommending actions to manage those threats, including goals for each priority value

5. Monitoring & review – allowing changes and adaptation to new needs and ways of thinking.

Community-based management planning:

1. Undertake a desktop assessment and prepare a Background Paper
2. Guided by the Background Paper, establish a Community Reference Group (CRG) and Scientific and Technical Advisory Group (STAG)
3. Consult with the CRG and STAG on the Background Paper via a facilitated workshop
4. Undertake a values, condition and threat assessment (desktop and/or on-ground) and prepare an Issues Paper
5. Develop a Communication Strategy to disseminate information in the Issues Paper to raise broad awareness in the community
6. Consult with the CRG and STAG on the Issues Paper and Communication Strategy, via focus groups and a facilitated workshop
7. Implement the Communication Strategy
8. Develop the Draft Management Plan in consultation with the STAG and following feedback from the CRG and broader community (through the Communications Strategy)
9. Consult with the CRG and STAG on the Draft Management Plan, via a facilitated workshop
10. Public release of the Draft Management Plan

Two critical components of the management planning process are:

- Values Mapping - a tool for building management partnerships
- Issues Paper

Values Mapping – a Tool for Building Management Partnerships

The Values Mapping process uses identification strategies from business marketing and consensus-building strategies from Alternative Dispute Resolution, as a tool for bringing together the diversity of interests in a range of aspects of planning for sustainable living.

The Values Mapping process involves:

- Background research directed to understanding the issues, the language relevant to the area and its issues, and the history of the issues
- Identifying the key players – their interests and roles in management of the area
- Designing the process so that it is accessible and meaningful to all who need to be involved
- Establishing 'buy in' – encouraging participation and building trust
- Mapping values - reporting on the outcomes

Four key activities in Values Mapping

1. Telephone Survey: People with an interest in the area, whether for conservation reasons or as recreational or commercial users, are

asked to complete a telephone survey addressing the values of the area and management issues.

2. Focus Group Sessions: A series of information gathering sessions (usually of 1--1½ hours duration) with interest groups (e.g. farmers & graziers, commercial fishers, recreational fishers, other recreational users, scientific researchers, government staff with management responsibilities in the area, and community conservation representatives).
   These focus group sessions are directed to gathering and confirming local and technical knowledge of the area – what places are special, what makes them special, what are the threats to those values and what management actions are possible.
3. Field Trip: A field trip, which all participants are strongly encouraged to attend, looks at key sites and the management issues of concern for retaining those values, helps all participants gain a shared understanding of the area and the differing values it holds for people in the area.
4. Facilitated Workshop: A professionally facilitated Values Mapping workshop, which brings together the knowledge and experience of the different sectors with an interest in the area, shares values and concerns, and seeks to find common ground which will help achieve the best possible future management for the area.

Both the focus group sessions and the Values Mapping workshop use topographical or other suitable maps of the area, with overlays to depict visually the areas valued and the management issues of concern.

Issues Paper

The objectives of an Issues Paper (focused on shorebirds, as opposed to broader natural, social and economic values) should be to:

- Review the status of knowledge on shorebirds and their habitat.
- Investigate and identify threats to important shorebird habitat, rank threats and identify sites/habitats with the highest level of threat.
- Investigate and identify options for mitigating threats and prioritise these options.
- Recommend opportunities for collaborative approaches to manage threats among local stakeholder groups.

A Shorebird Issues Paper developed for the Clarence Estuary in NSW took the following approach to meeting the objectives stated above:

Review the status of knowledge on shorebirds and their habitat

To review the status of knowledge on shorebirds and their habitat it is necessary to evaluate the data and identify gaps in the data/data collection.

Data evaluation – things to consider:

- Survey duration – the period over which surveys were undertaken.
- Survey frequency – the number of survey periods (individual surveys).

- Survey effort – the number of survey days/survey period.
- Methods used – general indication of how data were collected.
- Number of personnel – number of counters involved in the survey.
- Number of sites sampled – the number of sites listed in the data and sites within the area sampled.
- Survey coverage – general appraisal of the area surveyed.
- Data presentation – notes on the manner in which data are presented. This information is important for assessing the utility of data in identifying important roost and feeding sites.

Potential gaps – things to consider:

- Temporal coverage of surveys to document use of the site during northwards and southwards migration.
- Number of high tide surveys that encompass the entire site.
- Number of low tide surveys that encompass the entire site.
- Management of data i.e. specific information for each site sampled.
- Nocturnal surveys to identify night roost and feeding sites.
- Accessibility of information on methods and timing.
- Use of standard site names.

Assessing the Importance of Habitat

Things to consider in assessing (and comparing) the importance of habitat:

Roost Sites

- Maximum spring/summer counts,
- Average spring/summer counts,
- Species diversity and occurrence of threatened species between sites/ locations

Note: This provides a broad indication of the relative importance of known roost sites, however, there are important issues such as nocturnal habitat use, nesting and feeding sites and roost function (i.e. spring, neap or staging; spring tide roosts given a higher ranking than either neap roosts or staging areas).

Investigate and identify threats to important shorebird habitat, rank threats and identify sites/habitats with the highest level of threat.

Threats to shorebirds and their habitat can be broadly categorised as:

- Habitat Loss – removal of habitat through reclamation and in severe cases erosion.
- Habitat Modification – changes in the characteristics of habitat that reduces its utility for shorebirds.
- Habitat Disturbance – activities that often result in disturbance to roosting and foraging birds (including. sources of disturbance i.e. location of infrastructure and types of disturbance i.e. activities that may affect shorebirds)

- Habitat Pollution – accumulation of pollutants in body fat that reduces life span and potentially reproductive ability and abundance of food.
- Mortality – death of individuals through hunting by humans for food, recreation or site protection.

To rank threats, their occurrence and proximity to shorebird habitat was assessed and a matrix developed to allow comparisons among sites.

The method adopted to rank threats included:

- Each threat was given a score of 1, 5 or 10 depending on its proximity to a site.
- A score of 10 was given to threats that occur on-site, 5 for threats within 100m of a site and 1 for threats within 1km of a site.
- A score of 20 was given to sites approved for development. Such a high score was deemed necessary to reflect the strong likelihood that the site would be removed once the development proceeds.
- Threat scores were then added together to give a combined threat score. Sites were then ranked from highest to lowest based on the total threat score.
- The higher the score the greater level of threat experienced.
- A general indication of which threats are most prevalent was obtained by adding threats across sites to obtain a total threat score.
- Comparing the importance of each site to the threat scores gave an indication of where conflicts between habitat values and threats exist.

Investigate and Identify Options for Mitigating Threats

Options for managing threats to shorebirds/their habitat were broadly categorised as follows:

- Further research to clearly identify threats
- Community awareness and involvement
- Improved environmental planning and regulation
- Habitat conservation and remediation.
- On-ground works

Further Information

Clarence Estuary Shorebird Issues Paper

THE ENTREPRENEUR PLAN

This is otherwise known as business plan. It is a written explanation of the company's business model for the venture in question. Business plans are developed for ventures in both business and government.

Business plans are used internally for management and planning and are also used to convince outsiders such as banks or venture capitalists to invest money into a venture.

Business plans are noted for often quickly becoming out of date. One common belief within business circles is that the actual plan may have little value, but what is more important is the process of planning, through which the manager gains a greater understanding of the business and of the options available.

Business plan is prepared for customers for they need to know whether the product serves the purpose or not and the utility of the product, for government because it is necessary to know for government whether the legal economical and subsidy concerns are met or the like. Business plans can be divided roughly into four separate types. They require very different amounts of labour and not always with proportionately different results.

- The Miniplan: A miniplan, better known as the Executive Summary, may consist of one to 10 pages and should include at least cursory attention to such key matters as business concept, financing needs, marketing plan and financial statements, especially cash flow, income projection and balance sheet. It's a great way to quickly test a business concept or measure the interest of a potential partner or minor investor. It can also serve as a valuable prelude to a full-length plan later on.
- The Working Plan: A working plan is a tool to be used to operate the business. It has to be long on detail but may be short on presentation. As with a miniplan, one can probably afford a somewhat higher degree of candor and informality when preparing a working plan.
- The Presentation Plan: If a working plan is twisted to boost the amount of attention paid to its looks, it will become a presentation plan. This plan is suitable for showing to bankers, investors and others outside the company.
- The Electronic Plan: The majority of business plans are composed on a computer of some kind, then printed out and presented in hard copy. But more and more business information that once was transferred between parties only on paper is now sent electronically. An electronic plan can be handy for presentations to a group using a computer-driven overhead projector, for example, or for satisfying the demands of a discriminating investor who wants to be able to delve deeply into the underpinnings of complex spreadsheets.

A solid strategic plan delivers the following benefits:

- You focus your time and energy on activities that are most likely to achieve your goals.
- You know how to allocate resources.
- You put a solid strategy in place to set your business apart from the competition.
- You can communicate your plan to employees, and hold them accountable for results.

- You can track the results of your efforts and make mid-course corrections to get back on track if you need to.
- You can adapt your plan to create a second business plan to raise investment capital or get a business loan.

For an effective business plan, the following steps can be followed:

- Idea Generation
- Environment Scanning
- Feasibility Analysis
- Drawing up a Functional Plan
- Project Report Preparation
- Evaluation, Control & Review

A business plan can be seen as a collection of sub-plans including a marketing plan, financial plan, production plan, and human resource plan.

The business plan has many forms. There is however a format that is typical:

- Executive summary
  - Explains the basic business model
  - Gives rationale for the strategy
- Background
  - Gives short history of company (unless it is a new company)
  - Provides background details such as:
    - Age of company
    - Number of employees
    - Annual sales figures
    - Location of facilities
    - Form of ownership including
    - Sole proprietor
    - Partnership
    - Entrepreneurial startup
    - Private corporate startup
    - Publicly traded corporation
    - Limited liability company
    - Public utility
    - Non-profit organization
  - Background of key personnel including
    - Owners
    - Senior managers
    - Managing partners
    - Head scientists and researchers
- Marketing
  - The macroenvironment
  - The competitive environment
  - The industry
  - The customer priorities

  - Product strategy
  - Pricing strategy
  - Promotion strategy
  - Distribution strategy
- Production and manufacturing
  - Describe all processes
  - Production facility requirements - size, layout, capacity, location
  - Inventory requirements - raw materials inventory, finished goods inventory, warehouse space requirements
  - Equipment requirements
  - Supply chain requirements
  - Fixed cost allocation
- Finance
  - Source of funds
  - Existing loans and liabilities
  - Projected sales and costs
  - Break even analysis
  - Expected return
  - Monthly pro-forma cash flow statement
- Human resources
  - Assign responsibilities
  - Training required
  - Skills required
  - Union issues
  - Compensation
  - Skills availability
  - New hiring

Specialized sections such as product research and development, legal strategies, marketing research, or inter-company collaborations, are added to deal with unique features or characteristics of the business or its markets.

Cost and revenue estimates are central to any business plan for deciding the viability of the planned venture. But costs are often underestimated and revenues overestimated resulting in later cost overruns, revenue shortfalls, and possibly non-viability. During the dot-com bubble 1997-2001 this was a problem for many technology start-ups. However, the problem is not limited to technology or the private sector; public works projects also routinely suffer from cost overruns and/or revenue shortfalls. The main causes of cost overruns and revenue shortfalls are optimism bias and strategic misrepresentation. Reference class forecasting was developed to curb optimism bias and strategic misrepresentation and thus arrive at more accurate cost and revenue estimates in business plans.

Marketing Plan

A Marketing Plan is a written document that details the actions necessary to achieve a specified marketing objective(s). It can be for a product or service, a brand, or a product line. It can cover one year (referred to as an annual marketing plan), or cover up to 5 years.

A marketing plan may be part of an overall business plan. Solid marketing strategy is the foundation of a well-written marketing plan. While a marketing plan contains a list of actions, a marketing plan without a sound strategic foundation is of little use.

There are many formats for marketings plans and every company does it a little differently, but the outline that follows is a very complete format. Using this format will produce a 30 to 40 page plan. Many companies prefer an abridged format that would yield a 10 to 20 page plan.

1. Title page
2. Executive Summary
3. Current Situation - Macroenvironment
   - Economy
   - Legal
   - Government
   - Technology
   - Ecological
   - Sociocultural
   - Supply chain
4. Current Situation - Market Analysis
   - Market definition
   - Market size
   - Market segmentation
   - Industry structure and strategic groupings
   - Porter 5 forces analysis
   - Competition and market share
   - Competitors' strengths and weaknesses
   - Market trends
5. Current Situation - Consumer Analysis
   - Nature of the buying decision
   - Participants
   - Demographics
   - Psychographics
   - Buyer motivation and expectations
   - Loyalty segments
6. Current Situation - Internal
   - Company resources
     - Financial
     - People
     - Time
     - Skills
   - Objectives

  - Mission statement and vision statement
  - Corporate objectives
  - Financial objective
  - Marketing objectives
  - Long term objectives
- Corporate culture

7. Summary of Situation Analysis
   - External threats
   - External opportunities
   - Internal strengths
   - Internal weaknesses
   - Key success factors in the industry
   - our sustainable competitive advantage
8. Marketing research
   - Information requirements
   - Research methodology
   - Research results
9. Marketing Strategy - Product
   - Product mix
   - Product strengths and weaknesses
     - Perceptual mapping
   - Product life cycle management and new product development
   - Brand name, brand image, and brand equity
   - The augmented product
   - Product portfolio analysis
     - B.C.G. Analysis
     - contribution margin analysis
     - G.E. Multi Factoral analysis
     - Quality Function Deployment
10. Marketing Strategy - Market share objectives
    - By products,
    - By customer segments,
    - By geographical markets
11. Marketing Strategy - Price
    - Pricing objectives
    - Pricing method (eg.: cost plus, demand based, or competitor indexing)
    - Pricing strategy (eg.: skimming, or penetration)
    - Discounts and allowances
    - Price elasticity and customer sensitivity
    - Price zoning
    - Break even analysis at various prices

12. Marketing Strategy - promotion
    - Promotional goals
    - Promotional mix
    - Advertising reach, frequency, flights, theme, and media
    - Sales force requirements, techniques, and management
    - Sales promotion
    - Publicity and public relations
    - Electronic promotion (eg.: Web, or telephone)
13. Marketing Strategy - Distribution
    - Geographical coverage
    - Distribution channels
    - Physical distribution and logistics
    - Electronic distribution
14. Implementation
    - Personnel requirements
        - Assign responsibilities
        - Give incentives
        - Training on selling methods
    - Financial requirements
    - Management information systems requirements
    - Month-by-month agenda
        - PERT or critical path analysis
    - Monitoring results and benchmarks
    - Adjustment mechanism
    - Contingencies (What if's)
15. Financial Summary
    - Assumptions
    - Pro-forma monthly income statement
    - Contribution margin analysis
    - Breakeven analysis
    - Monte Carlo method
    - ISI: Internet Strategic Intelligence
16. Scenarios
    - Prediction of Future Scenarios
    - Plan of Action for each Scenario
17. Appendix
    - Pictures and specifications of the new product
    - Results from research already completed

The final stage of any marketing planning process is to establish targets (or standards) so that progress can be monitored. Accordingly, it is important to put both quantities and timescales into the marketing objectives (for example, to capture 20 per cent by value of the market within two years) and into the corresponding strategies.

Changes in the environment mean that the forecasts often have to be changed. Along with these, the related plans may well also need to be changed. Continuous monitoring of performance, against predetermined targets, represents a most important aspect of this. However, perhaps even more important is the enforced discipline of a regular formal review. Again, as with forecasts, in many cases the best (most realistic) planning cycle will revolve around a quarterly review. Best of all, at least in terms of the quantifiable aspects of the plans, if not the wealth of backing detail, is probably a quarterly rolling review - planning one full year ahead each new quarter. Of course, this does absorb more planning resource; but it also ensures that the plans embody the latest information, and - with attention focused on them so regularly - forces both the plans and their implementation to be realistic. Plans only have validity if they are actually used to control the progress of a company: their success lies in their implementation, not in the writing.

Most organizations track their sales results; or, in non-profit organizations for example, the number of clients. The more sophisticated track them in terms of 'sales variance' - the deviation from the target figures - which allows a more immediate picture of deviations to become evident. `Micro- analysis', which is a nicely pseudo-scientific term for the normal management process of investigating detailed problems, then investigates the individual elements (individual products, sales territories, customers and so on) which are failing to meet targets.

Relatively few organizations, however, track market share. In some circumstances this may well be a much more important measure. Sales may still be increasing, in an expanding market, while share is actually decreasing - boding ill for future sales when the market eventually starts to drop. Where such market share is tracked, there may be a number of aspects which will be followed:

- Overall market share
- Segment share - that in the specific, targeted segment
- Relative share -in relation to the market leaders

The key ratio to watch in this area is usually the 'marketing expense to sales ratio'; although this may be broken down into other elements (advertising to sales, sales administration to sales, and so on).

The 'bottom line' of marketing activities should at least in theory, be the net profit (for all except non-profit organizations, where the comparable emphasis may be on remaining within budgeted costs). There are a number of separate performance figures and key ratios which need to be tracked:

- Gross contribution<>net profit
- Gross profit<>return on investment
- Net contribution<>profit on sales

There can be considerable benefit in comparing these figures with those achieved by other organizations (especially those in the same industry); using, for instance, the figures which can be obtained (in the UK) from 'The Centre for Interfirm Comparison'. The most sophisticated use of this approach, however, is typically by those making use of PIMS (Profit Impact of Management Strategies), initiated by the General Electric Company and then developed by Harvard Business School, but now run by the Strategic Planning Institute. The above performance analyses concentrate on the quantitative measures which are directly related to short-term performance. But there are a number of indirect measures, essentially tracking customer attitudes, which can also indicate the organization's performance in terms of its longer-term marketing strengths and may accordingly be even more important indicators. Some useful measures are:

- Market research - including customer panels (which are used to track changes over time)
- Lost business - the orders which were lost because, for example, the stock was not available or the product did not meet the customer's exact requirements
- Customer complaints - how many customers complain about the products or services, or the organization itself, and about what

A formal, written marketing plan is essential; in that it provides an unambiguous reference point for activities throughout the planning period. However, perhaps the most important benefit of these plans is the planning process itself. This typically offers a unique opportunity, a forum, for 'information-rich' and productively focused discussions between the various managers involved. The plan, together with the associated discussions, then provides an agreed context for their subsequent management activities, even for those not described in the plan itself.

The classic quantification of a marketing plan appears in the form of budgets. Because these are so rigorously quantified, they are particularly important. They should, thus, represent an unequivocal projection of actions and expected results.

What is more, they should be capable of being monitored accurately; and, indeed, performance against budget is the main (regular) management review process.

The purpose of a marketing budget is, thus, to pull together all the revenues and costs involved in marketing into one comprehensive document. It is a managerial tool that balances what is needed to be spent against what can be afforded, and helps make choices about priorities. It is then used in monitoring performance in practice.

The marketing budget is usually the most powerful tool by which you think through the relationship between desired results and available means. Its starting point should be the marketing strategies and plans, which have already been formulated in the marketing plan itself; although, in practice, the two will run in parallel and will interact. At the very least, the rigorous, highly quantified, budgets may cause a rethink of some of the more optimistic elements of the plans.

Many budgets are based on history. They are the equivalent of 'time-series' forecasting. It is assumed that next year's budgets should follow some trend that is discernible over recent history. Other alternatives are based on a simple 'percentage of sales' or on 'what the competitors are doing'.

However, there are many other alternatives:

- Affordable - This may be the most common approach to budgeting. Someone, typically the managing director on behalf of the board, decides what is a 'reasonable' promotional budget; what can be afforded. This figure is most often based on historical spending. This approach assumes that promotion is a cost; and sometimes is seen as an avoidable cost.
- Percentage of revenue - This is a variation of 'affordable', but at least it forges a link with sales volume, in that the budget will be set at a certain percentage of revenue, and thus follows trends in sales. However, it does imply that promotion is a result of sales, rather than the other way round.

Both of these methods are seen by many managements to be 'realistic', in that they reflect the reality of the business strategies as those managements see it. On the other hand, neither makes any allowance for change. They do not allow for the development to meet emerging market opportunities and, at the other end of the scale, they continue to pour money into a dying product or service.

- Competitive parity - In this case, the organization relates its budgets to what the competitors are doing: for example, it matches their budgets, or beats them, or spends a proportion of what the brand leader is spending. On the other hand, it assumes that the competitors know best; in which case, the service or product can expect to be nothing more than a follower.
- Zero-based budgeting - In essence, this approach takes the objectives, as set out in the marketing plan, together with the resulting planned activities and then costs them out.

Environmental Scanning

For a company to gain or maintain a sustainable competitive advantage, it must be ever vigilant, watching for changes in the business environment. It must also be agile enough to alter its strategies and plans when the need arises.

Methods

There are three ways of scanning the business environment:

- Ad-hoc scanning - Short term, infrequent examinations usually initiated by a crisis
- Regular scanning - Studies done on a regular schedule (say, once a year)

- Continuous scanning - (also called continuous learning) - continuous structured data collection and processing on a broad range of environmental factors

Most commentators feel that in today's turbulent business environment the best scanning method available is continuous scanning. This allows the firm to act quickly, take advantage of opportunities before competitors do, and respond to environmental threats before significant damage is done.

Environmental scanning usually refers just to the macroenvironment, but it can also include industry and competitor analysis, consumer analysis, product innovations, and the company's internal environment. Macroenvironmental scanning involves analysing:

- The Economy
  - GNP or GDP per capital
  - GNP or GDP growth
  - Unemployment rate
  - Inflation rate
  - Consumer and investor confidence
  - Inventory levels
  - Currency exchange rates
  - Merchandise trade balance
  - Financial and political health of trading partners
  - Balance of payments
  - Future trends
- Government
  - Political climate - amount of government activity
  - Political stability and risk
  - Government debt
  - Budget deficit or surplus
  - Corporate and personal tax rates
  - Payroll taxes
  - Import tariffs and quotas
  - Export restrictions
  - Restrictions on international financial flows
- Legal
  - Minimum wage laws
  - Environmental protection laws
  - Worker safety laws
  - Union laws
  - Copyright and patent laws
  - Anti- monopoly laws
  - Sunday closing laws
  - Municipal licences
  - Laws that favour business investment
- Technology

- Efficiency of infrastructure, including: roads, ports, airports, rolling stock, hospitals, education, healthcare, communication, etc.
- Industrial productivity
- New manufacturing processes
- New products and services of competitors
- New products and services of supply chain partners
- Any new technology that could impact the company
- Cost and accessibility of electrical power

- Ecology
  - Ecological concerns that affect the firms production processes
  - Ecological concerns that affect customers' buying habits
  - Ecological concerns that affect customers' perception of the company or product
- Socio-Cultural
  - Demographic factors such as:
    - Population size and distribution
    - Age distribution
    - Education levels
    - Income levels
    - Ethnic origins
    - Religious affiliations
  - Attitudes towards:
    - Materialism, capitalism, free enterprise
    - Individualism, role of family, role of government, collectivism
    - Role of church and religion
    - Consumerism
    - Environmentalism
    - importance of work, pride of accomplishment
- Cultural structures including:
    - Diet and nutrition
    - Housing conditions
- Potential Suppliers
  - Labour supply
    - Quantity of labour available
    - Quality of labour available
    - Stability of labour supply
    - Wage expectations
    - Employee turn-over rate
    - Strikes and labour relations
    - educational facilities
  - Material suppliers
    - Quality, quantity, price, and stability of material inputs

  - Delivery delays
  - Proximity of bulky or heavy material inputs
  - Level of competition among suppliers
- Service Providers
  - Quantity, quality, price, and stability of service facilitators
  - Special requirements

Scanning these macroenvironmental variables for threats and opportunities requires that each issue be rated on two dimensions. It must be rated on its potential impact on the company, and rated on its likeliness of occurrence. Multiplying the potential impact parameter by the likeliness of occurrence parameter gives us a good indication of its importance to the firm.

When an issue is detected, there are generally six (6) ways of responding to them:

- Opposition strategy - try to influence the environmental forces so as to negate their impact - this is only successful where you have some control over the environmental variable in question
- Adaptation strategy - adapt your marketing plan to the new environmental conditions
- Offensive strategy - try to turn the new influence into an advantage - quick response can give you a competitive advantage
- Redeployment strategy - redeploy your assets into another industry
- Contingency strategies - determine a broad range of possible reactions - find substitutes
- Passive strategy - no response - study the situation further

Market Segment

Market segmentation is the process in marketing of dividing a market into distinct subsets (segments) that behave in the same way or have similar needs. Because each segment is fairly homogeneous in their needs and attitudes, they are likely to respond similarly to a given marketing strategy. That is, they are likely to have similar feeling and ideas about a marketing mix comprised of a given product or service, sold at a given price, distributed in a certain way, and promoted in a certain way.

Broadly, markets can be divided according to a number of general criteria, such as by industry or public versus private sector. Small segments are often termed niche markets or specialty markets. However, all segments fall into either consumer or industrial markets. Although it has similar objectives and it overlaps with consumer markets in many ways, the process of Industrial market segmentation is quite different.

The process of segmentation is distinct from targeting (choosing which segments to address) and positioning (designing an appropriate marketing mix for each segment). The overall intent is to identify groups of similar customers and potential customers; to prioritise the groups to address; to understand their behaviour; and to respond with appropriate marketing strategies that satisfy the different preferences of each chosen segment.

The requirements for successful segmentation are:

- Homogeneity within the segment
- Heterogeneity between segments
- Segments are measurable and identifiable
- Segments are accessible and actionable
- Segment is large enough to be profitable

These criteria can be summarized by the word SADAM:

- S Substantial: the segment has to be large and profitable enough
- A Accessible: it must be possible to reach it efficiently
- D Differential: it must respond differently to a different marketing mix
- A Actionable: you must have a product for this segment
- M Measurable: size and purchasing power can be measured

Currently a college student studying the marketing mix is introduced to the Four Ps of the Marketing Mix; Product, Place, Promotion, Price.

Product (service) is whatever it may be that is being sold/marketed.

Price refers to not only the actual price but also price elasticity.

Place has evidently replaced distribution simply by where or what area the marketing campaign is going to cover, as well as what types of distribution channel (retail, wholesale, online, etc) will be used. Today the idea of place is not limited to geographic profiling but also demographics and other categorizing variables. This has only occurred over the last ten years with the expansion of internet use and its ability to target specific types of people and not just people in a geographic area.

Promotion simply refers to what medium will deliver the message and what the overall marketing strategy is offering as a benefit.

The variables used for segmentation include:

- Geographic variables
  - Region of the world or country, East, West, South, North, Central, coastal, hilly, etc.
  - Country size/country size : Metropolitian Cities, small cities, towns.
  - Density of Area Urban, Semi-urban, Rural.
  - climate Hot, Cold, Humid, Rainy.
- Demographic variables
  - Age
  - Gender Male and Female
  - Sexual orientation
  - Family size
  - Family life cycle
  - Education Primary, High School, Secondary, College, Universities.

- Income
- Education
- Religion
- Language
- Occupation
- Socioeconomic status
- Nationality/race

- Psychographic variables
  - Personality
  - Life style
  - Value
  - Attitude
- Behavioural variables
  - Benefit sought
  - Product usage rate
  - Brand loyalty
  - Product end use
  - Readiness-to-buy stage
  - Decision making unit

When numerous variables are combined to give an in-depth understanding of a segment, this is referred to as depth segmentation. When enough information is combined to create a clear picture of a typical member of a segment, this is referred to as a buyer profile. When the profile is limited to demographic variables it is called a demographic profile (typically shortened to "a demographic"). A statistical technique commonly used in determining a profile is cluster analysis.

George Day describes model of segmentation as the top-down approach: You start with the total population and divide it into segments. He also identified an alternative model which he called the bottom-up approach. In this approach, you start with a single customer and build on that profile. This typically requires the use of customer relationship management software or a database of some kind. Profiles of existing customers are created and analysed.

Various demographic, behavioural, and psychographic patterns are built up using techniques such as cluster analysis. This process is sometimes called database marketing or micro-marketing. Its use is most appropriate in highly fragmented markets. McKenna claims that this approach treats every customer as a "micromajority". Pine used the bottom-up approach in what he called "segment of one marketing". Through this process mass customization is possible.

Where a monopoly exists, the price of a product is likely to be higher than in a competitive market and the quantity sold less, generating monopoly profits for the seller. These profits can be increased further if the market can be segmented with different prices charged to different segments, charging higher prices to those segments willing and able to pay more and charging less to those whose demand is price elastic. The price discriminator might need to create rate fences that will prevent members of a higher price segment from purchasing at the prices available to members of a lower price segment. This behaviour is rational on the part of the monopolist, but is often seen by competition authorities as an abuse of a monopoly position, whether or not the monopoly itself is sanctioned.

Competitor Analysis

Competitor analysis in marketing and strategic management is an assessment of the strengths and weaknesses of current and potential competitors.

One common and useful technique is constructing a competitor array. The steps include:

- Define your industry - scope and nature of the industry
- Determine who your competitors are
- Determine who your customers are and what benefits they expect
- Determine what the key success factors are in your industry
- Rank the key success factors by giving each one a weighting - The sum of all the weightings must add up to one.
- Rate each competitor on each of the key success factors - this can best be displayed on a two dimensional matrix - competitors along the top and key success factors down the side.
- Multiply each cell in the matrix by the factor weighting.
- Sum columns for a weighted assessment of the overall strength of each competitor relative to each other.

We can learn a lot about the competitive environment by scanning our competitors' ads. Changes in a competitor's advertising message can reveal new product offerings, new production processes, a new branding strategy, a new positioning strategy, a new segmentation strategy, line extensions and contractions, problems with previous positions, insights from recent marketing or product research, a new strategic direction, a new source of sustainable competitive advantage, or value migrations within the industry. It might also indicate a new pricing strategy such as penetration, price discrimination, price skimming, product bundling, joint product pricing, discounts, or loss leaders.

It may also indicate a new promotion strategy such as push, pull, balanced, short term sales generation, long term image creation, informational, comparative, affective, reminder, new creative objectives, new unique selling proposition, new creative concepts, appeals, tone, and themes, or a new advertising agency. It might also indicate a new distribution strategy, new distribution partners, more extensive distribution, more intensive distribution, a change in geographical focus, or exclusive distribution. Little of this intelligence is definitive : additional information is needed before conclusions should be drawn.

A competitor's media strategy reveals budget allocation, segmentation and targeting strategy, and selectivity and focus. From a tactical perspective, it can also be used to help a manager implement his/her own media plan. By knowing the competitor's media buy, media selection, frequency, reach, continuity, schedules, and flights, the manager can arrange his/her own media plan so that they do not coincide.

Other sources of corporate intelligence include trade shows, patent filings, mutual customers, annual reports, and trade associations.

Some firms hire competitor intelligence professionals to obtain this information.

In addition to analysing current competitors, it is necessary to estimate future competitive threats. The most common sources of new competitors are:

- Companies competing in a related product/market
- Companies using related technologies
- Companies already targeting your prime market segment but with unrelated products
- Companies from other geographical areas and with similar products
- New start-up companies organised by former employees and/or managers of existing companies

The entrance of new competitors is likely when:

- There are high profit margins in the industry
- There is unmet demand (insufficient supply) in the industry
- There are no major barriers to entry
- There is future growth potential
- Competitive rivalry is not intense
- Gaining a competitive advantage over existing firms is feasible

Demographic Profiles in Marketing

Marketers typically combine several variables to define a demographic profile. A demographic profile (often shortened to "a demographic") provides enough information about the typical member of this group to create a mental picture of this hypothetical aggregate. For example, a marketer might speak of the single, female, middle-class, age 18 to 24 demographic.

Marketing researchers typically have two objectives in this regard: first to determine what segments or subgroups exist in the overall population; and secondly to create a clear and complete picture of the characteristics of a typical member of each of these segments. Once these profiles are constructed, they can be used to develop a marketing strategy and marketing plan. A demographic or demographic profile is a term used in marketing and broadcasting, to describe a demographic grouping or a market segment. This typically involves age bands (as teenagers do not wish to purchase denture fixant), social class bands (as the rich may want different products than middle and poorer classes and may be willing to pay more) and gender (partially because different physical attributes require different hygiene and clothing products, and partially because of the male/female mindsets).

A demographic profile can be used to determine when and where advertising should be placed so as to achieve maximum results. In all such cases, it is important that the advertiser get the most results for their money, and so careful research is done to match the demographic profile of the target market to the demographic profile of the advertising medium.

A good way to figure out the intended demographic of a television show, TV channel, or magazine is to study the ads that accompany it. For example, in the United States the television programme The Price is Right most frequently airs from 11 a.m. to Noon. The commercials on it (besides the use of product placement in the show itself) are often for things like arthritis pain relievers and diapers. This indicates that the target demographics are senior citizens and parents with young children, both of which would be home at that time of day and see that show.

Research Marketing

Research is the search for and retrieval of existing, discovery or creation of new information or knowledge for a specific purpose. Research has many categories, from medical research to literary research. 'Marketing research is a form of business research. and Business-to-Business (B2B)Marketing Research, or Business Marketing Research, previously known as Industrial Marketing Research.

B2B Marketing Research investigates the markets for products sold by one business to another, rather than to consumers.

Consumer Marketing Research is a form of applied sociology which concentrates on understanding the behaviours, whims and preferences, of consumers in a market-based economy. The field of consumer marketing research as a statistical science was pioneered by Arthur Nielsen with the founding of the ACNielsen Company in 1923.

In addition to marketing research, other forms of business research include:

- Market research is broader in scope and examines all aspects of a business environment. It asks questions about competitors, market structure, government regulations, economic trends, technological advances, and numerous other factors that make up the business environment. Sometimes the term refers more particularly to the financial analysis of companies, industries, or sectors. In this case, financial analysts usually carry out the research and provide the results to investment advisors and potential investors.
- Product research - This looks at what products can be produced with available technology, and what new product innovations near-future technology can develop.
- Advertising research - This attempts to assess the likely impact of an advertising campaign in advance, and also measure the success of a recent campaign..

Types of Marketing Research

Marketing research techniques come in many forms, including:

- Test marketing - A small-scale product launch used to determine the likely acceptance of the product when it is introduced into a wider market
- Concept testing - To test the acceptance of a concept by target consumers
- Mystery shopping - An employee or representative of the market research firm anonymously contacts a salesperson and indicates he or she is shopping for a product. The shopper then records the entire experience. This method is often used for quality control or for researching competitors' products.
- Store audit - To measure the sales of a product or product line at a statistically selected store sample in order to determine market share, or to determine whether a retail store provides adequate service
- Demand estimation - To determine the approximate level of demand for the product
- Commercial Eye tracking research - examine advertisements, package designs, websites, etc by analyzing visual behaviour of the consumer
- Sales forecasting - To determine the expected level of sales given the level of demand. With respect to other factors like Advertising expenditure, sales promotion etc.
- Customer satisfaction studies - Exit interviews or surveys that determine a customer's level of satisfaction with the quality of the transaction
- Distribution channel audits - To assess distributors' and retailers' attitudes toward a product, brand, or company
- Price elasticity testing - To determine how sensitive customers are to price changes
- Segmentation research - To determine the demographic, psychographic, and behavioural characteristics of potential buyers
- Consumer decision process research - To determine what motivates people to buy and what decision-making process they use
- Positioning research - How does the target market see the brand relative to competitors? - what does the brand stand for?
- Brand name testing - What do consumers feel about the names of the products?
- Brand equity research - How favorably do consumers view the brand?
- Advertising and promotion research - How effective are ads - do potential customers recall the ad, understand the message, and does the ad influence consumer purchasing behaviour?
- Internet Strategic Intelligence - Searching for customer opinions in

the internet: chats, forums, web pages, blogs... where people express freely about their experiences with products, becoming strong "opinion formers"

All of these forms of marketing research can be classified as either problem-identification research or as problem-solving research.

A company collects primary research by gathering original data. Secondary research is conducted on data published previously and usually by someone else. Secondary research costs far less than primary research, but seldom comes in a form that exactly meets the needs of the researcher.

A similar distinction exists between exploratory research and conclusive research. Exploratory research provides insights into and comprehension of an issue or situation. It should draw definitive conclusions only with extreme caution. Conclusive research draws conclusions: the results of the study can be generalized to the whole population.

Exploratory research is conducted to explore a problem to get some basic idea about the solution at the preliminary stages of research. It may serve as the input to conclusive research. Exploratory research information is collected by focus group interviews, reviewing literature or books, discussing with experts, etc. This is unstructured and qualitative in nature. If a secondary source of data is unable to serve the purpose, a convenience sample of small size can be collected. Conclusive research is conducted to draw some conclusion about the problem. It is primary, structured and quantitative research, and the output of this research is the input to Management information systems (MIS).

Marketing Research Methods

Methodologically, marketing research uses four types of research designs, namely:

- Qualitative marketing research - generally used for exploratory purposes - small number of respondents - not generalizable to the whole population - statistical significance and confidence not calculated - examples include focus groups, in-depth interviews, and projective techniques
- Quantitative marketing research - generally used to draw conclusions - tests a specific hypothesis - uses random sampling techniques so as to infer from the sample to the population - involves a large number of respondents - examples include surveys and questionnaires
- Observational techniques - the researcher observes social phenomena in their natural setting - observations can occur cross-sectionally (observations made at one time) or longitudinally (observations occur over several time-periods) - examples include product-use analysis and computer cookie traces
- Experimental techniques - the researcher creates a quasi-artificial environment to try to control spurious factors, then manipulates

at least one of the variables - examples include purchase laboratories and test markets

Researchers often use more than one research design. They may start with secondary research to get background information, then conduct a focus group (qualitative research design) to explore the issues. Finally they might do a full nation-wide survey (quantitative research design) in order to devise specific recommendations for the client.

Business to business (b2b) research is inevitably more complicated than consumer research. The researchers need to know what type of multi-faceted approach will answer the objectives, since seldom is it possible to find the answers using just one method. Finding the right respondents is crucial in b2b research since they are often busy, and may not want to participate. Encouraging them to "open up" is yet another skill required of the b2b researcher. Last, but not least, most business research leads to strategic decisions and this means that the business researcher must have expertise in developing strategies that are strongly rooted in the research findings and acceptable to the client.

There are four key factors that make b2b market research special and different to consumer markets:

- The decision making unit is far more complex in b2b markets than in consumer markets
- B2b products and their applications are more complex than consumer products
- B2b marketers address a much smaller number of customers who are very much larger in their consumption of products than is the case in consumer markets
- Personal relationships are of critical importance in b2b markets.

Market research techniques resemble those used in political polling and social science research. Meta-analysis (also called the Schmidt-Hunter technique) refers to a statistical method of combining data from multiple studies or from several types of studies. Conceptualization means the process of converting vague mental images into definable concepts. Operationalization is the process of converting concepts into specific observable behaviours that a researcher can measure. Precision refers to the exactness of any given measure. Reliability refers to the likelihood that a given operationalized construct will yield the same results if re-measured. Validity refers to the extent to which a measure provides data that captures the meaning of the operationalized construct as defined in the study. It asks, "Are we measuring what we intended to measure?"

Applied research sets out to prove a specific hypothesis of value to the clients paying for the research. For example, a cigarette company might commission research that attempts to show that cigarettes are good for one's health. Many researchers have ethical misgivings about doing applied research.

Sugging (or Selling Under the Guise of market research) forms a sales technique in which sales people pretend to conduct marketing research, but with the real purpose of obtaining buyer motivation and buyer decision-making information to be used in a subsequent sales call.

Frugging comprises the practice of soliciting funds under the pretense of being a research organization.

Experimental research designs are used for the controlled testing of causal processes. The general procedure is one or more independent variables are manipulated to determine their effect on a dependent variable. These designs can be used where: 1) There is time priority in a causal relationship (cause precedes effect), 2) There is consistency in a causal relationship (a cause will always lead to the same effect), and 3) The magnitude of the correlation is great. The most common applications of these designs in marketing research and experimental economics are test markets and purchase labs. The techniques are commonly used in other social sciences including sociology and psychology.

One of the most important requirements of experimental research designs is the necessity of eliminating the effects of spurious, intervening, and antecedent variables. In the most basic model, cause (X) leads to effect (Y). But there could be a third variable (Z) that influences (Y), and X might not be the true cause at all. Z is said to be a spurious variable and must be controlled for. The same is true for intervening variables (a variable in between the supposed cause (X) and the effect (Y)), and anteceding variables (a variable prior to the supposed cause (X) that is the true cause). When a third variable is involved and has not been controlled for, the relation is said to be a [zero order] relationship. In most practical applications of experimental research designs there are several causes (X1,X2,X3). In most designs only one of these causes is manipulated at a time.

A true experimental design requires an artificial environment so as to control for all spurious, intervening, and antecedent variables. A purchase laboratory approaches this ideal. Participants are given money, script, or credit to purchase products in a simulated store. Researchers modify one variable at a time (for example; price, packaging, shelf location, size, or competitors' offerings) and determine what effect that has on sales volume. Internet based purchase labs (called virtual purchase labs) are becoming more common.

Simplified versions of the purchase laboratory are often used for pragmatic reasons. An example of this would be to use tachistocopes for testing packaging and shelf location.

Quasi-experimental designs control some, but not all, of the extraneous factors. A test market is an example of this. A new product is typically introduced in a select number of cities. These cities must be representative of the overall national (or international) population. They should also be relatively unpolluted by outside influences (for example : media from other cities). The marketer has some control over the marketing mix variables, but almost no control over the broader business environment variables. Competitors could change their prices during the test. Government could change the level of taxes.

New competing products could be introduced. An advertising campaign could be initiated by competitors. Any of these spurious variables could contaminate the test market.

In an attempt to control for extraneous factors, several experimental research designs have been developed, including:

- Classical pretest-post test - The total population of participants is randomly divided into two samples; the control sample, and the experimental sample. Only the experimental sample is exposed to the manipulated variable. The researcher compares the pretest results with the post test results for both samples. Any divergence between the two samples is assumed to be a result of the experiment.
- Solomon four group design - The population is randomly divided into four samples. Two of the groups are experimental samples. Two groups experience no experimental manipulation of variables. Two groups receive a pretest and a post test. Two groups receive only a post test. This is an improvement over the classical design because it controls for the effect of the pretest.
- Factorial design - This is similar to a classical design except additional samples are used. Each group is exposed to a different experimental manipulation.

Pricing Objectives

Pricing objectives or goals give direction to the whole pricing process. Determining what your objectives are is the first step in pricing. When deciding on pricing objectives you must consider: 1) the overall financial, marketing, and strategic objectives of the company; 2) the objectives of your product or brand; 3) consumer price elasticity and price points; and 4) the resources you have available.

Some of the more common pricing objectives are:

- Maximize long-run profit
- Maximize short-run profit
- Increase sales volume (quantity)
- Increase dollar sales
- Increase market share
- Obtain a target rate of return on investment (ROI)
- Obtain a target rate of return on sales
- Stabilize market or stabilize market price: an objective to stabilize price means that the marketing manager attempts to keep prices stable in the marketplace and to compete on nonprice considerations. Stabilization of margin is bascially a cost-plus approach in which

the manager attemptes to maintain the same margin regradless of changes in cost.

- Company growth
- Maintain price leadership
- Desensitize customers to price
- Discourage new entrants into the industry
- Match competitors prices
- Encourage the exit of marginal firms from the industry
- Survival
- Avoid government investigation or intervention
- Obtain or maintain the loyalty and enthusiasm of distributors and other sales personnel
- Enhance the image of the firm, brand, or product
- Be perceived as "fair" by customers and potential customers
- Create interest and excitement about a product
- Discourage competitors from cutting prices
- Use price to make the product "visible"
- Build store traffic
- Help prepare for the sale of the business (harvesting)
- Social, ethical, or ideological objectives
- Get competitive advantage

5

Entrepreneurship in Tourism Industry

Hospitality management is the name given to the collegiate academic major in which students are taught the business of running hotels, restaurants, and travel and tourism-related business.

The most famous hospitality school in management is located in Ithaca, NY: The Hotel School at Cornell University.

Another notable hospitality school is in Switzerland: the École hôtelière de Lausanne (EHL).The school currently offers three types of degrees. The primary programme, where students are educated in international hospitality management, leads to a Bachelor of Science (BOS) degree. Additionally, a prestigious MBA, the MHA (Master in Hospitality Administration) is offered. EHL has educated more than 25,000 hospitality industry executives who now make up a prestigious network for every member of the EHL community.

Entrepreneurship

Entrepreneurship is the practice of starting new organizations, particularly new businesses generally in response to identified opportunities. Entrepreneurship is often a difficult undertaking, as a majority of new businesses fail. Entrepreneurial activities are substantially different depending on the type of organization that is being started. Entrepreneurship ranges in scale from solo projects (even involving the entrepreneur only part-time) to major undertakings creating many job opportunities.

Many "high-profile" entrepreneurial ventures seek venture capital or angel funding in order to raise capital to build the business. Many kinds of organizations now exist to support would-be entrepreneurs, including specialized government agencies, business incubators, science parks, and some NGOs.

The understanding of entrepreneurship owes a lot to the work of economist Joseph Schumpeter and the Austrian School of economics. In Schumpeter (1950), an entrepreneur is a person who is willing and able to convert a new idea or invention into a successful innovation. Entrepreneurship forces "creative destruction" across markets and industries, simultaneously creating new products and business models others. In this way, creative destruction is largely responsible for the dynamism of industries and long-run economic growth. Despite Schumpeter's early 20th-century contributions, the traditional microeconomic theory of economics has had little room for entrepreneurs in their theoretical frameworks (instead assuming that resources would find each other through a price system).

Entrepreneurship received a boost in the formalized creation of so-called incubators and science parks where businesses can start at a small scale, share services and space while they grow, and eventually move into space of their own when they have achieved a large enough scale to be viable stand-alone businesses. Also, entrepreneurship is being employed to revitalize fading downtowns and inner cities, which may have excellent resources but suffer from a lack of spirited development.

For Frank H. Knight and Peter Drucker entrepreneurship is about taking risk. The behaviour of the entrepreneur reflects a kind of person willing to put his or her career and financial security on the line and take risks in the name of an idea, spending much time as well as capital on an uncertain venture.

Still another view of entrepreneurship is that it is the process of discovering, evaluating, and exploiting opportunities, which go on to reify themselves in the form of new business ventures. In this model an entrepreneur could be defined as "someone who acts with ambition beyond that supportable by the resources currently under his control, in relentless pursuit of opportunity" (a definition common to entrepreneurship professors Howard Stevenson and Jeffry Timmons). Pinchot coined the term Intrapreneurship to describe entrepreneurial-like activities inside organizations and government. The concept is commonly referred to as Corporate Entrepreneurship.

The place of the disharmony-creating and idiosyncratic entrepreneur in traditional economic theory (which describes many efficiency-based ratios assuming uniform outputs) presents theoretic quandaries. William Baumol has added greatly to this area of economic theory and was recently honored for it at the 2006 annual meeting of the American Economic Association.

The Entrepreneur

Entrepreneurs have many of the same character traits as leaders. Similarly to the early great man theories of leadership, however, trait-based theories of entrepreneurship are increasingly being called into question. Entrepreneurs are often contrasted with managers and administrators who are said to be more methodical and less prone to risk-taking. Although such person-centric models of entrepreneurship have shown to be of questionable validity, a vast but clearly dated literature studying the entrepreneurial personality found that certain traits seem to be associated with entrepreneurs:

- For example, in 1961, David McClelland described the entrepreneur as primarily motivated by an overwhelming need for achievement and strong urge to build.

- Collins and Moore (1970) studied 150 entrepreneurs and concluded that they are tough, pragmatic people driven by needs of independence and achievement. They seldom are willing to submit to authority.
- Bird sees entrepreneurs as mercurial, that is, prone to insights, brainstorms, deceptions, ingeniousness and resourcefulness. They are cunning, opportunistic, creative, and unsentimental.
- Busenitz and Barney claim entrepreneurs are prone to overconfidence and over generalisations.
- According to Cole, there are four types of entrepreneur: the innovator, the calculating inventor, the over-optimistic promoter, and the organisation builder. These types are not related to the personality but to the type of opportunity the entrepreneur faces.
- Burton W. Folsom, Jr. distinguishes between what he calls a political entrepreneur and a market entrepreneur. The political entrepreneur uses political influences to gain income through subsidies, protectionism, government-granted monopoly, government contracts, or other such favorable arrangements with governments. The market entrepreneur operates without special favors from government.

Characteristics of Entrepreneurship

- The entrepreneur has an enthusiastic vision, the driving force of an enterprise.
- The entrepreneur's vision is usually supported by an interlocked collection of specific ideas not available to the marketplace.
- The overall blueprint to realize the vision is clear, however details may be incomplete, flexible, and evolving.
- The entrepreneur promotes the vision with enthusiastic passion.
- With persistence and determination, the entrepreneur develops strategies to change the vision into reality.
- The entrepreneur takes the initial responsibility to cause a vision to become a success.
- Entrepreneurs take prudent risks. They assess costs, market/customer needs and persuade others to join and help.
- An entrepreneur is usually a positive thinker and a decision maker.

Entrepreneur

An entrepreneur (a loanword from French) is a person who undertakes and operates a new enterprise or venture and assumes some accountability for the inherent risks. In the context of the creation of for-profit enterprises, entrepreneur is often synonymous with founder.

Most commonly, the term entrepreneur applies to someone who establishes a new entity to offer a new or existing product or service into a new or existing market, whether for a profit or not-for-profit outcome. Business entrepreneurs often have strong beliefs about a market opportunity and are willing to accept a high level of personal, professional or financial risk to pursue that opportunity. Business entrepreneurs are often highly regarded in U.S. culture as critical components of its capitalistic society.

- An entrepreneur is a person who organizes and manages any enterprise, esp. a business, usually with considerable initiative and risk.
- An employer of productive labour; contractor.
- Is the one to deal with or initiate as an entrepreneur.

Role of Entrepreneur in an Organization

An entrepreneur is someone who organizes a system. He is the person who creates and/or sells a product or service in order to gain profit. However, there is a general sense that entrepreneurship involves the establishment of a new venture while adopting some of the risk and being ready for failure. There is no general definition for the word, as it has been used in a large variety of ways. Some scholars of entrepreneurship, such as Prof. W. Long have tried to develop a specific definition by studying the evolution of the word's usage.

Entrepreneur as a Risk Bearer

An entrepreneur is an agent who buys factors of production at certain prices in order to combine them into a product with a view to selling it at uncertain prices in future. Uncertainty is defined as a risk, which cannot be insured against and is incalculable. There is a distinction between ordinary risk and uncertainty. A risk can be reduced through the insurance principle, where the distribution of the outcome in a group of instances is known. On the contrary, uncertainty is a risk, which cannot be calculated. The entrepreneur, according to Knight, is the economic functionary who undertakes such responsibility of uncertainty, which by its very nature cannot be insured, or capitalized or salaried to. Mark Casson has extended this notion to characterize entrepreneurs as decision makers who improvise solutions to problems which cannot be solved by routine alone.

Entrepreneur as an Organizer

An entrepreneur is one who combines the land of one, labour of another and the capital of yet another, and, thus, produces a product.

By selling the product in the market, he pays interest on capital, rent on land and wages to laborers and what remains is his or her profit.

Entrepreneur as a Leader

Scholar R. B. Reich considers leadership, management ability, and team-building as essential qualities of an entrepreneur.

Entrepreneur is sometimes mistakenly equated with "opportunist". An entrepreneur may be considered one who creates an opportunity rather than merely exploits it, though that distinction is difficult to make precise.

Supply vs Demand Theories

Business academics have two classes of theories of how people become entrepreneurs, called supply and demand theories, after Economics. In the supply theory, entrepreneurs arise as they are born, with personality traits which drive them to become entrepreneurs. In the demand theory, anyone could be recruited by circumstance or opportunity to become an entrepreneur.

Several research studies have shown that entrepreneurs are convinced that they can command their own destinies. Behaviourial scientists express this by saying that entrepreneurs perceive the "locus of control" to be within themselves. It is this self-belief which stimulates the entrepreneur, according to supply-side theorists.

A more generally held theory is that entrepreneurs emerge from the population on demand, from the combination of opportunities and people well-positioned to take advantage of them. The entrepreneur may perceive that they are among the few to recognize or be able to solve a problem. In this view, one studies on one side the distribution of information available to would-be entrepreneurs and on the other, how environmental factors (access to capital, competition, etc.) change the rate of a society's production of entrepreneurs.

Personality Characteristics

John G. Burch lists the following traits typical of entrepreneurs:

- A desire to achieve: The push to conquer problems, and give birth to a successful venture.
- Hard work: It is often suggested that many entrepreneurs are workaholics.
- Desire to work for themselves: Entrepreneurs like to work for themselves rather than working for an organization or any other individual. They may work for someone to gain the knowledge of product or service that they may want to produce.
- Nurturing quality: Willing to take charge of, and watch over a venture until it can stand alone.
- Acceptance of responsibility: Are morally, legally, and mentally accountable for their ventures. Some entrepreneurs may be driven more by altruism than by self-interest.
- Reward orientation: Desire to achieve, work hard, and take responsibility, but also with a commensurate desire to be rewarded handsomely for their efforts; rewards can be in forms other than money, such as recognition and respect.
- Optimism: Live by the philosophy that this is the best of times, and that anything is possible.

- Orientation to excellence: Often desire to achieve something outstanding that they can be proud of.
- Organization: Are good at bringing together the components (including people) of a venture.
- Profit orientation: Want to make a profit; but the profit serves primarily as a meter to gauge their success and achievement.

FUNCTIONS OF MANAGEMENT

Planning

Planning is the (psychological) process of creating and refining a plan, or integrating it with other plans. The term is also used to describe the formal procedures used in such an endeavour, such as the creation of documents, diagrams, or meetings to discuss the important issues to be addressed, the objectives to be met, and the strategy to be followed. Beyond this, planning has a different meaning depending on the political or economic context in which it is used.

Planning refers to the practice and profession associated with land use planning, urban planning or spatial planning. In many countries, the operation of town and country planning system is often referred to as 'planning' and the professionals which operate the system are known as 'planners'.It is a process which is decided in advance what is to be done in the coming future.

Objectives for Non-profit-making Organizations

In the case of non-profit organizations the objectives may be less than clear. Keith Blois suggested five main reasons for the differences from 'commercial' organizations:

1. Ambiguous Goals [more actors and groups of actors are involved
2. Lack of Agreement in Means-End Relationships [even where there is consensus on the goal there may be disagreement on how to get there]
3. Environmental Turbulence [non-profit organizations seem to be exposed more to turbulence than commercial ones
4. Unmeasurable Outputs [unfortunately, by definition, non-profit organizations do not have the classically convenient simplicity of 'bottom-line profit'
5. The Effects of Management Intervention are Unknown [the lack of precision caused by factors 1-4 is problem enough, but the 'culture' seems to add further barriers to managing these organizations

Even so, Kotler and Andreasen suggested some possible objectives for such organizations:

1. Surplus Maximization [equivalent to profit maximization]
2. Revenue Maximization [as for profit-making organizations]

3. Usage Maximization [maximizing the numbers of users and their usage]
4. Usage Targeting [matching the capacity available]
5. Full Cost Recovery [breaking even]
6. Partial Cost Recovery [minimizing the subsidy]
7. Budget Maximization [maximizing what is offered]
8. Producer Satisfaction Maximization [satisfying the wants of staff]

Planning in Organizations

Planning is also a management function, concerned with defining goals for future organizational performance and deciding on the tasks and resources to be used in order to attain those goals. To meet the goals, managers will invest significant resources for training and incentives to motivate employees. Planning is the process of setting objectives and determining how to accomplish them

Simply it is the act of thinking before doing. It access us in predecting the about the future. So,it serve as the standard for the function of controlling if there is any devation.

The Marketing Planning Process

In most organizations 'strategic planning' is an annual process, typically covering just the year ahead. Occasionally, a few organizations may look at a practical plan which stretches three or more years ahead.

To be most effective, the plan has to be formalized, usually in written form, as a formal 'marketing plan'. The essence of the process is that it moves from the general to the specific; from the overall objectives of the organization down to the individual action plan for a part of one marketing programme. It is also an iterative process, so that the draft output of each stage is checked to see what impact it has on the earlier stages - and is amended accordingly.

The Corporate Plan

The starting point for the marketing plan, and the context within which it is set, is the corporate plan. In most marketing-oriented organizations the contents of the corporate plan will closely match those of the marketing plan itself; but it will also include the plans for the disposition of the other internal resources of the organization. Thus, the corporate plan is likely to contain three main components:

The first category is intimately involved with the customers. In marketing terms, although there are many other factors to take into account, the most important definition of where the company is revolves around where it is in the market (and hence where it is with its consumers). The same is largely true of the second stage as well; since, no matter how much its managers may wish otherwise, where the company can realistically expect to go is totally in the hands of its customers. It is only at the third stage that the 4 Ps come into play as vehicles for moving the company to reach its objectives.

Corporate Objectives

The overall objectives of commercial organizations are conventionally supposed to be financial. However, other aims are also possible. Many companies choose long-term growth (which may be quite different to revenue maximization in the short term). Almost all have an implicit, and very powerful, aim of survival.

One of the best known 'alternatives', that of 'satisficing' (rather than profit maximization), came from Herbert Simon: "In one way or another, they [alternative theories] incorporate the notions of bounded rationality: the need to search for decision alternatives, the replacement of optimization [profit-based objectives] by targets and satisficing [minimal] goals, and mechanisms of learning and adaptation."

Pfeffer and Salancik said that: "We prefer to view organizations as coalitions altering their purposes and domains to accommodate new interests, sloughing off parts of themselves to avoid some interests, and when necessary, becoming involved in activities far afield from their stated central purposes. Organizations are social instruments of tremendous power and energy, and the critical issue becomes who will control this energy and for what purpose."

If we accept the traditional assumption, as to the financial basis of the objectives behind the corporate plan, these objectives are ideally meant to be quantified in numerical and, in particular, financial terms.

In the most general terms, though, the 'objectives' behind a strategy address two questions: ''Where' do we want to be?' and ''When' do we expect to be there?'

Forecasting

This can be a very complex topic but can, in general, be roughly divided into two parts;

Short-Term Forecasting

This is the type of forecasting you will recognise. It is normally based upon a projection of historical trends, usually focused on sales volumes. There are many sophisticated techniques, increasingly using large amounts of computing power, but in essence all of these try to separate out the four main components:

1. Long term trends probably represent the most important information you are trying to extract from the mass of data before you.
2. Medium term cycles are supposed to result from regular economic ups and downs (from boom to bust) which used to be encapsulated in a 5 year 'business cycle' which, unfortunately, became unpredictable in the 1980s. The much quoted 'Kondratieff Cycles' are much longer, if they exist at all, being of the order of 25 - 50 years; and hence do not normally enter into shorter term forecasts.

3. Seasonal is the pattern within a single year, a pattern which most suppliers who are affected by it know well.
4. Random fluctuations, which do not fit regular patterns, afflict all products and services, and make computer analysis a very difficult proposition.

The end result of all these patterns superimposed may appear very confusing indeed. Despite all the sophistication on offer, therefore, by far the best advice is to keep it as simple as possible. The human eye is much better at resolving the complications shown above than the most powerful computer. Thus, the best approach to forecasting (and certainly the best check on any more sophisticated technique) is 'eyeballing' the sales charts! With some practise you should be able to sort out the main features of what is happening - and that is better than most computer models achieve.

The evidence is that the sophistication adds little or nothing to the accuracy (though it does to the image of the forecasters, and the prices they charge). Worst of all, such unnecessary complexity hinders your understanding of what is going on under the covers of the computer (and hides the fact that most forecasts are really based on human judgement). In any case, even if historical trends are accurately analysed, there is no guarantee that the future will be the same as the past. It is much better that you surface all the assumptions, and make your own judgements in full knowledge of what is involved.

Two very simple techniques to use (if nothing else but as a check on the forecasts others are trying to sell to you);

- Eyeballing - the technique I mentioned above is the first, and best, method. It merely requires you to plot historical results graphically; and then look for the patterns. Trust your own judgement - until you are proved wrong.
- Exponential Smoothing - this is the mathematical technique which reportedly gives the best results; probably because it is so simple, and consequently easily understood. Indeed, it is a very impressive title for a simple, but useful, mathematical technique; which can quite easily be handled manually. It just allows greater weight to be given to recent periods. Instead of, for example, the average trend over the whole of the last year being calculated, the sales data for each of the months is given a weighting, depending on how recent that month was. It simply takes the previous forecast, and adds on the latest 'actual' sales figure; except that it does this in a fixed proportion, which is chosen to reflect the weighting to be given to the latest period. The general form is; $Ft+1 = Ft + aEt$ where $Ft+1$ is the new forecast you are calculating, Ft is the previous one and Et is the deviation (or 'error') of the actual performance recorded against that previous period forecast; and 'a' is the weighting to be given to the most recent events. Exponential smoothing will not,

in this simple form, allow for seasonality; though more sophisticated (but less easily understood) versions can do this.

Long-Term Forecasting

This tends to be qualitative (as compared with the quantitative, numeric, focus of short term forecasts). It is even more dependent on judgement; and most of the more complicated approaches to it (such as Delphi, or Jury methods) aim to reduce the risks implicit in the judgement by spreading the process over panels of experts. It does not, in the final analysis, absolve the manager from backing his or her own judgement (which is probably better informed, in terms of the specific situation, than that of the 'experts').

Of all the techniques the most useful involves developing complementary scenarios, which allow for the uncertainties involved; as well as expanding the viewpoint of all the managers involved in the process. Unfortunately, in the form most often described it can also be the most complex and sophisticated of these techniques - and in this form perhaps only the very large corporate planning team at Shell have used it really effectively. A much simplified approach, based on the version which Shell recommend for their line managers who are not part of their corporate planning group, is more practical for most organisations. In this simplified version of the form originally described by Shell[1] the four steps to this process are:

1. Identify the important variables
2. Brainstorm to find the possible outcomes
3. Link these together in a series of alternative scenarios
4. Refine these scenarios
    1. Identify the important variables - what (in the whole of the external environment, not just the marketing environment) are the most important factors which will determine the future of the organisation.
    2. Brainstorm to find the possible outcomes - work through the different outcomes which different alternatives for these variables may lead to.
    3. Link these together in a series of alternative scenarios - start to build six or seven scenarios ('stories' about the future of the organisation, or more importantly its market) which are able to contain these different alternatives.
    4. Refine these scenarios - then work on the scenarios until they are condensed to two or three meaningful alternative (but complementary) descriptions of the future.

Corporate Mission

Behind the corporate objectives, which in themselves offer the main context for the marketing plan, will lie the "corporate mission; which in turn provides the context for these corporate objectives. This 'corporate mission' can be thought of as a definition of what the organization is; of what it does: 'Our business is...'.

This definition should not be too narrow, or it will constrict the development of the organization; a too rigorous concentration on the view that 'We are in the business of making meat-scales', as IBM was during the early 1900s, might have limited its subsequent development into other areas. On the other hand, it should not be too wide or it will become meaningless; 'We want to make a profit' is not too helpful in developing specific plans.

Abell suggested that the definition should cover three dimensions: 'customer groups' to be served, 'customer needs' to be served, and 'technologies' to be utilized.

Thus, the definition of IBM's 'corporate mission' in the 1940s might well have been: 'We are in the business of handling accounting information [customer need] for the larger US organizations [customer group] by means of punched cards [technology].' Fortunately, as the name itself (International Business Machines) indicates, IBM already had a wider perspective (and its corporate mission was virtually defined by its name).

Corporate Vision

Perhaps the most important factor in successful marketing is the 'corporate vision'. Surprisingly, it is largely neglected by marketing textbooks; although not by the popular exponents of corporate strategy - indeed, it was perhaps the main theme of the book by Peters and Waterman, in the form of their 'Superordinate Goals'. Theodore Levitt said: "Nothing drives progress like the imagination. The idea precedes the deed."

If the organization in general, and its chief executive in particular, has a strong vision of where its future lies, then there is a good chance that the organization will achieve a strong position in its markets (and attain that future). This will be not least because its strategies will be consistent; and will be supported by its staff at all levels. In this context, all of IBM's marketing activities were underpinned by its philosophy of 'customer service'; a vision originally promoted by the charismatic Watson dynasty.

Henry Mintzberg explained: "... in some cases, in addition to the mission there is the `sense of mission', that is, a feeling that the group has banded together to create something new and exciting. This is common in new organizations".

What a worthwhile vision consists of is, however, usually open to debate; hence the reason why such visions tend to be associated with strong, charismatic leaders. But the vision must be relevant. The message for the marketer is that, to be most effective, the marketing strategies must be converted into a powerful long-term vision; if such a vision does not already exist.

Marketing Audit

The first formal step in the marketing planning process is that of conducting the marketing audit. Ideally, at the time of producing the marketing plan, this should only involve bringing together the source material which has already been collected throughout the year - as part of the normal work of the marketing department.

The emphasis at this stage is on obtaining a complete and accurate picture. In a single organization, however, it is likely that only a few aspects will be sufficiently important to have any significant impact on the marketing plan; but all may need to be reviewed to determine just which 'are' the few.

In this context some factors related to the customer, which should be included in the material collected for the audit, may be:

- Who are the customers?
- What are their key characteristics?
- What differentiates them from other members of the population?
- What are their needs and wants?
- What do they expect the 'product' to do?
- What are their special requirements and perceptions?
- What do they think of the organization and its products or services?
- What are their attitudes?

A 'traditional' - albeit product-based - format for a 'brand reference book' (or, indeed, a 'marketing facts book') was suggested by Godley more than three decades ago:

1. Financial data —Facts for this section will come from management accounting, costing and finance sections.
2. Product data —From production, research and development.
3. Sales and distribution data - Sales, packaging, distribution sections.
4. Advertising, sales promotion, merchandising data - Information from these departments.
5. Market data and miscellany - From market research, who would in most cases act as a source for this information.

His sources of data, however, assume the resources of a very large organization. In most organizations they would be obtained from a much smaller set of people (and not a few of them would be generated by the marketing manager alone). It is apparent that a marketing audit can be a complex process, but the aim is simple: 'it is only to identify those existing (external and internal) factors which will have a significant impact on the future plans of the company'.

It is clear that the basic material to be input to the marketing audit should be comprehensive. Accordingly, the best approach is to accumulate this material continuously, as and when it becomes available; since this avoids the otherwise heavy workload involved in collecting it as part of the regular, typically annual, planning process itself - when time is usually at a premium. Even so, the first task of this 'annual' process should be to check that the material held in the current 'facts book' or 'facts files' actually 'is' comprehensive and accurate, and can form a sound basis for the marketing audit itself.

The structure of the facts book will be designed to match the specific needs of the organization, but one simple format - suggested by Malcolm McDonald - may be applicable in many cases. This splits the material into three groups:

1. 'Review of the marketing environment'. A study of the organization's markets, customers, competitors and the overall economic, political, cultural and technical environment; covering developing trends, as well as the current situation.
2. 'Review of the detailed marketing activity'. A study of the company's marketing mix; in terms of the 4 Ps - product, price, promotion and place.
3. 'Review of the marketing system'. A study of the marketing organization, marketing research systems and the current marketing objectives and strategies.

The last of these is too frequently ignored. The marketing system itself needs to be regularly questioned, because the validity of the whole marketing plan is reliant upon the accuracy of the input from this system, and 'garbage in, garbage out' applies with a vengeance.

The analysis of this material will, no doubt, require significant effort. In the first instance it is a matter of selection, of sorting the wheat from the chaff. What is important, and will need to be taken into account in the marketing plan that will eventually emerge from the overall process, will be different for each product or service in each situation. One of the most important skills to be learned in marketing is that of being able to concentrate on just what is important.

It is important to say not just what happened but why. The process of marketing planning encompasses all of the marketing skills. However, a number of these may be particularly relevant at this stage:

- 'Positioning'. The starting point of the marketing plan must be the consumer. It is a matter of definition that his or her needs should drive the whole marketing process. The techniques of positioning and segmentation therefore usually offer the best starting point for what has to be achieved by the whole planning process.
- 'Portfolio planning'. In addition, the coordinated planning of the individual products and services can contribute towards the balanced portfolio.
- '80:20 rule'. To achieve the maximum impact, the marketing plan must be clear, concise and simple. It needs to concentrate on the 20 per cent of products or services, and on the 20 per cent of customers, which will account for 80 per cent of the volume and 80 per cent of the 'profit'.
- '4 Ps'. The 4 Ps can sometimes divert attention from the customer, but the framework they offer can be very useful in building the action plans.

Marketing Objectives

It is only at this stage (of deciding the marketing objectives) that the active part of the marketing planning process begins'.

This next stage in marketing planning is indeed the key to the whole marketing process. The marketing objectives state just where the company intends to be; at some specific time in the future. James Quinn succinctly defined objectives in general as: "Goals (or objectives) state 'what' is to be achieved and 'when' results are to be accomplished, but they do not state 'how' the results are to be achieved".

They typically relate to what products (or services) will be where in what markets (and must be realistically based on customer behaviour in those markets). They are essentially about the match between those 'products' and 'markets'. Objectives for pricing, distribution, advertising and so on are at a lower level, and should not be confused with marketing objectives. They are part of the marketing strategy needed to achieve marketing objectives.

To be most effective, objectives should be capable of measurement and therefore 'quantifiable'. This measurement may be in terms of sales volume, money value, market share, percentage penetration of distribution outlets and so on. An example of such a measurable marketing objective might be `to enter the market with product Y and capture 10 per cent of the market by value within one year'. As it is quantified it can, within limits, be unequivocally monitored; and corrective action taken as necessary.

The marketing objectives must usually be based, above all, on the organization's financial objectives; converting these financial measurements into the related marketing measurements.

It is conventionally assumed that marketing objectives will be designed to maximize volume or profit (or to optimize the utilization of resources in the non-profit sector), by creating demand or rejuvenating existing demand, say; although the various sub-objectives may indicate many different routes to achieving such optimization. However, as Kotler suggested (in the earlier edition of his book), there may be a number of other objectives:

- Synchromarketing
- Demarketing
- Counter-marketing

1. Synchromarketing - The aim may be to 'redistribute' existing sales (which are already at optimum levels) so that they occur at times, or in places, which the supplier prefers. Thus, for example, organizations which have highly seasonal sales (which make inefficient use of resources) may want to increase non-seasonal sales. Walls achieved this by balancing its summer sales of ice-cream with pies and sausages, demand for which peaks in winter. The suppliers of central-heating oil offer special deals for those customers willing to restock their tanks in summer.

2. Demarketing' - Demand may sometimes exceed supply. In these circumstances the emphasis will be on rationing scarce supplies. Occasionally the supplier, rather than bring on-stream expensive new plant, may seek to persuade customers to buy less (or be less dissatisfied with the scarcity). Some suppliers of electrical energy (electricity generators in Europe and the USA) have heavily advertised energy conservation measures to achieve this end (otherwise, the cost of meeting the peak winter loads would be very high - and unprofitable).
3. Counter-marketing - In what is usually a public-sector activity (but is occasionally undertaken by the private sector, where some uses of a product are damaging the corporate image), there may be an objective of stopping consumption completely. The anti-tobacco and anti-drug campaigns are the most obvious examples; but McDonald's campaigns to stop its customers dropping litter, or the brewers' campaigns to stop drinking and driving, fall into this category.

Emergent Strategy

In this case, the intended strategy, decided upon traditionally or incrementally, is overtaken by events in two main ways. One, which will probably be recognised by the organisation, is that of unrealised strategy; where it proves impossible to implement the chosen strategy in practice.

Less obvious is the emergent strategy which is decided by events in the external environment; and, thus, forced upon the organisation. This may not necessarily be recognised, in its totality, by the organisation - since many of its implications may be hidden. As markets become more complex, however, such emergent strategies are becoming more common.

Many organizations see both these processes in terms of failure - they have been forced, usually by unpredictable events, to abandon their own strategy. There is, accordingly, a tendency for these unwelcome facts to be ignored until they are so obvious that they cannot be avoided. This is a major error. Such deviations must be recognised (probably through one or other form of environmental analysis coupled with networking) as soon as possible- so that the organisation can react in good time.

A much more powerful approach is, though, to be proactive; so seize upon these deviations as the basis for future developments. What needs to be recognised is that emergent strategies are the most powerful of all. They must, by definition, be dierctly derived from the needs of the market - where even successful deliberate strategies may not ideally match market needs but may achieve their targets by sheer force (especially where conviction marketing lies behind them). Emergent strategies are, thus, likely to be vigorous ones.

There are two main approaches to capitalising on such emergent strategies. The first of these, favoured in the West, is the umbrella strategy. This is a form of very positive delegation, in that the overall strategies, the umbrella, are very general in nature - and allow the lower level managers, who are closest to the external environment, the freedom to react to these changes.

A much more direct, and hence even more powerful, approach is that favoured by the Japanese corporations. They integrate emergent strategies with their own. Indeed it is arguable that, in terms of marketing, to a large extent they use emergent strategies instead of their own deliberate strategies. This is evidenced as much by an attitude of mind as by any other feature. They deliberately go out to look for symptoms of such emergent trends which can be detected in the performance of their own products. More than that, though, they often deliberately launch a range of products rather than a single one to see which is most successful. It is almost as if they deliberately seek out the emergent strategies by offering the best environment for them to develop - the very reverse of the Western approach which seeks to avoid them! The Japanese then go on to build on these emergent strategies with a number of very effective tools - most of which are designed to overcome the major problem which accompanies emergent strategies, that they emerge on the scene much later than deliberate ones (and are likely to be visible to all the competitors at the same time) so that time is the essence. Thus, time management techniques (including parallel development along with flexible manufacturing and JIT) which have been developed by the Japanese offer them a significant competitive advantage in handling such emergent strategies.

Marketing Strategies

There are numerous definitions of what strategy is, but again James Quinn again gave a succinct general definition: "A strategy is a 'pattern' or 'plan' that 'integrates' an organization's 'major' goals, policies and action sequences into a 'cohesive' whole"

He went on to explain his view of the role of 'policies', with which strategy is most often confused: "Policies are rules or guidelines that express the 'limits' within which action should occur.

Simplifying somewhat, marketing strategies can be seen as the means, or 'game plan', by which marketing objectives will be achieved and, in the framework that we have chosen to use, are generally concerned with the 4 Ps. Examples are:

Product

- Developing new products, repositioning or relaunching existing ones and scrapping old ones
- Adding new features and benefits
- Balancing product portfolios
- Changing the design or packaging

Price

- Setting the price to skim or to penetrate

- Pricing for different market segments
- Deciding how to meet competitive pricing

Promotiom

- Specifying the advertising platform and media
- Deciding the public relations brief
- Organizing the salesforce to cover new products and services or markets

Place

- Choosing the channels
- Deciding levels of customer service

In principle, these strategies describe how the objectives will be achieved. The 4 Ps are a useful framework for deciding how the company's resources will be manipulated (strategically) to achieve the objectives. It should be noted, however, that they are not the only framework, and may divert attention from the real issues. The focus of the strategies must be the objectives to be achieved - not the process of planning itself. Only if it fits the needs of these objectives should you choose, as we have done, to use the framework of the 4 Ps.

The strategy statement can take the form of a purely verbal description of the strategic options which have been chosen. Alternatively, and perhaps more positively, it might include a structured list of the major options chosen.

One aspect of strategy which is often overlooked is that of 'timing'. Exactly when it is the best time for each element of the strategy to be implemented is often critical. Taking the right action at the wrong time can sometimes be almost as bad as taking the wrong action at the right time. Timing is, therefore, an essential part of any plan; and should normally appear as a schedule of planned activities.

Having completed this crucial stage of the planning process, you will need to re-check the feasibility of your objectives and strategies in terms of the market share, sales, costs, profits and so on which these demand in practice. As in the rest of the marketing discipline, you will need to employ judgement, experience, market research or anything else which helps you to look at your conclusions from all possible angles.

At this stage, you will need to develop your overall marketing strategies into detailed plans and programmes. Although these detailed plans may cover each of the 4 Ps, the focus will vary, depending upon your organization's specific strategies. A product-oriented company will focus its plans for the 4 Ps around each of its products. A market or geographically oriented company will concentrate on each market or geographical area. Each will base its plans upon the detailed needs of its customers, and on the strategies chosen to satisfy these needs.

Again, the most important element is, indeed, that of the detailed plans; which spell out exactly what programmes and individual activities will take place over the period of the plan (usually over the next year). Without these specified - and preferably quantified - activities the plan cannot be monitored, even in terms of success in meeting its objectives.

It is these programmes and activities which will then constitute the 'marketing' of the organization over the period. As a result, these detailed marketing programmes are the most important, practical outcome of the whole planning process. These plans should therefore be:

- Clear - They should be an unambiguous statement of 'exactly' what is to be done.
- Quantified - The predicted outcome of each activity should be, as far as possible, quantified; so that its performance can be monitored.
- Focused - The temptation to proliferate activities beyond the numbers which can be realistically controlled should be avoided. The 80:20 Rule applies in this context too.
- Realistic - They should be achievable.
- Agreed - Those who are to implement them should be committed to them, and agree that they are achievable.

The resulting plans should become a working document which will guide the campaigns taking place throughout the organization over the period of the plan. If the marketing plan is to work, every exception to it (throughout the year) must be questioned; and the lessons learned, to be incorporated in the next year's plan.

Organizing

Organizing is the act of rearranging elements following one or more rules. It can also be seeing as the opposite of messing up.

One organized opposite could be disordered, since ordered is almost synonymous. The difference between ordered and organized is that something is only ordered as long as it is both organized and standardized.

Anything is commonly considered organized when it looks like everything has a correct order of placement. But it's only ultimately organized if any element has no difference on time taken to find it. In that sense, organizing can also be defined as the act to place different objects in sequential arrangement for better searching.

Organizations are groups of people frequently trying to organize some specific subject, such as political issues. So, even while organizing can be viewed as a simple definition, it can get as complex as organizing the world's information.

Historically, humans have always tried to organize ourselves. Be it on religion, through books and spoken word, or in science, through journals and studies, or in many other ways. Writing ideas in a book, not to talk to someone, but to specific catalog is also an attempt to organize information.

Science books are notable by their organization attempt of a specific subject. Encyclopedias, instead, usually try to organize any subject into one place, for faster indexing and seeking of meanings.

Recently there was the advent of computers and in the last decade, a huge Internet usage world wide. Notably, the Internet growth is directly related to the advent of websites to search the internet, which also means organizing the internet, since nobody would know how to get anywhere without either guessing, hints or those websites.

Organizing, in companies point of view, is the management function that usually follows after planning. And it involves the assignment of tasks, the grouping of tasks into departments and the assignment of authority and allocation of resources across the organization.

Leading

Management skills are a subset of leadership skills. I've often heard people try to separate them by saying that they are leaders, but not managers. In my experience the people who say this are generally failures when it comes to attracting followers which makes it difficult to consider them successful leaders.

A leader is someone who knows where to go. Management skills are how they actually get there. A college student who gets a bunch of friends together to take a weekend trip skiing is acting not only as a leader, but also as a manager. The student must take into account how much gas they have in their car, how much lift tickets are going to cost, invite people who have a reasonable chance of getting along with each other, etc.

Someone who is trying to act as a leader, but wants nothing to do with management is like a 7 year old who has found the keys to the family car and is overcome with the desire to drive to Disney World. Vision, a goal, and a sense of purpose are all present, but the ability to plan and execute is lacking.

That is a pretty good description of someone who wants to lead, but not manage. They may have wonderful ideas, but without the ability to plan and oversee the necessary work their ideas are not going to be realized—at least not by them. If their ideas do get implemented it will be done by another leader who embraces the management function.

While management is an important part of leadership, the reverse is not necessarily true. There are many people who are very skilled at implementing someone else's vision who are not leaders. The fact that these people exist can make some leaders feel justified in abdicating their responsibility to manage.

In its simplest form, management is the process of defining and measuring success. The leader who attempts to pass these responsibilities off to a different individual is unlikely to achieve 100% alignment between their vision and the actual work done by the organization. This doesn't mean that the organization will necessarily be ineffective, but if only 80% of the work being done is actually aligned with the vision, there is going to be a decrease in productivity overall.

A leader who sets the vision, defines success, and determines the measurements of success will be more effective than the same leader who wants to set the vision but refuses to undertake any work in the management area.

The word leadership can refer to:

1. The process of leading
2. The concept of leading
3. Those entities that perform one or more acts of leading.

The various meanings can lead to some confusion.

House defines "leadership" organizationally and narrowly as "the ability of an individual to influence, motivate, and enable others to share contribute toward the effectiveness and success of the organizations of which they are members". One can also characterize leadership by the period of the authority, as in "During the 1940s Russia was under Stalinist leadership". In formal hierarchies the term can also serve to describe the position or relationships which allow and legitimize the exercising of what one might term "leadership behaviour".

In some languages the term for a leader and the term for the principle of leadership have very different meanings. Furthermore, note the different connotations of a synonym of the word "leader" adopted from the German: the word Führer, and its accompanying ideas on the Führerprinzip.

In would-be controlling groups such as the military, political parties, ruling élites, and other belief-based enterprises like religions or businesses, the idea of leadership can become a Holy Grail and people can come to expect transformational change stemming from the leader; such entities may encourage their followers and believers to worship leadership, to respect it, and to strive (whether realistically or not) to become proficient in it. Ideally, one cannot buy or sell leadership in the military (or elsewhere); instead, leaders must ratify their position of command in the hearts and minds of their soldiers in order to obtain the best from them. Followers in such a situation may become uncritically obedient. Personal strategies that one can use to guard against the unrealistic expectations associated with belief in leaders include:

- Maintaining a questioning and skeptical attitude
- Bolstering confidence in one's own decision-making abilities

Categories and types of Leadership

One can categorize the exercise of leadership as either actual or potential:

- Actual - giving guidance or direction, as in the phrase "the emperor has provided satisfactory leadership".
- Potential - the capacity or ability to lead, as in the phrase "she could have exercised effective leadership"; or in the concept "born to lead".

In both cases, as a result of the constancy of change some people detect within the late 20th and early 21st centuries, the act of learning appears fundamental to certain types of leading and leadership. When learning and leadership coalescee, one could characterize this as "learnership".

Leadership can have a formal aspect (as in most political or business leadership) or an informal one (as in most friendships). Speaking of "leadership" (the abstract term) rather than of "leading" (the action) usually implies that the entities doing the leading have some "leadership skills" or competencies. Several types of entities may provide or exhibit leadership, actual or potential, including:

- A person in a position or office of authority, such as a President or a chairperson
- A person in a position or office associated with expertise, skill, or experience, such as a team leader, a ship's captain, a chief engineer, a chief, or a parent
- A group or person in the vanguard of some trend or movement, as in fashion trend-setters
- A group of respected people, (called a "reference group" by sociologists) such as business commentators or union spokespersons
- A product that influences other product offerings in a competitive marketplace

Leadership can come from an individual, a collective group of leaders, or even from the disincarnate — if not mystical — characteristics of a celebrity figurehead (compare hero). Yet other usages have a "leadership" which does little active leading, but to which followers show great (often traditional) respect (compare the courtesy title reverend). Followers often endow the leader with status or prestige. Aside from the prestige-role sometimes granted to inspirational leaders, a more mundane usage of the word "leadership" can designate current front-runners that exercise influence over competitors, for example, a corporation or a product can hold a position of "market leadership" without any implication of permanence or of merited respect. Note that the ability to influence others does form an integral part of the "leadership" of some but not all front-runners. A front-runner in a sprint may "lead" the race, but does not have a position of "leadership" if he does not have the potential to influence others in some way. Thus one can make an important distinction between "being in the lead" and the process of leadership. Leadership implies a relationship of power — the power to guide others.

Analyzing the inspirational leader (one who can instill passion and direction into a group of individuals) requires an understanding of how the psychology of a group can affect the members of the group.

Different approaches to group dynamics (for example: Arthur F Carmazzi's ideas on "directive communication"; and Sigal Barsade's theory of "the ripple effect", see leadership as a product of awareness and command of the reactions and influences of a group on the emotions of the individual.

According to Arthur F Carmazzi, leadership does not involve changing the mindset of the group, but the cultivation of an environment that brings out the best (inspires) the individuals in that group... Each individual has various environments that bring out different facets from their own identity, and emotionally charged perceptions drive each facet within each environment. To lead, Carmazzi says, one must build a platform through education and awareness where individuals fill each others needs. Leaders accomplish this by knowing why people may react favorably to a situation in environment A, but get frustrated or disillusioned in environment B.

When leaders change their actions in accordance with their awareness of what those actions really mean, they affect the emotional and perceptive affects on a group. By taking control of the "standard" reactions to the actions of the group, a leader can in effect change the psychology of the group and change the culture of an organization.

Leadership Associated with Positions of Authority

In On Heroes, Hero-Worship, and the Heroic in History, Thomas Carlyle demonstrated the concept of leadership associated with a position of authority (auctoritas in Latin). In praising Oliver Cromwell's use of power to bring King Charles I to trial and eventual beheading, he wrote the following: "Let us remark, meanwhile, how indispensable everywhere a King is, in all movements of men. It is strikingly shown, in this very War, what becomes of men when they cannot find a Chief Man, and their enemies can."

From this viewpoint, leadership emerges when an entity as "leader" contrives to receive deference from other entities who become "followers". And as the passage from Carlyle demonstrates, the process of getting deference can become competitive in that the emerging "leader" draws "followers" from the factions of the prior or alternative "leaders".

In representative democracies the people retain sovereignty (popular sovereignty) but delegate day-to-day administration and leadership to elected officials. In the United States, for example, the Constitution provides an example of recycling authority. In the Constitutional Convention of 1787, the American Founders rejected the idea of a monarch. But they still proposed leadership by people in positions of authority, with the authority split into three powers: in this case the legislative, the executive, and the judiciary. Under the American theory, the authority of the leadership derives from the power of the voters as conveyed through the electoral college. Many individuals share authority, including the many legislators in the Senate and the House of Representatives.

If a group or an organization wants or expects identifiable leadership, it will require processes for appointing/acquiring and replacing leaders.

Traditional closed groups rely on bloodlines or seniority to select leaders and/or leadership candidates: monarchies, tribal chiefdoms, oligarchies and aristocratic societies rely on (and often define their institutions by) such methods.

Competence or perceived competence provides a possible basis for selecting leadership elites from a broader pool of potential talent. Political lobbying may prove necessary in electoral systems, but immediately demonstrated skill and character may secure leadership in smaller groups such as gangs.

Many organizations and groups aim to identify, foster and promote what they see as leadership potential or ability - especially among younger members of society.

The issues of succession planning or of legitimation become important at times when leadership (particularly individual leadership) might or must change due to term-expiry, accident or senescence.

Some cultures, especially those with a reverence for age and wisdom, see leadership as a standard part of the life-cycle of a person. Just as a youth becomes initiated into adulthood, so an adult may gain initiation as a leader. Such societies may require special reinforcement of the respect and kudos due to such senior members in order to maintain their position. If aged adults can no longer hunt or fight or play a full part in physical labour, for example, those adults' positions in society must rest on respect and implied wisdom and teaching roles, whether or not they show identified "leadership traits".

At certain stages in their development, the hierarchies of social ranks implied different degrees or ranks of leadership in society. Thus a knight led fewer men in general than did a duke; a baronet might in theory control less land than an earl.

In the course of the 19th and 20th centuries, several political operators took non-traditional paths to become dominant in their societies. They or their systems often expressed a belief in strong individual leadership, but existing titles and labels ("King", "Emperor", "President" and so on) often seemed inappropriate, insufficient or downright inaccurate in some circumstances. The formal or informal titles or descriptions they or their flunkeys employed express and foster a general veneration for leadership of the inspired and autocratic variety.

The whole structure of military hierarchies and the idea and the titles of an officer corps tend to reinforce the importance attached to leadership and to the chain of command in the military. Thus (for example) other ranks defer to Lieutenants who defer to Majors who defer to Colonels who defer to Generals who defer to Marshals. Similar elaborate structures of hierarchical leadership titles can occur in Christian churches (Deacon - Priest - Bishop - Archbishop - Cardinal) or in commercial enterprises (team leader - supervisor - line manager/ middle manager - staff manager/senior manager - vice president etc).

Informal, often spontaneously-generated titles or descriptions can provide informative insights. The use of "boss" in work-places and crime-syndicates may suggest a relatively loose hierarchy, while dubbing someone "chief" can express either instantaneous readiness to follow of an acknowledgment of collegiality.

Some titles can outstay their use. "Divine Augustus" fell prey to religious changes in the later Roman Empire. "Master" (or "Massa") has fallen out of general use in the American South, and "Baas" has new connotations in the new South Africa since the late 20th century.

Other honorifics can also change in accordance with social circumstances. Britons whose remote ancestors paid due deference to the local "lord" will now find that title more concentrated in the areas of politics and the law. Their American cousins have virtually confined the word "lord" to religious usage.

Richard Wrangham and Dale Peterson, in Demonic Males: Apes and the Origins of Human Violence present empirical evidence that only humans and chimpanzees, among all the animals living on earth, share a similar tendency for a cluster of behaviours: violence, territoriality, and competition for uniting behind the one chief male of the land.

By comparison, bonobos, the second-closest species-relatives of man, do not unite behind the chief male of the land. The bonobos show deference to an alpha or top-ranking female that, with the support of her coalition of other females, can prove as strong as the strongest male in the land. Thus, if leadership amounts to getting the greatest number of followers, then among the bonobos, a female almost always exerts the strongest and most effective leadership.

Some have argued that, since the bonobo pattern inverts the dominant pattern among chimpanzees and men with regard to whether a female can get more followers than a male, humans and chimpanzees both likely inherited gender-bias against women from the ancestors of the chimpanzees; gender-bias features as a genetic condition of men. And the bias against women having leadership as a position of authority occurs in most cultures in the world. As of 2002, Sweden had the highest percentage of women in the legislature: but only 43%. And the United States, Andorra, Israel, Sierra Leone, and Ireland tied for 57th place with less than 15% of the legislature women. Admittedly, those percentages significantly outclass the occurrence of female chimpanzees becoming alpha of the community by getting the most followers, but similar trends exist in manifesting a general gender-bias across cultures against females gaining leadership as a position of authority over followers.

An alternative explanation suggests that those individuals best suited to lead the a group will somehow rise to the occasion and that followers (for some reason) will accept them as leaders or as proto-leaders. In this scenario, the traits of the leaders (such as gender, aggressiveness, etc.) will depend on the requirements of a given situation, and ongoing leadership may become extrapolated from a series of such situations.

In cultural anthropology, much speculation on the origins of human leadership relates to the perceived increasing need for dispute resolution in increasingly densely-populated and increasingly complex societies.

Sometimes followership can occur without intentional leadership. Despite (or because of) its mythical origin, the image of swarms of lemmings which follow the first lemming off a cliff appears frequently in characterizing followers. The animal kingdom also provides the actual model of the bellwether function in a mob of sheep. And human society also offers many examples of emulation. The fashion industry, for example, depends on it. Fashion marketers design clothing for celebrities, then offer less expensive variations/ imitations for those who emulate the celebrities.

Unintentional leadership can also occur from more pro-active forms followership. For example, in organizations which punish both leadership inaction and mistakes, and in which a predicament has no good solution, a common tendency involves declaring oneself a follower of someone else — metaphorically passing the buck.

Another example of followership without intentional leadership comes with the market leadership of a pioneering company, or the price leadership of a monopolist. Other companies will emulate a successful strategy, product, or price, but originators may certainly not desire this — in fact they often do all they can legally do to prevent such direct competition.

The term "leadership" sometimes applies (confusingly) to a winning position in a race. One can speak of a front-runner in a sprint or of the "leader" in an election or poll as in a position of leadership.

But such "leadership" does not involve any influence processes, and the "leader" will have followers who may not willingly choose to function as followers. Once again: one can make an important distinction between "in the lead" and the process of leadership. Once again, leadership implies a relationship of power - the power to guide others.

Leading from the front, in a military sense, may imply foolhardiness and unnecessary self-exposure to danger: these do not necessarily make for successful long-term leadership strategies.

Scope of Leadership

One can govern oneself, or one can govern the whole earth. In between, we may find leaders who operate primarily within:

- Families
- Bands
- Tribes
- States and nations
- Empires

Intertwined with such categories, and overlapping them, we find (for example) religious leaders (potentially with their own internal hierarchies), work-place leaders (executives, officers, senior/upper managers, middle managers, staff-managers, line-managers, team-leaders, supervisors...) and leaders of voluntary associations.

Some anthropological ideas envisage a widespread (but by no means universal) pattern of progression in the organisation of society in ever-larger groups, with the needs and practices of leadership changing accordingly. Thus simple dispute resolution may become legalistic dispensation of justice before developing into proactive legislative activity.

Some leadership careers parallel this sort of progression: today's school-board chairperson may become tomorrow's city councillor, then take in (say) a mayordom before graduating to nation-wide politics. Compare the cursus honorum in ancient Rome.

Those who sing the praises of leadership or of certain types of leadership may encounter problems in implementing consistent leadership structures. For example, a pyramidical structure in which authority consistently emanates from the summit can stifle initiative and leave no path for grooming future leaders in the ranks of subordinate levels. Similarly, a belief in universal direct democracy may become unwieldy, and a system consisting of nothing but representative leaders may well become stymied in committees.

Thus many leadership systems promote different rules for different levels of leadership. Hereditary autocrats meet in the United Nations on equal representative terms with elected governments in a collegial leadership. Or individual local democracies may assign some of their powers to temporary dictators in emergencies, as in ancient Rome. Hierarchies intermingle with equality of opportunity at different levels.

Though advocates of the "big man" school of visionary leadership would have us believe that charisma and personality alone can work miracles, most leaders operate within a structure of supporters and executive agents who carry out and monitor the expressed or filtered-down will of the leader. This undercutting of the importance of leadership may serve as a reminder of the existence of the follower: compare followership. A more or less formal bureaucracy (in the Weberian sense) can throw up a colourless nonentity as an entirely effective leader: this phenomenon may occur (for example) in a politburo environment. Bureaucratic organizations can also raise incompetent people to levels of leadership.

In modern dynamic environments formal bureaucratic organizations have started to become less common because of their inability to deal with fast-changing circumstances. Most modern business organizations (and some government departments) encourage what they see as "leadership skills" and reward identified potential leaders with promotions. According to B. Nanus, the forces that shape today's leading-edge organizations and their implications provide the key to visionary leadership. To underline his point we can examine the success-story of Bill Gates: in brief he built Microsoft from the start as a twenty-first-century organization, and he allegedly runs it with a highly-developed sense of visionary leadership.

In a potential down-side to this sort of development, a big-picture grand-vision leader may foster another sort of hierarchy: a fetish of leadership amongst subordinate sub-leaders, encouraged to seize resources for their own sub-empires and to apply to the supreme leader only for ultimate arbitration.

Some leaders build coalitions and alliances: political parties abound with this type of leader. Still others depend on rapport with the masses: they labour on the shop-floor or stand in the front-line of battle, leading by example.

In comparing various leadership styles in many cultures, academic studies have examined the patterns in which leadership emerges and then fades, sometimes by natural succession according to established rules and sometimes by the imposition of brute force.

The simplest way to measure the effectiveness of leadership involves evaluating the size of the following that the leader can muster. By this standard, Adolf Hitler became a very effective leader for a period — even if through delusional promises and coercive techniques. However, this approach may measure power rather than leadership. To measure leadership more specifically, one may assess the extent of influence on the followers, that is, the amount of leading. This may involve testing the results of leadership activities against a goal, vision, or objective.

James MacGregor Burns introduced a normative element: an effective Burnsian leader will unite followers in a shared vision that will improve an organization and society at large. Burns calls leadership that delivers "true" value, integrity, and trust transformational leadership. He distinguishes such leadership from "mere" transactional leadership that builds power by doing whatever will get more followers. But problems arise in quantifying the transformational quality of leadership - evaluation of that quality seems more difficult to quantify than merely counting the followers that the straw man of transactional leadership James MacGregor Burns has set as a primary standard for effectiveness. Thus transformational leadership requires an evaluation of quality, independent of the market demand that exhibits in the number of followers.

Current assessments of transformational and transactional leadership commonly make use of the Multifactor Leadership Questionnaire (MLQ), developed by Bass and Avolio in 1990 and revised in 1995. It measures five dimensions of transformational leadership:

The functional leadership model conceives leadership as a set of behaviours that helps a group perform a task, reach their goal, or perform their function. In this model, effective leaders encourage functional behaviours and discourage dysfunctional ones.

In the path-goal model of leadership, developed jointly by Martin Evans and Robert House and based on the "Expectancy Theory of Motivation", a leader has the function of clearing the path toward the goal(s) of the group, by meeting the needs of subordinates.

Some commentators use the metaphor of an orchestral conductor to describe the quality of the leadership process. An effective leader resembles an orchestra conductor in some ways. He/she has to somehow get a group of potentially diverse and talented people - many of whom have strong personalities - to work together toward a common output. Will the conductor harness and blend all the gifts his or her players possess? Will the players accept the degree of creative expression they have? Will the audience enjoy the sound they make? The conductor may have a clear determining influence on all of these questions.

Suggested Qualities of Leadership

Studies of leadership have suggested qualities that people often associate with leadership. They include:

- Guiding others through modeling (in the sense of providing a role model) and through willingness to serve others first (compare followership)
- Talent and technical/specific skill at some task at hand
- Initiative and entrepreneurial drive
- Charismatic inspiration - attractiveness to others and the ability to leverage this esteem to motivate others
- Preoccupation with a role - a dedication that consumes much of leaders' life - service to a cause
- A clear sense of purpose (or mission) - clear goals - focus - commitment
- Results-orientation - directing every action towards a mission - prioritizing activities to spend time where results most accrue
- Optimism - very few pessimists become leaders
- Rejection of determinism - belief in one's ability to "make a difference"
- Ability to encourage and nurture those that report to them - delegate in such a way as people will grow
- Role models - leaders may adopt a persona that encapsulates their mission and lead by example
- Self-knowledge (in non-bureaucratic structures)
- Self-awareness - the ability to "lead" (as it were) one's own self prior to leading other selves similarly
- With regards to people and to projects, the ability to choose winners - recognizing that, unlike with skills, one cannot (in general) teach attitude. Note that "picking winners" ("choosing winners") carries implications of gamblers' luck as well as of the capacity to take risks, but "true" leaders, like gamblers but unlike "false" leaders, base their decisions on realistic insight (and usually on many other factors partially derived from "real" wisdom).
- Understanding what others say, rather than listening to how they say things - this could partly sum this quality up as "walking in someone else's shoes" (to use a common cliché).

The approach of listing leadership qualities, often termed "trait theory", assumes certain traits or characteristics will tend to lead to effective leadership. Although trait theory has an intuitive appeal, difficulties may arise in proving its tenets, and opponents frequently challenge this approach.

The "strongest" versions of trait theory see these "leadership characteristics" as innate, and accordingly labels some people as "born leaders" due to their psychological makeup. On this reading of the theory, leadership development involves identifying and measuring leadership qualities, screening potential leaders from non-leaders, then training those with potential.

David McClelland, a Harvard-based researcher in the psychology of power and achievement, saw leadership skills, not so much as a set of traits, but as a pattern of motives. He claimed that successful leaders will tend to have a high need for power, a low need for affiliation, and a high level of what he called activity inhibition (one might call it self-control).

Situational leadership theory offers an alternative approach. It proceeds from the assumption that different situations call for different characteristics. According to this group of theories, no single optimal psychographic profile of a leader exists. The situational leadership model of Hersey and Blanchard, for example, suggest four leadership-styles and four levels of follower-development.

For effectiveness, the model posits that the leadership-style must match the appropriate level of followership-development. In this model, leadership behaviour becomes a function not only of the characteristics of the leader, but of the characteristics of followers as well. Other situational leadership models introduce a variety of situational variables. These determinants include:

- The nature of the task (structured or routine)
- Organizational policies, climate, and culture
- The preferences of the leader's superiors
- The expectations of peers
- The reciprocal responses of followers

The contingency model of Vroom and Yetton uses other situational variables, including:

- The nature of the problem
- The requirements for accuracy
- The acceptance of an initiative
- Time-constraints
- Cost constraints

However one determines leadership behaviour, one can categorize it into various leadership styles. Many ways of doing this exist. For example, the Managerial Grid Model, a behavioural leadership-model developed by Robert Blake and Jane Mouton in 1964, suggests five different leadership styles, based on leaders' strength of concern for people and their concern for goal achievement.

Kurt Lewin, Ronald Lipitt, and R. K. White identified three leadership styles: authoritarian, democratic, and laissez-faire, based on the amount of influence and power exercised by the leader.

The Fiedler contingency model bases the leader's effectiveness on what Fred Fiedler called situational contingency. This results from the interaction of leadership style and situational favourableness (later called "situational control").

In 1994 House and Podsakoff attempted to summarize the behaviours and approaches of "outstanding leaders" that they obtained from some more modern theories and research findings. These leadership behaviours and approaches do not constitute specific styles, but cumulatively they probably characterize the most effective style of today's leaders/managers. The listed leadership "styles" cover:

1. Vision. Outstanding leaders articulate an ideological vision congruent with the deeply-held values of followers, a vision that describes a better future to which the followers have an alleged moral right.
2. Passion and self-sacrifice. Leaders display a passion for, and have a strong conviction of, what they regard as the moral correctness of their vision. They engage in outstanding or extraordinary behaviour and make extraordinary self-sacrifices in the interest of their vision and mission.
3. Confidence, determination, and persistence. Outstanding leaders display a high degree of faith in themselves and in the attainment of the vision they articulate. Theoretically, such leaders need to have a very high degree of self-confidence and moral conviction because their mission usually challenges the status quo and, therefore, may offend those who have a stake in preserving the established order.
4. Image-building. House and Podsakoff regard outstanding leaders as self-conscious about their own image. They recognize the desirability of followers perceiving them as competent, credible, and trustworthy.
5. Role-modeling. Leader-image-building sets the stage for effective role-modeling because followers identify with the values of role models whom they perceived in positive terms.
6. External representation. Outstanding leaders act as spokespersons for their respective organizations and symbolically represent those organizations to external constituencies.
7. Expectations of and confidence in followers. Outstanding leaders communicate expectations of high performance from their followers and strong confidence in their followers' ability to meet such expectations.
8. Selective motive-arousal. Outstanding leaders selectively arouse those motives of followers that the outstanding leaders see as of special relevance to the successful accomplishment of the vision and mission.
9. Frame alignment. To persuade followers to accept and implement change, outstanding leaders engage in "frame alignment". This refers to the linkage of individual and leader interpretive orientations such that some set of followers' interests, values, and beliefs, as well as the leader's activities, goals, and ideology, becomes congruent and complementary.

10. Inspirational communication. Outstanding leaders often, but not always, communicate their message in an inspirational manner using vivid stories, slogans, symbols, and ceremonies.

Even though these ten leadership behaviours and approaches do not really equate to specific styles, evidence has started to accumulate that a leader's style can make a difference. Style becomes the key to the formulation and implementation of strategy and plays an important role in work-group members' activity and in team citizenship. Little doubt exists that the way (style) in which leaders influence work-group members can make a difference in their own and their people's performance.

Leadership and Vision

Many definitions of leadership involve an element of vision — except in cases of involuntary leadership and often in cases of traditional leadership. A vision provides direction to the influence process. A leader (or group of leaders) can have one or more visions of the future to aid them to move a group successfully towards this goal. A vision, for effectiveness, should allegedly:

- Appear as a simple, yet vibrant, image in the mind of the leader
- Describe a future state, credible and preferable to the present state
- Act as a bridge between the current state and a future optimum state
- Appear desirable enough to energize followers
- Succeed in speaking to followers at an emotional or spiritual level (logical appeals by themselves seldom muster a following)

For leadership to occur, according to this theory, some people ("leaders") must communicate the vision to others ("followers") in such a way that the followers adopt the vision as their own. Leaders must not just see the vision themselves, they must have the ability to get others to see it also. Numerous techniques aid in this process, including: narratives, metaphors, symbolic actions, leading by example, incentives, and penalties.

Stacey has suggested that the emphasis on vision puts an unrealistic burden on the leader. Such emphasis appears to perpetuate the myth that an organization must depend on a single, uncommonly talented individual to decide what to do. Stacey claims that this fosters a culture of dependency and conformity in which followers take no pro-active incentives and do not think independently.

Leadership in Management

Some commentators link leadership closely with the idea of management. Some regard the two as synonymous, and others consider management a subset of leadership. If one accepts this premise, one can view leadership as:

- Centralized or decentralized
- Broad or focused
- Decision-oriented or morale-centred
- Intrinsic or derived from some authority

Any of the bipolar labels traditionally ascribed to management style could also apply to leadership style. Hersey and Blanchard use this approach: they claim that management merely consists of leadership applied to business situations; or in other words: management forms a sub-set of the broader process of leadership. They put it this way: "Leadership occurs any time one attempts to influence the behaviour of an individual or group, regardless of the reason. Management is a kind of leadership in which the achievement of organizational goals is paramount."

However, a clear distinction between management and leadership may nevertheless prove useful. This would allow for a reciprocal relationship between leadership and management, implying that an effective manager should possess leadership skills, and an effective leader should demonstrate management skills. One clear distinction could provide the following definition:

- Management involves power by position.
- Leadership involves power by influence.

Abraham Zaleznik, for example, delineated differences between leadership and management. He saw leaders as inspiring visionaries, concerned about substance; while managers he views as planners who have concerns with process. Warren Bennis (1989) further explicated a dichotomy between managers and leaders. He drew twelve distinctions between the two groups:

- Managers administer, leaders innovate
- Managers ask how and when, leaders ask what and why
- Managers focus on systems, leaders focus on people
- Managers do things right, leaders do the right things
- Managers maintain, leaders develop
- Managers rely on control, leaders inspire trust
- Managers have a short-term perspective, leaders have a longer-term perspective
- Managers accept the status-quo, leaders challenge the status-quo
- Managers have an eye on the bottom line, leaders have an eye on the horizon
- Managers imitate, leaders originate
- Managers emulate the classic good soldier, leaders are their own person
- Managers copy, leaders show originality

Paul Birch (1999) also sees a distinction between leadership and management. He observed that, as a broad generalization, managers concerned themselves with tasks while leaders concerned themselves with people. Birch does not suggest that leaders do not focus on "the task." Indeed, the things that characterise a great leader include the fact that they achieve. The difference lies in the leader realising that the achievement of the task comes about through the goodwill and support of others, while the manager may not.

This goodwill and support originates in the leader seeing people as people, not as another resource for deployment in support of "the task". The manager often has the role of organizing resources to get something done. People form one of these resources, and many of the worst managers treat people as just another interchangeable item. A leader has the role of causing others to follow a path he/she has laid out or a vision he/she has articulated in order to achieve a task. Often, people see the task as subordinate to the vision. For instance, an organization might have the overall task of generating profit, but a good leader may see profit as a by-product that flows from whatever aspect of their vision differentiates their company from the competition.

Leadership does not only manifest itself as purely a business phenomenon. Many people can think of an inspiring leader they have encountered who has nothing whatever to do with business: a politician, an officer in the armed forces, a Scout or Guide leader, a teacher, etc. Similarly, management does not occur only as a purely business phenomenon. Again, we can think of examples of people that we have met who fill the management niche in non-business organisations. Non-business organizations should find it easier to articulate a non-money-driven inspiring vision that will support true leadership. However, often this does not occur.

Differences in the mix of leadership and management can define various management styles. Some management styles tend to de-emphasize leadership. Included in this group one could include participatory management, democratic management, and collaborative management styles. Other management styles, such as authoritarian management, micro-management, and top-down management, depend more on a leader to provide direction. Note, however, that just because an organisation has no single leader giving it direction, does not mean it necessarily has weak leadership. In many cases group leadership (multiple leaders) can prove effective. Having a single leader (as in dictatorship) allows for quick and decisive decision-making when needed as well as when not needed. Group decision-making sometimes earns the derisive label "committee-itis" because of the longer times required to make decisions, but group leadership can bring more expertise, experience, and perspectives through a democratic process.

Patricia Pitcher has challenged the bifurcation into leaders and managers. She used a factor analysis technique on data collected over 8 years, and concluded that three types of leaders exist, each with very different psychological profiles. She characterises one group as imaginative, inspiring, visionary, entrepreneurial, intuitive, daring, and emotional, and calls them "artists". In a second grouping she places "craftsmen" as well-balanced, steady, reasonable, sensible, predictable, and trustworthy. Finally she identifies "technocrats" as cerebral, detail-oriented, fastidious, uncompromising, and hard-headed. She speculates that no one profile offers a preferred leadership style. She claims that if we want to build, we should find an "artist leader"; if we want to solidify our position, we should find a "craftsman leader"; and if we have an ugly job that needs to get done (like downsizing), we should find a "technocratic leader." Pitcher also observed that a balanced leader exhibiting all three sets of traits occurs extremely rarely: she found none in her study.

Leadership by a Group

In contrast to individual leadership, some organizations have adopted group leadership. In this situation, more than one person provides direction to the group as a whole. Some organizations have taken this approach in hopes of increasing creativity, reducing costs, or downsizing. Others may see the traditional leadership of a boss as costing too much in team performance. In some situations, the maintenance of the boss becomes too expensive - either by draining the resources of the group as a whole, or by impeding the creativity within the team, even unintentionally.

A common example of group leadership involves cross-functional teams. A team of people with diverse skills and from all parts of an organization assembles to lead a project. A team structure can involve sharing power equally on all issues, but more commonly uses rotating leadership. The team member(s) best able to handle any given phase of the project become(s) the temporary leader(s).

For example, the Orpheus orchestra has performed for over thirty years without a conductor — that is, without a sole leader. As a team of over 25 members, it has drawn discriminating audiences, and has produced over 60 recordings for Deutsche Grammophon in successful competition with other world-class orchestras.

Rather than an autocratic or charismatic conductor deciding the overall conception of a work and then dictating how each individual is to perform the individual tasks, the Orpheus team generally selects a different "core group" for each piece of music. The core group provides leadership in working out the details of the piece, and presents their ideas to the whole team. Members of the whole team then participate in refining the final conception, rehearsal, and product, including checking from various places in the auditorium how the sound balances and verifying the quality of the final recording.

At times the entire Orpheus team may follow a single leader, but whom the team follows rotates from task to task, depending on the capabilities of its members.

The orchestra has developed seminars and training sessions for adapting the Orpheus Process to business.

Co-leadership

As a compromise between individual leadership and an open group, leadership structures of two or three people or entities occur commonly. Ancient Rome preferred two consuls to a single king, and the Roman Empire grew to accommodate two Emperors - those of the East and of the West -

simultaneously. The Middle Ages saw leadership divided between the secular and spiritual realms - between Emperor and Pope. Some groups - often left-wing or Green in orientation - employ a co-leader structure today.

Triumvirates have long served to balance leadership ambitions - notably in Rome in the first century BC, but also as recently as in the Soviet Union troikas of the 20th century. Compare the separation of powers (legislative, judicial and executive) formalised (for example) in the constitution of the United States of America.

Divided Leadership

Whereas sometimes one can readily and definitively identify the locus of leadership, in other circumstances the situation remains obscured. Pre-modern Japan offers a classical example: the emperors provided symbolic and religious leadership, but the shoguns embodied virtually all political and administrative leadership.

Similar dichotomies appear in many places and in many periods. Any constitutional monarch has a potentially confusing relationship with the day-to-day leader (typically a prime minister) who remains (at least theoretically) subordinate - socially as well as politically. Regents may stand against monarchs (and their supporters) during the minority or absence of those monarchs. Heads of state may operate at cross-purposes with heads of government. Political leaders may or may not align closely with religious leaders. And in federal-type systems, regional leadership and its potentially different systems may cross swords with national leaders. Not to mention the potentially conflicting leadership manifestations of boards of directors and of Chief Executives.

Greiner's study of the language of U.S. Presidents examined the relationship between leader and followers and observed that changes have taken place in the presidential use of words that define the leader and the community as one. Modern US presidents have an observed tendency to make more use of inclusive words like we, us and our in their inaugural speeches. The use of inclusive words may suggest an effort by these democratically selected leaders to make the community work together to solve problems collectively.

Aristocratic thinkers have postulated that leadership depends on one's blue blood or genes: monarchy takes an extreme view of the same idea, and may prop up its assertions against the claims of mere aristocrats by invoking divine sanction: see the divine right of kings. Contrariwise, more democratically-inclined theorists have pointed to examples of meritocratic leaders, such as the Napoleonic marshals profiting from careers open to talent.

In the autocratic/paternalistic strain of thought, traditionalists recall the role of leadership of the Roman pater familias. Feminist thinking, on the other hand, may damn such models as patriarchal and posit against them emotionally-attuned, responsive, and consensual empathetic guidance and matriarchies.

Comparable to the Roman tradition, the views of Confucianism on "right living" relate very much to the ideal of the (male) scholar-leader and his benevolent rule, buttressed by a tradition of filial piety.

Within the context of Islam, views on the nature, scope and inheritance of leadership have played a major role in shaping sects and their history.

In the 19th century, the elaboration of anarchist thought called the whole concept of leadership into question. (Note that the Oxford English Dictionary traces the word "leadership" in English only as far back as the 19th century.) One response to this denial of élitism came with Leninism, which demanded an élite group of disciplined cadres to act as the vanguard of a socialist revolution, bringing into existence the dictatorship of the proletariat.

Other historical views of leadership have addressed the seeming contrasts between secular and religious leadership. The doctrines of Caesaro-papism have recurred and had their detractors over several centuries. Christian thinking on leadership has often emphasized stewardship of divinely-provided resources - human and material - and their deployment in accordance with a Divine plan. Compare servant leadership.

Specific Theories of Leadership

In State of Exception, Agamben reads Carl Schmitt's theory of sovereignty in the light of Walter Benjamin. Agamben traces Schmitt's definition of sovereignty as the power to decide the state of exception to the Roman concept of auctoritas - the power to declare justitium. Agamben writes: "It is significative that modern specialists were so enclined to admit that auctoritas was inherent to the living person of the pater or the princeps. What was evidently an ideology or a fictio aiming to be the groundwork of auctoritas ' preeminence or, at least, specific rank compared to potestas thus became a figure of right's immanence to life. Although it is evident that there can't be an eternal human type that would incarnate itself each time in Augustus, Napoleon, Hitler, but only more or less similar mechanisms {"dispositif", a term often used by Foucault} - the state of exception, justitium, the auctoritas principis, the Führertum - put in use in more or less different circumstances, in the 1930s - overall, but not only - in Germany, the power that Weber had defined as "charismatic" is related to the concept of auctoritas and elaborated in a Führertum doctrine as the original and personal power of a leader. In 1933, in a short article intending to define the fundamental concepts of national-socialism, Schmitt defines the Führung principal by the "root identity between the leader and his entourage" {"identité de souche entre le chef et son entourage"} (we shall note the use of Weberian concepts)."

James MacGregor Burns wrote that a study of the definition of the word leadership revealed 130 definitions. However, several generally-accepted variations on the definition appear in the management and leadership literature.

Ronald Heifetz described the difference between a descriptive view and a prescriptive view of leadership. A descriptive view describes leadership and how it occurs, and a prescriptive view suggests how it should occur. The notion of "adaptive work" forms a central concept of Heifetz's prescriptive view. Heifetz pointed out (p. 37) that people fail to adapt to new and unsettling situations through six avoidance mechanisms:

1. Blaming others
2. Finding scapegoats (to the extent that this differs from blaming)
3. Externalizing the enemy
4. Denying that a problem exists
5. Jumping to conclusions
6. Finding a distracting issue

In a prescriptive view, the leader would squarely face the problem and avoid the six surface-level solutions of the non-leader. A true leader would help a community face reality and deal with the issues: finding solutions where none previously existed. Using the 1950s television character, the Lone Ranger, as an example, we see the Ranger in a weekly episode, moving from frontier town to frontier town, discovering problems wherever he goes, fixing the problems and riding off into the sunset. In this metaphor, the Ranger fixes the symptom, but not the problem. A Lone Ranger non-leader would catch fish to feed the poor while a true leader would teach the poor how to catch fish and would motivate them to do so. The true leader finds a way to help the community engage the problem and collectively find a solution.

George Terry has defined leadership as: "the activity of influencing people to strive willingly for group objectives". If we define leadership simply as "influencing others to some purpose" and we define followership as "becoming influenced by others to accept (willingly or un willingly) some purpose", then leadership and followership emerge as two sides of the same coin. In this scenario, leadership - whether successful or not - has not occurred until at least one follower joins in. Likewise, no followership exists without someone or something (not necessarily a leader) to follow. However, in this latter case, a "leader" need not exercise deliberate or even conscious leadership - that is, followers can follow someone who is not trying to lead. Some see "unconscious leadership" as a dubious concept, however. Many, using a different definition of leadership, would claim that it does not classify as leadership at all - simply because no deliberate intention to lead exists. Unconscious "leading by example" (as the phrase has it) may nevertheless exemplify such "leadership".

Conscious Leadership

Dr. James Farr argued not for any one "correct leadership style" but for the style that each situation requires. Great leaders require the use of nearly every leadership style: one must apply the correct style to meet the situation. Farr terms this "Conscious Leadership".

"Conscious Leadership" consists of the art and science of leading change from a self-aware perspective, with clarity of purpose and an acute insight into others' perspectives and state of mind. This fully-aware state uniquely allows leaders to properly inspire motivation in others and to choose the most appropriate course of action both to solve pressing problems and to effectively achieve long-term organizational goals.

Futurist John Renesch has written extensively on conscious leadership, which he advocates for everyone — not only those in positions of authority or holding designated titles. As he wrote in early 2001:

Conscious leaders don't tolerate conditions or processes where people feel the need to compromise their values — to "sell their souls" for the task at hand. Conscious leadership includes conscious discernment, a principle that demands performance, integrity, competence and a noncalloused form of spiritual toughness. The conscious leader does not sit with his or her head in the clouds, dreaming of utopian schemes and professing New Age idealism. The conscious leader walks in the spiritual and physical domains concurrently, remaining simultaneously grounded and comfortable in both.

Renesch also writes about "The Conscious Organization" which he defines as "one which continually examines itself, committed to becoming as conscious as it can. In other words, it has very low tolerance for unconsciousness. It possesses the collective will to be vigilant, the collective commitment to continuous evolution, and the collective courage to act."

Alternatives to Leadership

Within groups, alternatives to the cult of leadership include using decision-making structures such as co-operative ventures, collegiality, consensus, anarchism and applied democracy. One can down play the ubiquitous idea of leadership by using structures such as information clearing houses or stressing functions such as administration. Note the different implications and connotations of the two phrases "coalition of the willing" and "US-led coalition". The Orpheus Chamber Orchestra, which practises a form of distributed leadership, provides a extbook example of alternative leadership.

Control and Co-ordination

A concise and clear general definition is from: "Coordination is the act of managing interdependencies between activities."

Coordination or Co-Ordination is "the ability to reduce all-together, in oder to generate an only one all."

Coordination, co-ordination is the regulation of diverse elements into an integrated and harmonious operation. Coordination means integrating or linking together different parts of an organization to accomplish a collective set of tasks.

New, more "organic" forms or organizations (self-organizing organizations, self-managed teams, network organizations, etc.) allow organizations to be more responsive and adaptable in today's rapidly changing world. These forms also cultivate empowerment among employees, much more than the hierarchical, rigidly structured organizations of the past.

Many people assert that as the nature of organizations has changed, so must the nature of management control. Some people go so far as to claim that management shouldn't exercise any form of control whatsoever. They claim that management should exist to support employee's efforts to be fully productive members of organizations and communities — therefore, any form of control is completely counterproductive to management and employees.

Some people even react strongly against the phrase "management control". The word itself can have a negative connotation, e.g., it can sound dominating, coercive and heavy-handed. It seems that writers of management literature now prefer use of the term "coordinating" rather than "controlling".

Regardless of the negative connotation of the word "control", it must exist or there is no organization at all. In its most basic form, an organization is two or more people working together to reach a goal. Whether an organization is highly bureaucratic or changing and self-organizing, the organization must exist for some reason, some purpose, some mission (implicit or explicit) — or it isn't an organization at all. The organization must have some goal. Identifying this goal requires some form of planning, informal or formal. Reaching the goal means identifying some strategies, formal or informal. These strategies are agreed upon by members of the organization through some form of communication, formal or informal. Then members set about to act in accordance with what they agreed to do. They may change their minds, fine. But they need to recognize and acknowledge that they're changing their minds.

This form of ongoing communication to reach a goal, tracking activities toward the goal and then subsequent decisions about what to do is the essence of management coordination. It needs to exist in some manner — formal or informal.

The following are rather typical methods of coordination in organizations. They are used as means to communicate direction and guide behaviours in that direction. The function of the following methods is not to "control", but rather to guide. If, from ongoing communications among management and employees, the direction changes, then fine. The following methods are changed accordingly.

Note that many of the following methods are so common that we often don't think of them as having anything to do with coordination at all. No matter what one calls the following methods — coordination or control — they're important to the success of any organization.

Administrative Controls

Organizations often use standardized documents to ensure complete and consistent information is gathered. Documents include titles and dates to detect different versions of the document. Computers have revolutionized administrative controls through use of integrated management information systems, project management software, human resource information systems, office automation software, etc. Organizations typically require a wide range of reports, e.g., financial reports, status reports, project reports, etc. to monitor what's being done, by when and how.

DELEGATION

Delegation is an approach to get things done, in conjunction with other employees. Delegation is often viewed as a major means of influence and therefore is categorized as an activity in leading (rather than controlling/ coordinating).

Delegation generally includes assigning responsibility to an employee to complete a task, granting the employee sufficient authority to gain the resources to do the task and letting the employee decide how that task will be carried out. Typically, the person assigning the task shares accountability with the employee for ensuring the task is completed.

Delegating is a critical skill for supervisors. Delegating involves working with an employee to establish goals, granting them sufficient authority and responsibility to achieve the goals, often giving them substantial freedom in deciding how the goals will be achieved, remaining available as a resource to help them achieve the goals, assessing their performance (the quality of their effort and attainment of the goals), addressing performance issues and/or rewarding their performance. Ultimately, the supervisor retains responsibility for the attainment of the goals, but chooses to achieve the goals by delegating to someone else.

Delegation can sometimes be a major challenge for new supervisors to learn because they are concerned about giving up control or struggle to have confidence in the abilities of others. Supervisors that can effectively delegate can free up a great deal of their own time, help their direct reports to cultivate expertise in learning, and can develop their own leadership skills — skills that are critical for problem solving, goal attainment and learning.

The hallmark of good supervision is effective delegation. Delegation is when supervisors give responsibility and authority to subordinates to complete a task. Effective delegation develops people who are ultimately more fulfilled and productive. Managers become more fulfilled and productive themselves as they learn to count on their staffs and are freed up to attend to more strategic issues.

Delegation is often very difficult for new supervisors, particularly if they have had to scramble to start the nonprofit or start a major new service themselves. Many managers want to remain comfortable, making the same decisions they have always made.

They believe they can do a better job themselves. They don't want to risk losing any of their power and stature (ironically, they do lose these if they don't learn to delegate effectively). Often, they don't want to risk giving authority to subordinates in case they fail and impair the organization.

However, there are basic approaches to delegation that, with practice, become the backbone of effective supervision and development. Thomas R. Horton, in Delegation and Team Building: No Solo Acts Please suggests the following general steps to accomplish delegation:

1. Delegate the whole task to one person.
   This gives the person the responsibility and increases their motivation.
2. Select the right person.
   Assess the skills and capabilities of subordinates and assign the task to the most appropriate one.
3. Clearly specify your preferred results.
   Give information on what, why, when, who, where and how. Write this information down.
4. Delegate responsibility and authority
   Assign the task, not the method to accomplish it. Let the subordinate complete the task in the manner they choose, as long as the results are what the supervisor specifies. Let the employee have strong input as to the completion date of the project. Note that you may not even know how to complete the task yourself — this is often the case with higher levels of management.
5. Ask the employee to summarize back to you.
   Ask to hear their impressions of the project and the results that you prefer.
6. Get ongoing non-intrusive feedback about progress on the project.
   This is a good reason to continue to get weekly, written status reports from all direct reports. Reports should cover what they did last week, plan to do next week and any potential issues. Regular staff meetings provide this ongoing feedback, as well.
7. Maintain open lines of communication.
   Don't hover over the subordinate, but sense what they're doing and support their checking in with you along the way.
8. If you're not satisfied with the progress, don't immediately take the project back.
   Continue to work with the employee and ensure they perceive the project as their responsibility.
9. Evaluate and reward performance.
   Evaluate results, not methods. Address insufficient performance and reward successes (including the manager's).

Poor Delegation

Signs that you are not borrowing enough brains or that your delegation is failing include:

- Team Motivation / Morale is down
- You are always working late
- Your team is confused / conflicting / tense
- You get questions about delegated tasks too often

How to Delegate

1. Identify a suitable person for the task.
2. Prepare the person. Explain the task clearly. Make sure that you are understood. Leave room in the task description for ingenuity / initiative.
3. Make sure the person has the necessary authority to do the job properly.
4. Keep in touch with the person for support and monitoring progress. Do not get to close. Accept alternative approaches.
5. Praise / Acknowledge a job well done.

Responsibility

Even though you have delegated a task to someone else, you are still responsible for making sure the task is done on time and correctly. If the task fails, you can not point the finger. You delegated. It is your fault. You may have picked the wrong person for the job.

Authority

The amount of authority you delegate is up to you, although it should be enough to complete the task. It is no good giving Bob the task of opening the safe every morning at 10am if you do not give him the authority required to do it. Bob needs the key to open the safe with.

Tasks You Should not Delegate

Obviously some aspects of leadership are sensitive and should not be delegated. For example:

- Hiring
- Firing
- Pay issues
- Policy

Your Task after Delegating

After delegating:

- Plan - goals, meeting, tasks
- Direct - your team, keep them on track
- Encourage - boost morale

THE ART OF DELEGATION

Delegation is a skill of which we have all heard - but which few understand. It can be used either as an excuse for dumping failure onto the shoulders of subordinates, or as a dynamic tool for motivating and training your team to realize their full potential.

Everyone knows about delegation. Most managers hear about it in the cradle as mother talks earnestly to the baby-sitter: "just enjoy the television... this is what you do if... if there is any trouble call me at"; people have been writing about it for nearly half a millennium; yet few actually understand it.

Delegation underpins a style of management which allows your staff to use and develop their skills and knowledge to the full potential. Without delegation, you lose their full value.

As the ancient quotation above suggests, delegation is primarily about entrusting your authority to others. This means that they can act and initiate independently; and that they assume responsibility with you for certain tasks. If something goes wrong, you remain responsible since you are the manager; the trick is to delegate in such a way that things get done but do not go (badly) wrong.

Objective

The objective of delegation is to get the job done by someone else. Not just the simple tasks of reading instructions and turning a lever, but also the decision making and changes which depend upon new information. With delegation, your staff have the authority to react to situations without referring back to you.

If you tell the janitor to empty the bins on Tuesdays and Fridays, the bins will be emptied on Tuesdays and Fridays. If the bins overflow on Wednesday, they will be emptied on Friday. If instead you said to empty the bins as often as necessary, the janitor would decide how often and adapt to special circumstances. You might suggest a regular schedule (teach the janitor a little personal time management), but by leaving the decision up to the janitor you will apply his/her local knowledge to the problem. Consider this frankly: do you want to be an expert on bin emptying, can you construct an instruction to cover all possible contingencies? If not, delegate to someone who gets paid for it.

To enable someone else to do the job for you, you must ensure that:

- They know what you want
- They have the authority to achieve it
- They know how to do it.

These all depend upon communicating clearly the nature of the task, the extent of their discretion, and the sources of relevant information and knowledge.

Information

Such a system can only operate successfully if the decision-makers (your staff) have full and rapid access to the relevant information. This means that you must establish a system to enable the flow of information. This must at least include regular exchanges between your staff so that each is aware of what the others are doing. It should also include briefings by you on the information which you have received in your role as manager; since if you need to know this information to do your job, your staff will need to know also if they are to do your (delegated) job for you.

One of the main claims being made for computerized information distribution is that it facilitates the rapid dissemination of information. Some protagonists even suggest that such systems will instigate changes in managerial power sharing rather than merely support them: that the "enknowledged" workforce will rise up, assume control and innovate spontaneously.

You may not believe this vision, but you should understand the premise. If a manager restricts access to information, then only he/she is able to make decisions which rely upon that information; once that access is opened to many others, they too can make decisions - and challenge those of the manager according to additional criteria.

The manager who fears this challenge will never delegate effectively; the manager who recognizes that the staff may have additional experience and knowledge (and so may enhance the decision-making process) will welcome their input; delegation ensures that the staff will practise decision-making and will feel that their views are welcome.

Effective Control

One of the main phobias about delegation is that by giving others authority, a manager loses control. This need not be the case. If you train your staff to apply the same criteria as you would yourself (by example and full explanations) then they will be exercising your control on you behalf.

And since they will witness many more situations over which control may be exercised (you can't be in several places at once) then that control is exercised more diversely and more rapidly than you could exercise it by yourself. In engineering terms: if maintaining control is truly your concern, then you should distribute the control mechanisms to enable parallel and autonomous processing.

Staggered Development

To understand delegation, you really have to think about people. Delegation cannot be viewed as an abstract technique, it depends upon individuals and individual needs. Let us take a lowly member of staff who has little or no knowledge about the job which needs to be done.

Do you say: "Jimmy, I want a draft tender for contract of the new Hydro Powerstation on my desk by Friday"? No. Do you say: "Jimmy, Jennifer used to do the tenders for me. Spend about an hour with her going over how she did them and try compiling one for the new Hydro Powerstation.

She will help you for this one, but do come to me if she is busy with a client. I want a draft by Friday so that I can look over it with you"? Possibly.

The key is to delegate gradually. If you present someone with a task which is daunting, one with which he/she does not feel able to cope, then the task will not be done and your staff will be severely demotivated. Instead you should build-up gradually; first a small task leading to a little development, then another small task which builds upon the first; when that is achieved, add another stage; and so on. This is the difference between asking people to scale a sheer wall, and providing them with a staircase. Each task delegated should have enough complexity to stretch that member of staff - but only a little.

Jimmy needs to feel confident. He needs to believe that he will actually be able to achieve the task which has been given to him. This means that either he must have the sufficient knowledge, or he must know where to get it or where to get help. So, you must enable access to the necessary knowledge. If you hold that knowledge, make sure that Jimmy feels able to come to you; if someone else holds the knowledge, make sure that they are prepared for Jimmy to come to them. Only if Jimmy is sure that support is available will he feel confident enough to undertake a new job.

You need to feel confident in Jimmy: this means keeping an eye on him. It would be fatal to cast Jimmy adrift and expect him to make it to the shore: keep an eye on him, and a lifebelt handy. It is also a mistake to keep wandering up to Jimmy at odd moments and asking for progress reports: he will soon feel persecuted. Instead you must agree beforehand how often and when you actually need information and decide the reporting schedule at the onset. Jimmy will then expect these encounters and even feel encouraged by your continuing support; you will be able to check upon progress and even spur it on a little.

When you do talk to Jimmy about the project, you should avoid making decisions of which Jimmy is capable himself. The whole idea is for Jimmy to learn to take over and so he must be encouraged to do so. Of course, with you there to check his decisions, Jimmy will feel freer to do so. If Jimmy is wrong - tell him, and explain very carefully why. If Jimmy is nearly right - congratulate him, and suggest possible modifications; but, of course, leave Jimmy to decide. Finally, unless your solution has significant merits over Jimmy's, take his: it costs you little, yet rewards him much.

Constrained Availability

There is a danger with "open access" that you become too involved with the task you had hoped to delegate. One successful strategy to avoid this is to formalize the manner in which these conversation take place. One formalism is to allow only fixed, regular encounters (except for emergencies) so that Jimmy has to think about issues and questions before raising them; you might even insist that he draw-up an agenda. A second formalism is to refuse to make a decision unless Jimmy has provided you with a clear statement of alternatives, pros and cons, and his recommendation. This is my favourite. It allows Jimmy to rehearse the full authority of decision making while secure in the knowledge that you will be there to check the outcome. Further, the insistence upon evaluation of alternatives promotes good decision making practices. If Jimmy is right, then Jimmy's confidence increases - if you disagree with Jimmy, he learns something new (provided you explain your criteria) and so his knowledge increases. Which ever way, he benefits; and the analysis is provided for you.

Outcomes and Failure

Let us consider your undoubtedly high standards. When you delegate a job, it does not have to be done as well as you could do it (given time), but only as well as necessary: never judge the outcome by what you expect you would do (it is difficult to be objective about that), but rather by fitness for purpose. When you delegate a task, agree then upon the criteria and standards by which the outcome will be judged.

You must enable failure. With appropriate monitoring, you should be able to catch mistakes before they are catastrophic; if not, then the failure is yours. You are the manager, you decided that Jimmy could cope, you gave him enough rope to hang himself, you are at fault. Now that that is cleared up, let us return to Jimmy. Suppose Jimmy gets something wrong; what do you want to happen?

Firstly, you want it fixed. Since Jimmy made the mistake, it is likely that he will need some input to develop a solution: so Jimmy must feel safe in approaching you with the problem. Thus you must deal primarily with the solution rather than the cause (look forward, not backwards). The most desirable outcome is that Jimmy provides the solution.

Once that is dealt with, you can analyse the cause. Do not fudge the issue; if Jimmy did something wrong say so, but only is very specific terms. Avoid general attacks on his parents: "were you born this stupid?", and look to the actual event or circumstance which led to the error: "you did not take account of X in your decision". Your objectives are to ensure that Jimmy:

- Understands the problem
- Feels confident enough to resume
- Implements some procedure to prevent recurrence.

The safest ethos to cultivate is one where Jimmy actually looks for and anticipates mistakes. If you wish to promote such behaviour, you should always praise Jimmy for his prompt and wise action in spotting and dealing with the errors rather that castigate him for causing them. Here the emphasis is placed upon checking/testing/monitoring of ideas. Thus you never criticise Jimmy for finding an error, only for not having safe-guards in place.

There is always the question of what to delegate and what to do yourself, and you must take a long term view on this: you want to delegate as much as possible to develop you staff to be as good as you are now.

The starting point is to consider the activities you used to do before you were promoted. You used to do them when you were more junior, so someone junior can do them now. Tasks in which you have experience are the easiest for you to explain to others and so to train them to take over. You thus use your experience to ensure that the task is done well, rather than to actually perform the task yourself. In this way you gain time for your other duties and someone else becomes as good as your once were (increasing the strength of the group).

Tasks in which your staff has more experience must be delegated to them. This does not mean that you relinquish responsibility because they are expert, but it does mean that the default decision should be theirs. To be a good manager though, you should ensure that they spend some time in explaining these decisions to you so that you learn their criteria.

Decisions are a normal managerial function: these too should be delegated - especially if they are important to the staff. In practice, you will need to establish the boundaries of these decisions so that you can live with the outcome, but this will only take you a little time while the delegation of the remainder of the task will save you much more.

In terms of motivation for your staff, you should distribute the more mundane tasks as evenly as possible; and sprinkle the more exciting onces as widely. In general, but especially with the boring tasks, you should be careful to delegate not only the performance of the task but also its ownership. Task delegation, rather than task assignment, enables innovation. The point you need to get across is that the task may be changed, developed, upgraded, if necessary or desirable. So someone who collates the monthly figures should not feel obliged to blindly type them in every first-Monday; but should feel empowered to introduce a more effective reporting format, to use Computer Software to enhance the data processing, to suggest and implement changes to the task itself.

Negotiation

Since delegation is about handing over authority, you cannot dictate what is delegated nor how that delegation is to be managed. To control the delegation, you need to establish at the beginning the task itself, the reporting schedule, the sources of information, your availability, and the criteria of success. These you must negotiate with your staff: only by obtaining both their input and their agreement can you hope to arrive at a workable procedure.

Once you have delegated everything, what do you do then? You still need to monitor the tasks you have delegated and to continue the development of your staff to help them exercise their authority well.

There are managerial functions which you should never delegate - these are the personal/personnel ones which are often the most obvious additions to your responsibilities as you assume a managerial role. Specifically, they include: motivation, training, team-building, organization, praising, reprimanding, performance reviews, promotion.

As a manager, you have a responsibility to represent and to develop the effectiveness of your group within the company; these are tasks you can expand to fill your available time - delegation is a mechanism for creating that opportunity.

Delegation Tips

- Delegation helps people grow underneath you in an organization and thus pushes you even higher in management. It provides you with more time, and you will be able to take on higher priority projects.
- Delegate whole pieces or entire job pieces rather than simply tasks and activities.
- Clearly define what outcome is needed, then let individuals use some creative thinking of their own as to how to get to that outcome.
- Clearly define limits of authority that go with the delegated job. Can the person hire other people to work with them? Are there spending constraints?
- Clear standards of performance will help the person know when he or she is doing exactly what is expected.
- When on the receiving end of delegation, work to make your boss' job easier and to get the boss promoted. This will enhance your promotability also.
- Assess routine activities in which you are involved. Can any of them be eliminated or delegated?
- Never underestimate a person's potential. Delegate slightly more than you think the person is capable of handling. Expect them to succeed, and you will be pleasantly surprised more frequently than not.
- Expect completed staff work from the individuals reporting to you. That is, they will come to you giving you alternatives and suggestions when a problem exists rather than just saying "Boss, what should we do?"
- Do not avoid delegating something because you cannot give someone the entire project. Let the person start with a bite size piece, then after learning and doing that, they can accept larger pieces and larger areas of responsibility.
- Agree on a monitoring or measurement procedure that will keep you informed as to progress on this project because you are ultimately still responsible for it and need to know that it is progressing as it should. In other words-If you can't measure it don't delegate it.

Evaluations

Evaluation is carefully collecting and analyzing information in order to make decisions. There are many types of evaluations in organizations, for example, evaluation of marketing efforts, evaluation of employee performance, programme evaluations, etc. Evaluations can focus on many aspects of an organization and its processes, for example, its goals, processes and outcomes.

Evaluation, in the context of management activities, is carefully collecting information about something in order to make necessary decisions about it. There are a large number and wide variety of evaluations that can occur in businesses, whether for-profit or nonprofit. Evaluation is closely related to performance management (whether about organizations, groups, processes or individuals), which includes identifying measures to indicate results. Evaluation often includes collecting information around these measures to conclude the extent of performance.

Financial Statements

Once the organization has establish goals and associated strategies (or ways to reach the goals), funds are set aside for the resources and labour to the accomplish goals and tasks. As the money is spent, statements are changed to reflect what was spent, how it was spent and what it obtained. Review of financial statements is one of the more common methods to monitor the progress of programmes and plans. The most common financial statements include the balance sheet, income statement and cash flow statement. Financial audits are regularly conducted to ensure that financial management practices follow generally accepted standards, as well.

Performance management focuses on the performance of the total organization, including its processes, critical subsystems (departments, programmes, projects, etc.) and employees. Most of us have some basic impression of employee performance management, including the role of performance reviews. Performance reviews provide an opportunity for supervisors and their employees to regularly communicate about goals, how well those goals should be met, how well the goals are being met and what must be done to continue to meet (or change) those goals. The employee is rewarded in some form for meeting performance standards, or embarks on a development plan with the supervisor in order to improve performance.

Policies help ensure that behaviours in the workplace conform to federal and state laws, and also to expectations of the organization. Often, policies are applied to specified situations in the form of procedures. Personnel policies and procedures help ensure that employee laws are followed (e.g., laws such as the Americans with Disabilities Act, Occupational Health and Safety Act, etc.) and minimize the likelihood of costly litigation. A procedure is a step-by-step list of activities required to conduct a certain task. Procedures ensure that routine tasks are carried out in an effective and efficient fashion.

Quality Control and Operations in Management

The concept of quality control has received a great deal of attention over the past twenty years. Many people recognize phrases such as "do it right the first time, "zero defects", "Total Quality Management", etc. Very broadly, quality includes specifying a performance standard (often by benchmarking, or comparing to a well-accepted standard), monitoring and measuring results, comparing the results to the standard and then making adjusts as necessary. Recently, the concept of quality management has expanded to include organization-wide programmes, such as Total Quality Management, ISO9000, Balanced Scorecard, etc. Operations management includes the overall activities involved in developing, producing and distributing products and services.

6

Employment Facilities and Hospitality for Business Tourism

DEVELOPMENT OF EMPLOYMENT RELATIONS

Interest in employment, now the preserve of many individuals, but not all, in western economies, derives from the fact that 'Work dominates the lives of men and women ... the management of employees both individually and collectively remains a central feature of organisational life'. Before beginning an examination of employment relations in the HI, it is useful to outline the historical development of employment relations and their relevance as a field of study, thereby introducing the reader to some of the key terms used throughout the book.

According to Hyman (1989) academic interest in employment relations was prompted when the potential stability of social order was put under threat by militant behaviour among a growing number of unionized industrial manual workers, who were no longer prepared to tolerate very bad terms and conditions of employment. This challenge to social order, which began in the late nineteenth century, was met by two responses. First, the social welfare reformers, in keeping with their predecessors who had successfully campaigned for health and safety legislation earlier in the nineteenth century, urged legal intervention to improve the conditions under which work was performed and the terms under which it was undertaken. They achieved limited success, notably the introduction of minimum wages in four manufacturing industries in 1906.

The second and main response, which was to characterize public policy on employment relations until 1979, was that voluntary collective bargaining provided the best means to secure order within employer-employee relations. Collective bargaining is a process whereby employers and trade unions negotiate the substantive terms and conditions of employment, such as pay and hours of work, and procedural agreements that facilitate the resolution of disputes between the parties. Industrial relations, the term in usage at the time, focused on the institutions of collective bargaining in fixing these 'rules' of employment, largely within male-dominated manufacturing environments. Collective agreements were not legally enforceable.

While public services such as the health service, the railways and the coal mines came to assume importance in industrial relations following the mass nationalization programme after the Second World War, private services remained the 'Cinderella' of British industrial relations. Even though the growth of private services such as retailing and hospitality opened up more employment opportunities for women, whose main work opportunities had been in domestic service in the earlier part of the century, unregulated, female service work was deemed not to be part of industrial relations. Even so, the lack of collective bargaining arrangements prompted the Labour government to extend the scope of minimum wage legislation to embrace these sectors. Thus in 1945 the newly named wages councils, a form of 'state-sponsored' collective bargaining, were able to fix remuneration (any pay including basic pay, overtime and shift premiums) and paid holidays for many 'unprotected' workers in private services.

Collective Consensus and a More Active State

Greater state intervention in employment matters was a response by both Conservative and Labour governments to the mounting economic difficulties of the 1960s, e.g. statutory and voluntary incomes policies. State intervention also constituted a response to the perceived failure of voluntary collective bargaining to provide an effective regulatory mechanism for social order and social welfare, notably to protect the interests of the low-paid, many of whom were women. This perceived breakdown prompted the government to appoint a Royal Commission in 1965, the Donovan Commission (1968), to investigate the state of employer- worker relations, in order to recommend how the 'system' could be reformed. The Donovan prescription sought to maintain voluntarism, and placed the onus on employers to improve the rules of employment, and to introduce more formal procedures for the resolution of disputes.

Donovan's prescription was not universal, because it could not be applied to large parts of private services comprising small, informally managed, non-union workplaces, where female and part-time employment was concentrated. A different approach based on legal intervention in employment relations began to develop, based on employment protection for individual employees. Early employment protection rights of the 1960s included the right to a written statement of terms and conditions of employment, statutory redundancy pay and equal pay. Workers lacking the protection of a trade union and with no recourse to formal workplace procedures could resolve employment disputes, which are those in scope of the law, by going to an industrial (now employment) tribunal.

The 1970s represented a significant turning point for legal intervention in employment relations. Britain joined the European Economic Community

(EEC) in 1972. This heralded the start of a wide-ranging programme designed to establish a floor of new rights relating to matters including unfair dismissal, maternity leave, sex and race discrimination and health and safety at work. The main beneficiaries were to be those working in private services.

A Challenge to Tradition

Events of the 1980s and early 1990s effectively killed the model of voluntary collective bargaining. In pursuit of an overriding objective to deregulate the labour market and employment, successive Conservative governments systematically dismantled institutions deemed to interfere with the free working of the labour market, notably the trade unions and wages councils. Paradoxically, in spite of the government's antipathy to the EU's social action programme and subsequent opt out of the social chapter, the EU continued to influence British employment relations in a significant way. Rulings from the European Court of Justice (ECJ) obliged Britain to introduce new legislation, e.g. the transfer of undertakings or the amendment of existing legislation relating to equal pay and sex discrimination. The floor of employment rights was both strengthened and extended.

Managers reasserted the right to manage increasingly flexible and non-standard workers under the banner of 'managerialism', in workplaces that might be labelled 'bleak houses'. An alternative version of management thinking stressed the benefits of 'commitment' over 'control'. Both approaches came to signify the two variants of HRM. 'Soft' HRM emphasized fostering commitment, improving quality and developing the human resource, whereas 'hard' HRM was contingent and calculating in its utilization of the human resource. If organizations were to survive the effects of adverse economic conditions, globalization and increasing competition, the imperative was to integrate HRM within business strategy.

The impact of HRM on industrial relations was widely debated. Other key issues in the wider academic debate included the extent of continuity and change in industrial relations, the sharp decline in trade union membership, the impact of deregulation and whether employment relations could be re-regulated.

Labour

By the mid-1990s individual relationships were catapulted firmly to the forefront of analysis of the employment relationship.

Recognition of this change had been apparent from WIRS in 1990, perhaps most notably within the HI. HI managers are free to exercise a high degree of managerial prerogative in the absence of unorganized labour, termed 'unbridled individualism'.

The election of a Labour government for the first time in nearly 20 years in 1997 raised expectations that there would be a new agenda for employment relations, although Heery's assessment was that 'it is extremely doubtful whether New Labour will issue in a new industrial relations'. New Labour's stakeholder economy is based on fairness and partnership. Fairness at work is to be achieved in two ways. The government signed up to the EU social chapter and set about introducing a new floor of minimum employment standards, including a National Minimum Wage (NMW), and family-friendly measures. Social partnership between employers and workers is designed to foster a more consensual and cooperative relationship between employers and employees. The Low Pay Commission (LPC), whose first task was to recommend the initial rate of the NMW, provides an early manifestation of social partnership comprising employer, worker and independent representatives. Although many of the Conservatives' trade union reforms remain in place, the introduction of statutory trade union recognition procedures might help reverse the steep decline in trade union membership.

By the time of WERS in 1998 the system of collective representation had crumbled 'to such an extent that it no longer represented the dominant model'. In reality employment relations could conform to different and diverse patterns. Private service establishments employing 25 or more employees were numerically more important than private sector manufacturing and the public sector put together. Their share of employment increased from 26 per cent in 1980 to 44 per cent in 1998, reinforcing the point that alternative ways to view and reform employment relations were long overdue, particularly in circumstances of 'bleak house' or 'black hole' employment. Although we find these terms wanting in respect of the HI, they highlight the relevance of the industry as a unit of analysis. Consequently we shall show how these types of workplaces throw up major problems for employment relations reform.

Agenda for the Twenty-first Century

In calling for a new industrial relations paradigm, Ackers (2002) now argues that the new problem of social order focuses on links between employment and society, and that such a link provides an explicit ethical framework for policies like social partnership. He rejects the traditional industrial relations notion of workers as unattached individuals in their out-of-work lives, and argues that industrial relations can no longer ignore issues of work-life balance and corporate social responsibility. Indeed social concerns underpin 'Fairness at Work' and the 'Welfare to Work' programme, and family-friendly issues are a new addition to WERS. Hence a new definition of industrial relations as neo-pluralism:

Employment relations is the study of the social institutions involved in the normative regulation of the employment relationship and business's interaction with other stakeholders in society.

Thus Ackers rejects as inappropriate Kelly's (1997) industrial relations paradigm for the twenty-first century, which derives from a redefinition of Marxism based on socialism, workers' mobilization, economic militancy and strikes, and organized labour.

Edwards (2003a) identifies three pressing issues in contemporary employment relations: 'high commitment' or 'high involvement' work systems, the international context and economic performance. The first, although interesting, is very rarely found anywhere in Britain. Its alternative of 'low skills' and 'low wages' strikes right at the heart of much hospitality employment. This links to economic performance, where the absence of collective bargaining is likely to have contributed to income inequality and the perpetuation of low pay in the HI, although pay may be subsidized by the state through social security and taxation. The further subsidy of low pay through tips as a defensible employment practice is a matter of conjecture. We shall also explore if particular employment relations practices can be linked to successful performance outcomes. The international context and its implications for employment relations in the HI are considered below.

A fourth pressing issue can be added. Employment relations discourse needs to recognize that prejudice and bias have been built into much of the theoretical and practical analysis, thus distorting its perspective. Gender is not the only example, but may be the most obvious. In spite of an increasing interest in what may be described as 'women's issues', such as (un)equal pay and employment opportunities, family-friendly policies and sexual harassment, one major barrier to understanding employment relations is an assumption that they are gender neutral. The argument is that adding women's issues to the agenda is simply not good enough. Management, trade unions and the state are not gender neutral, and therefore we need to recognize the gendered characteristics of the employment relationship and work and integrate this into our understanding of the field of employment relations. Other 'omissions' include age, ethnicity and the role of customers. We shall explore these issues throughout the book where it is possible or relevant to do so.

All these issues were placed under review in The Future of Work Programme launched by the ESRC in 1998. The Programme has supported 27 projects designed to rectify gaps in our understanding and improve the quality of information available to the policy-makers in the UK. Topics under investigation have included the future of unskilled work, business re-engineering and performance, the changing position of ethnic minorities and women in the labour market, the future for trade unions and the changing nature of the employment relationship.

Three terms denote the relations between managers and workers in the employment relationship - industrial relations, employee relations and employment relations. These terms are often used interchangeably, but can also convey subtle differences of meaning. They may coincide with other fields of academic inquiry and practical activity concerned with 'people management', namely personnel management and HRM. Edwards provides an insightful analysis of the employment relationship, taking as his starting point the distinction made by Fox (1966) and Flanders (1974) between market relations and managerial relations. At the root is an economic exchange between capital (the employer) and labour (the worker), in which the price of labour is set as a contract of employment.

In this economic exchange between the buyer (employer) and seller (worker) of labour, the parties do not share equal power resources. In common law the employer has the right to command and the employee has a duty to obey. The commodity at the heart of the bargain is the worker's labour power. The employer will seek to maximize control over that 'labour process' in order to generate a surplus as profit. The employment relationship, as an exchange and in recognition of its broader context, has also been termed the effort-reward bargain: 'an economic, social and political relationship, for which employees provide manual and mental labour in return for rewards allotted by employers'. Labour only becomes useful if it can be persuaded by management to work, but this is only the beginning. Workers must demonstrate commitment, continue working to the required standards, and not deviate from those standards.

In other words workers must follow 'rules', otherwise management may need to deploy corrective or punitive measures via the disciplinary procedure. Bonamy and May (1997) argue that a weakening of employment relationships since the 1970s has given rise to the emergence of employment as a service relationship. This relationship demands increased recognition of the professional qualities of the 'autonomous' worker, which poses problems of incompatibility with an employment contract built upon subordination. Pay is determined by time worked, whilst idle time due to poor organization and absenteeism is reduced. This is manifested in new forms of employment contract (fixed-term and part-time), externalization of employment to agencies and the sub-contracting of activities. Edwards notes that, if we were starting from scratch, 'employment relations' might be the best label. Employment relations do not rule out all variants within the employment relationship including:

- Trade unions and formal collective bargaining;
- Individually based management/workforce relations conducted informally;
- Managerialism;
- More democratic and highly participative non-union relations;
- Men, women and disadvantaged groups;
- Employees and workers, including atypical workers and the self-employed.

Further:

- Employment relations is the main term used in the WERS sourcebook;
- Industrial tribunals have been renamed employment tribunals;
- The cornerstone of New Labour's industrial relations policy is the Employment Relations Act 1999.

A necessary departure for this book, as noted earlier, is to relocate the nexus of the employment relationship to include a relatively ignored third actor in the employment relationship - the customer. The notion of the customer in the employment relationship has been increasingly incorporated into the sociology of work, but less so in employment relations. Front-line workers, such as receptionists and servers in bars and restaurants, have to serve two 'masters': their superior manager and the customer. Individual workers can have a simultaneous and coterminous employment relationship with the organization and the customer.

Organizations in services are best seen as inverted pyramids, with most workers in direct customer contact. Direct service workers engage directly with customers in an exchange that carries both economic and social connotations. Their ability to deliver successfully hinges upon a social relationship with indirect service workers, whose actions are also instrumental to the provision of good customer service, e.g. an enjoyable meal or clean bedrooms. Indirect service workers are not in regular customer contact, so customer influence may be more economic than social. Hence, customers cannot be excluded from an analysis of the employment relationship. As shown below and explained later, an earlier definition has been revised:

Employee relations in hotels and catering is about the management of employment and work relationships between managers and workers and, sometimes, customers; it also covers contemporary employment and work practices.

Frames of Reference

Before exploring the facets of the employment relationship, we need to outline why our attitude towards things influences the way in which we see any given situation, and how itTriplets watch a local football match from adjoining seats, getting an almost identical view of the game. The result is United 5 City 1. One triplet is deliriously happy, the second feels very low, while the third is able to provide a balanced analysis of events, conceding that the result was a fair one, although two of United's goals were the result of dubious refereeing and City deserved more than a single goal.

Why did their particular attitude affect their view of the game?

Fox proposed two frames of reference as a means by which 'the problems of industrial relations can be seen realistically and laid more open to solution'. The unitary perspective is a 'management ideology' built on the belief that everyone in the organization shares the same goals, and that 'conflict' is pathological and derives from deviance. Trade unions are seen as an intrusion, competing with management for worker loyalty. Fox's main argument was that the unitary perspective was a naive and unrealistic frame of reference that might 'distort reality and thereby prejudice solutions'. Yet in reality many managers do perceive their organizations in unitary terms, regarding themselves as the sole source of authority. Unitarism has underpinned the 'human relations school' of management, including Mayo, Likert, McGregor, Schein and Herzberg, and reasserted itself in 'managerialism' and HRM.

Fox suggested that the more realistic approach to managing people was to recognize that organizations are pluralistic, comprising various groups, each with their own basis of authority and sets of interests. The 'rules' of employment are not just the preserve of management. A new pay rate set by management will not necessarily be seen as fair by workers, creating an issue of potential dispute. Therefore conflict or differences between individuals and groups are inevitable. Management should recognize this inevitability, and find the ways and means to regulate such differences. As noted above, an institutional approach - collective bargaining between employers and trade unions, and the development of formal procedures to deal with disputes about pay, grievances and discipline - was considered to be the most appropriate solution. However, this is flawed to the extent that it implies both parties to the bargain have equal power resources at their disposal.

Later Fox revised his thinking and added a third perspective of radicalism, prompted by a wave of 'shop floor' discontent and 'wildcat' strikes at workplace level. Such worker behaviour was perceived as a reaction against exploitative and oppressive employers whose sole aim was to maximize profit. Conflict was caused by the economic disparity of society as a whole, with the principal disparity between capital and labour - employers who own and manage the means of production and workers who have their (human) capital to sell. This view underpins the labour process approach. This approach stresses the contradiction of managerial goals, with regulation and control having to be balanced by the need to gain workers' consent.

Even today Edwards (2003a) argues that unitarism cannot be written off as naive and outdated any more than radicalism because of the apparent disappearance of discontent. Ackers' (2002) neo-pluralism refocuses the employment relationship beyond the workplace by connecting the old pluralist and voluntary frames of reference with new questions raised by contemporary society. The health of society is put first, encouraging industrial relations policy initiatives that are driven by social concerns, not just a business agenda. Further he argues that the employment relationship bears hidden ethical considerations of trust and responsibility in relation to human beings.

As we shall show, both managers and workers in a variety of work and employment situations in the HI do see their workplaces in unitary terms, but this does not necessarily infer the absence of conflict. Areas of potential dispute, conflict and difference do exist between managers and workers, between managers and other managers, and between workers and customers, demonstrating that workplaces are pluralistic. In cases where workers 'fiddle' or 'pilfer' from their employer, the nature of their behaviour is more in keeping with a radical perspective. Thus it is possible to observe facets of unitarism, pluralism and radicalism in the same employment relationship in which management, for the most part, remains the more powerful.

Even so, areas of common interest self-evidently exist otherwise all these relationships would break down. Consent provides the basis for resolving conflict and achieving cooperation. Cooperation is built on trust between individuals engendered at workplace level rather than through elaborate organizational mechanisms. Yet securing workers' consent is neither a straightforward nor certain process. Therefore, a mix of overt and covert conflict and cooperation underpins all employment relationships and, as we shall argue, workplace harmony owes more to pragmatic acceptance and accommodation among the parties in the employment relationship than to ideological belief.

The rules of Employment and Power Relations

We have already noted that the employment relationship is underpinned by rules, hence the continuing validity of Clegg's definition of industrial relations as 'The study of the rules governing employment' which Edwards explains in more detail:

This does not limit the subject to the collective relations between managements and trade unions, for a rule can derive from other sources, and there are rules governing non-union groups; nor does it restrict analysis to one sector, for it covers all paid forms of employment. A rule is a social institution involving two or more parties which may have its basis in law, a written collective agreement, an unwritten agreement, a unilateral decree or merely an understanding that has the force of custom. In non-union settings, as much as union ones, rules determine rates of pay, hours of work, job descriptions and many other aspects of employment. The subject is about the ways in which the employment relationship is regulated. To regulate means to control, to adapt or adjust continuously or to adjust by rule.

Managerial Issues

While rules may be the substantive rules of employment, e.g. pay and conditions of employment, implicit in the notion of rules affecting people is the concept of behaviour. Management's job is to control and direct workers' behaviour to perform work to the desired standards, and thereby ensure that the rules of employment are adhered to.

Four key issues arise:

- Rules are not always absolute and may be gendered.
- Managerial control of workers' behaviour is underpinned by a power relationship.
- This power relationship is unequal and may be gendered.
- Managers have a choice of means to maximize control.

The first point is that one should caution against perceiving rules in too absolute a sense. At one end of the spectrum rules embodied in the law of the land provide a good example of formal rules. Any breach may incur very severe penalties, e.g. health and safety. In a workplace setting rules in practice may derive from informal understandings that can in one set of circumstances be interpreted by the worker as a permissive concession or in a different set of circumstances as something to be observed at all costs. Strawberries as a worker's perquisite during the Wimbledon lawn tennis championship are a good example. Experienced workers know that taking home unwanted strawberries is 'permitted' during busy periods. When fewer staff are needed, increased managerial surveillance will be deployed to dismiss staff caught in possession of company property.

Rule-learning is part of what Polanyi (1967) refers to as 'tacit skills'. As argued elsewhere:

Tacit skills, such as learning to deal with customers, are learnt in and through the very act of doing, often involving trial and error and not from following a body of procedurally-designed rules. They are seen as an interpretive achievement of the user as to how the 'rules' fit the task in hand. By mastery of the rules comes the power to extend them.

This example embracing the customer provides a developmental point to Edwards' observation that rule-making is difficult, and that rules have to be interpreted in action for them to have any real meaning. Specifically in the labour contract this is because the worker's ability to work is only realized as useful labour in the course of carrying out that work, hence 'a rule is a complex social institution'.

In service work physical appearance and 'personality', or 'aesthetic labour', are an implicit part of the employment contract. Only female flight attendants, not their male colleagues, are subjected to regular weigh-ins to ensure they comply to specified weight: height ratios. This demonstrates clearly how a rule may be gendered.

The second point to note is that the very essence of management seeking to control workers' behaviour is underpinned by a power relationship. Power is the capacity to pursue one's own interests individually and collectively, involving the capacity to oppose the actions of others and to pursue one's own objectives, and is embedded in continuing relationships. This does not mean power has to be exercised by either party in an overt sense. The threat of power may be sufficient to maintain broadly consensual employment relationships, such that any disputes or differences (conflicts) are resolved amicably without recourse to either party seeking to deploy sanctions against the other.

The third point assumes a power inequality in the employment relationship. Self-evidently an employer is more powerful than an individual worker. The employer's ability to terminate a worker's services is likely to be more detrimental to the worker than to the employer, in spite of employment protection legislation. Yet the individual behaviours of workers, such as high labour turnover, may be detrimental to an employer, even though they are not concerted. When workers combine collectively, with or without the backing of a trade union, there is some tilt in the balance of power, because collective sanctions may be imposed against the employer. Ultimately the outcome of the process by which each side seeks to gain concessions will depend on the relative power of the parties. For example, a plentiful supply of suitable workers in the labour market makes existing workers more readily dispensable and replaceable on the employer's terms. The opposite would be true for workers with scarce skills who can command high wages.

As Wajcman argues, gender relations are power-based and women's subordination in the workforce and workplace owes as much to trade unions as it does to managers. Spradley and Mann provide a graphic account of how the subordination of one group of female workers was brought about by another group of male workers who were the custodians of the male proprietor's trust. The male bartenders controlled the orders, and sought to make the cocktail waitresses' job difficult by giving orders in an inconsistent and confusing way. Any mistakes became the waitresses' responsibility, even if they had been caused by the bartenders. Such was the power of the bartenders that pleasing them became more important than pleasing the customers.

The fourth point is that managers have a choice of means to maximize control over workers. Friedman's 'direct control' is a variant of Taylorism (the separation of mental and manual labour or scientific management). Management is responsible for planning, designing and organizing the labour process, while cheap, unskilled workers perform standardized, simple repetitive tasks. Fast food is a good case in point, and also epitomizes McDonaldization, a social critique of how contemporary society and culture are being shaped by rationalist scientific management. While Taylorism sought to control the organization of work, McDonaldization is based on rationalization, replication, standardization of products and service, and quantification. In this low trust strategy worker behaviour is controlled through the use of standardized scripts in the service encounter. In Friedman's alternative of 'responsible autonomy', a high trust approach, managers delegate control to relatively privileged skilled workers who may already have elements of job control and discretion.

The objective is to get workers to identify with the competitive aims of the organization so they will behave responsibly with minimum supervision. An obvious example of where such an approach might be used is in a luxury hotel, but it is also associated with empowerment and much customer-service work. As we shall argue, and implied in the example of cocktail waitresses above, these and other similar approaches including 'hard' and 'soft' HRM provide a useful framework for analysis, but are not necessarily alternatives.

The history of hotel internationalization has been characterized by American chains that secure control and integration through highly standardized procedures and manuals of operational procedures. Yet a 'soft' focus on the service encounter as the driver of competitive advantage necessitates developing a culture of customized service. Mass customization illustrated by Burger King's 'have it your way' slogan as a challenge to McDonald's hold on the market is proposed as an alternative paradigm to McDonaldization.

Workers and Customers

Other tensions within the employment relationship impinge upon the rules of employment and power relationships. If management is about the achievement of organizational goals through people it can be argued that managers will be successful to the extent that these goals coincide with the aims and aspirations of those people, be they workers or customers. This 'matching' of broadly reciprocal needs between employers and workers may be referred to as a 'psychological contract'; or set of contracts. It suggests managers and workers can share goals, but this is not at all straightforward. There is not a necessarily clear cut distinction between boss and worker, or a 'them and us' scenario.

Further we must also account for a psychological contract with customers. Two key points are noteworthy:

- Organizations comprise people and are, therefore, social organizations.
- People, as social animals, may behave in unpredictable ways.

Workers

Human beings do not necessarily behave consistently or predictably, even in the same sets of circumstances. People are citizens and customers as well as employees, and these multiple identities bring different and sometimes conflicting expectations of the organization. This makes the management of the employment relationship an uncertain process within which there is a blend of contradictory principles around the need to control and to gain the consent of workers. Workers may seek to regain control individually or collectively when they perceive that management has operated outside the rules. At that point workers' consent has been withdrawn and management will need to find ways to restore order and regain consent.

In Lucas workers' individual response to organizational rules is seen in three main ways - to conform or be deviant in employment, or to terminate their employment. These responses are similar to Marchington's 'getting on', 'getting by' and 'getting back'. These are behaviours deployed in circumstances where customer care and service quality are dependent on workers' use of their tacit skills, which contain both technical and attitudinal elements. Limiting the definition of tacit skills to employer-employee relations is too narrow. Marchington overlooked how workers exhibit their tacit skills in ways other than in respect of their relationship with the employer, notably the customer. The point that 'getting back', 'getting by' and 'getting on' are as much resistance strategies in the labour process as coping mechanisms is developed. These behaviours can also be deployed collectively.

At workplace level personal relationships are likely to be closely connected to morale and success. Managers often 'muck in' when required. In small workplaces the existence of a single leader, often the owner, may serve to inspire loyalty from the workforce, but it is not a one-way process, as workers' respect has to be earned. Is it realistic to suggest that Mina, Jo and Sadie, who wait on table in the restaurant, share all the same goals as their boss? The hotel may not be doing very well, so there may be mutual concern for the survival of the business. Yet these ladies' main goal may be to serve their customers cheerfully and effectively, while at the same time enjoying some social banter among themselves and with their customers in the process of earning a reasonable wage.

Customers

Within the triadic employment relationship a simultaneous and coterminous relationship with the organization and the customer directly impinges on how workers carry out their work, and such interactions may be rewarding or stressful. The consequent effect on workers' performance may have positive or negative implications for the rules of employment: what they can earn (from good tips to no tips), their prospects of promotion (satisfactory manager and customer appraisal) or actually keeping their job (customer complaint leading to disciplinary sanctions or closure). Unequivocally the worker-customer relationship affects the rules governing employment and workplace behaviour. But so do employer- customer relationships, hence the employment relationship embodies a triadic set of power relations.

This relationship embodies a socio-economic exchange, and is not simply an economic exchange around the price of labour. Fox provides a useful starting point, since he noted that organizations are social organizations and how people behave is a crucial issue in the employment relationship. Even Edwards' point that 'a rule is a complex social institution' does not adequately encapsulate our position. The main justification for widening the scope of this relationship derives from the fact that the service encounter is the interaction of the producer and consumer of services, and is a more complex phenomenon where financial considerations are interwoven with social ones.

In hospitality the social function of service work derives from the provision of a 'home away from home'. The service encounter entails 'emotion work' - the assumption of a social-self, which effectively masks the individual's own personal dispositions to act, including the need to smile and be pleasant in an uninvolved way.

We have already noted that 'aesthetic' and sexual labour may also be inherent in service work. It is the 'normalizing' social role of service labour that distinguishes it from other wage labour. Service work cannot be understood in terms of economic rationality alone. Examination must be based on the supposition that service work is the intended outcome of a necessarily social process in which some social interaction occurs between one or more producers and one or more consumers.

The relations between three groups of people - managers, workers and customers - embody the potential for contradiction between, on the one hand, uncertainty, unpredictability, conflict and difference and, on the other hand, consent, team effort and concerted performance. The practical benefit this book seeks to convey accrues from an understanding of the nature and scope of the rules of employment in this triadic employment relationship, and how it is regulated, primarily at workplace level.

The Employment Relationship in a Wider Context

This concludes by considering some key external contextual influences on workplace employment relationships at two levels - internationally and, in more detail, nationally in Britain.

The International Context

The national context of British employment relations increasingly needs to be understood within a much wider international context.

Three international dimensions have particular resonance:

- International competition has created more open economies that have attracted investment from foreign-owned businesses. For example the French-owned groups Accor and Envergure have respectively opened hotels within their Novotel and Campanile brands in the United Kingdom (UK).
- On a larger scale American multinational corporations (MNCs) have created world brands. McDonald's, Burger King, KFC (formerly Kentucky Fried Chicken) and Marriott are among those that are now household names in many countries across the world.
- Spin-offs from European integration, especially on employment law in Britain, have provided an important underpinning to the employment relationship in the HI.

Foreign investment and MNCs are clearly important factors underpinning the expansion of hospitality and tourism not only in Britain but also in developing countries. Examples of 'better' employment practices, in so far as they may exist in the British HI, have been associated with foreign-owned businesses.

Aspects of the American model of employment relations, that are non-union and market-driven, may seem to reflect some aspects of observed employment relations practice in the British HI, but the similarity has been overstated. The United States (US) has substantially more legal regulation than Britain, which has benefited American HI workers, while the trade unions are not entirely powerless - issues we highlight in later. The European model based on social partnership designed to forge a common agenda between capital and labour is considerably more diverse and different across the member states than is often acknowledged. While we cannot expect it to reflect current developments in HI employment relations in most British workplaces, it has not necessarily produced wholesale benefits for HI workers across the EU either.

The British experience is not necessarily mirrored in other countries across the world. Differences in other countries' institutional arrangements and cultural considerations are among the factors that will affect their employment relations systems.

The British Context

Workplace employment relationships cannot be immune from wider economic, social, legal and political contextual influences. Contemporary examples, which may be influential in Britain today. The distinctions between these sets of influences are not always clear-cut as they can be interrelated.

Other Institutions

Many other institutions, some of which may have a political bias, offer a mixture of fact and opinion on employment relations. National bodies, which take either an employer or management view, include the Confederation of British Industry (CBI), the Institute of Directors (IOD), and the Chartered Institute of Personnel and Development (CIPD). The British Hospitality Association (BHA), Restaurant Association (RA), the British Beer and Pub Association (BBPA), the Hotel, Catering and International Management Association (HCIMA) and the British Institute of Innkeeping (BII) are specific to the HI.

The HtF, formerly the HI's National Training Organisation (NTO), is recognized by government as the employer-led voice on all issues relating to hospitality training, education and qualifications. The HtF also carries out research, and produces useful statistical information about the labour market.

The Trades Union Congress (TUC), Institute of Employment Rights (IER) and the Low Pay Network serve to defend workers' interests. The HCIMA can also be regarded as having a worker perspective since, as the professional body of hospitality managers, it serves to defend their interests as well as disseminating good management practice.

Three large unions have special sections for hospitality workers: the General, Municipal and Boilermakers' Union (GMB), the Transport and General Workers Union (TGWU) and the Union of Shop, Distributive and Allied Workers (USDAW). The National Association of Licensed House Managers (NALHM) was self-standing for many years, but has recently become part of the TGWU.

Viewing employment relations in the HIIndustrial relations are associated with trade unions and the formal institution of collective bargaining. Employee relations place emphasis on strong management often denoted by the term 'managerialist', but not all workers are afforded employee status.

- Specifically in relation to the HI, suggest why these labels may be problematic.

Frames of Reference

Take examples of different managers for whom you have worked:

- Which frame of reference guided their approach to employment relations?
- What specific instances of their behaviour or actions have led you to reach this conclusion?

Employment Rules

Drawing from your work experience:

- What were the main rules of employment?
- Which of these were formal written rules?
- Which of these rules were learnt in practice?
- Can you identify any rules that were ignored in particular circumstances and enforced in others, and explain why this occurred?

Power and Control

Drawing from your work experience, discuss examples of where:

- Managers sought to oppose the actions of others;
- Managers sought to pursue their own objectives;
- Workers sought to oppose the actions of others;
- Workers sought to pursue their own objectives;
- Managers sought to control workers through 'direct control';
- Managers sought to control workers through 'responsible autonomy'.

Workforce Behaviour

Based on your work experience:

- What were the circumstances when managers and customers operated outside the rules of employment?
- What was the workers' response, either as individuals or as groups?

The context of Employment Relations

Using data about the HI from elsewhere and from this book (e.g. trade union density is 2 per cent):

- Produce a new that more specifically outlines the national context of hospitality employment relations;
- See if you can add any new contextual influences;
- Analyse and evaluate the potential effects of these influences on workplace relations.

MAKING HOTEL SUCCESSFUL

Even when the U.S. economy was growing and prosperous, the hotel under its previous owner did not succeed in servicing its debt. Now, because of the current recession, its financial picture is even more bleak. As the hotel's new lender-owner, you may decide to retain it in your bank's portfolio, or to find a buyer on suitable terms as soon as possible (a period surely measured in months, and perhaps in years, due to the depressed condition of the hospitality marketplace).

Purchasers of hotels typically base the purchase price on the property's income stream, applying a capitalization rate to the cash flow before debt service. If the cash flow is a negative number, how can you make the hotel pay its own way? Evaluate management. We assume that the hotel you've taken back has management already in place-an in-house management team or representatives of a professional management firm engaged by the previous owner.

Begin by evaluating the basic documents that the management should have prepared as a guide to the hotel's focus and direction:

- The current-year marketing plan, which characterizes the hotel's customers and sets forth a strategy for securing their business.
- The current-year budget, which estimates the revenue and expense dollars.
- A long-range business plan, which projects the marketing and budget picture, ideally for three to five years into the future.
- A capital facilities plan, which anticipates any expansions or renovations the property may require.
- The operations manual, which outlines the duties of employees and sets standards for their performance.

Next, try to determine whether the manager and key department heads are actually using the plans. Those plans should be living documents. Increase revenue. In times like these, many hoteliers are tempted to save money by cutting back on marketing, but that is the worst thing to do. To put more bodies in the beds, you need creative marketing.

For instance, if your hotel has focused in the past on international leisure travellers, it has been especially hard-hit in recent months by the combination of worldwide recession and Middle East war.

As the threat of war mounted, your hotel should have been targeting domestic tour groups, corporate business, and frequent individual travellers. Your hotel may also have to reduce its room rates to a more competitive level, then increase the volume of business enough to generate a profit. How sophisticated is your hotel's marketing plan? It should begin with knowledge of the existing customer base. Many luxury hotels maintain a detailed guest history which allows them to respond to the specific whims and desires of each repeat guest, but even an economy property should maintain a guest tracking system that provides demographic data on the guests as well as the origin of their reservations.

Control expenses. Your hotel may be losing money because its expenses exceed its revenues.

A recession is a good time to take a fresh look at every conceivable expense. Most people want to start with wages and benefits, because payroll constitutes the largest single expense category. The hotel should trim its payroll where it can, but it must not cut back so far as to compromise service. Examine your hotel's contracts with outside vendors. Get competitive quotes from at least three sources, then negotiate with the suppliers of:

- goods used in the hotel, including food and beverage items, cleaning supplies, and office supplies;
- outside contract services such as pest control, pool cleaning, linen and laundry, and maintenance of indoor plants and outdoor landscaping; and
- maintenance contracts on major equipment such as the climate-control system, computers, and elevators.

Evaluate your hotel's preventive maintenance programme. In the short run you can save money by deferring maintenance, but letting the physical plant and equipment deteriorate will cost you more in the long run for repairs or replacement. What's more, breakdowns seem inevitably to occur at an inconvenient hour, creating emergencies when workers charge a premium for their time. Manage to quality standards. Service quality is particularly important in a recessionary economy, when you can't afford to lose a single guest.

Five ways exist to monitor quality:

- Personal inspection-You or your designated in-house hospitality executive should visit the property at regular intervals to observe and ask questions.
- Franchise inspections-If your hotel has a franchise, the franchise company will send inspectors to the property to assess its compliance with their company's quality standards.
- In-house market research-You can hire a market research firm to interview guests on a random basis during their stay or as they depart.
- Secret-shopper programmes-I use these programmes myself on my clients' behalf, and I recommend them to every absentee owner. Secret-shopper programmes can test the honesty of the staff and quality of service.
- Guest comment cards-While most comments reflect only the best and worst aspects of the guest experience, you should receive a summary of these cards at least every month and review the most egregious complaints with the hotel manager.

The keys to maintaining standards with lean staff are flexible staffing and cross-training. If the hotel has an extra clerk at the front desk when the dining room needs an extra server, that clerk should be able to fill in. As an owner, you should receive regular reports which allow you to track the relationship between staffing levels and the volume of business, and training reports that show who has learned what. Don't assume that hiring a management firm absolves you of the need to be an active owner. You must still hold the firm accountable.

Obtain assurances from each candidate firm that you will have veto power at all times over any manager or key department head the firm assigns to your property. If one of these individuals isn't fitting in, you want the right to have the management firm remove and replace that person rapidly.

The new world of appraisals set in motion by the Financial institutions Reform, Recovery and Enforcement Act continues to evolve. Meanwhile, the industry nears the July 1 deadline for states to have functioning licensing and certification programmes. Significant deliberations have been in the works on several fronts. To recap them:

- The Federal Financial Institutions Examination Council Appraisal Subcommittee, which has the power to extend the July 1 deadline on a state-by-state basis, has been considering a petition to grant more time to all states. Late last year the ABA and state bankers associations asked the subcommittee to grant a blanket extension to Dec. 31.

  While many states have passed laws setting up systems to address requirements of FIRREA, putting the systems in place and using them to qualify appraisers is a time-consuming task.
- The Federal Reserve Board has been reviewing comments on its proposal to cut the de minimis level for institutions it regulates to $50,000 from $100,000. While doing so would put the Fed in synch with the Comptroller's Office and FDIC, bankers have urged the agency to leave the limit where it stands.
- The Appraiser Qualifications Board was set to meet in late March to consider public comments and make a final decision on a restructuring of appraiser categories.

The board is part of the Appraisal Foundation, a private standards setting body with which the Exam Council's subcommittee works and to which states and the appraisal industry look for guidance. Late last December, the board proposed to expand to three categories the original two-category system of appraiser qualifications it envisioned under FIRREA. The board learned that in some states with significant quantities of high-priced homes, its original categories would have barred qualified residential appraisers from properties they are capable of appraising.

To remedy this, the board proposed creating three qualification levels-two certified and one licensed. Some changes in the latter category caused ABA to object, though it endorsed most other aspects of the proposal. For its part, in late January the Exam Council's Appraisal Subcommittee announced that it would be willing to accept a three-tier system in those states that considered it necessary for their real estate markets. The subcommittee noted that its agreement was general in nature and not a judgment on the qualification board's specific proposal. The government body also set several conditions for its actual approval.

Career in Hotel Management Involve

Hotel managers oversee the running of hotels. They are responsible for food and refreshments, accommodation and amenities, entertainment and conference facilities. Large hotels may have individual managers responsible for each department such as housekeeping, maintenance, and food and beverages who have to report to the hotel's general manager. Duties include analysing financial data and targets, managing staff, dealing with customer complaints and ensuring compliance with regulations such as licensing laws. You may also be required to "muck in" when short staffed.

You must have a good head for business and enjoy working with people, being able to manage staff. You need good written and spoken communication skills with the ability to keep calm under pressure and solve problems quickly. You need to be well organised with plenty of energy and enthusiasm and be prepared to work long, unsociable hours. Training normally takes place on the job, gaining experience in different areas of the business.

You may start work at a lower level on the career ladder, working towards NVQs or other vocational qualifications or you can enter at management trainee level. Relevant NVQs include hospitality service at level 2, leading on to hospitality supervision at level 3 and management at level 4. A variety of degrees and HNC/Ds are relevant to hotel management, including hospitality management, international hospitality management, hotel and hospitality management, and hospitality and licensed retail management. Foundation degrees are also available in relevant subjects, such as hospitality business management.

However, academic qualifications are not always necessary and many people work their way up to management. Hotel chains often have their own structured management training schemes for graduates. Apprenticeships may be available for those under 24. In hotel chains, promotion may be into a strategic role such as corporate marketing or training. Experienced managers may open their own hotels.

Training is an integral part of ISO 9002 implementation in a hotel or any organization. A planned, systematic training process is required, as the skills needed for the development of a quality management system are still new to most service organizations. Sufficient time must be set aside for training in such areas as procedure writing and quality auditing.

Training and orientation should be conducted for new staff (including temporary staff) to provide them with the knowledge and skills necessary for the completion of tasks to specified standards. Training for management and existing staff should be initiated after needs analysis of the organization has been conducted. The organization should define the competence needed for each task that affects the quality of products.

Having well trained people to become members of the working group and to become involved in developing, implementing, using and maintaining the Quality System is vital to the success of the project. This emphasizes the importance of training to gain ISO 9002 certification. The term ISO and 9002 are explained at the beginning and a hotel case study is used at the end to demonstrate the practical method of implementing ISO 9002 standards.

Organization for Standardization

The International Organization for Standardization (ISO) is made up of national standards institutes from countries large and small, industrialized and developing, in all regions of the world. ISO develops voluntary technical standards that add value to all types of business operations. These standards contribute to making the development, manufacturing and supply of products and services more efficient, safer and cleaner. "ISO is located in Switzerland and was established in 1947 to develop common international standards. Its members come from the standards bodies in over 135 countries". The ISO technical committee was formed in 1979 to harmonize the increasing international activity in quality management and quality assurance standards.

Organizations Involved with ISO

There are three main types of other organizations that are involved with various aspects of ISO standards. These are:

- Member bodies, the national organizations (or bureaus) of standards in 135 ISO member countries.
- Accreditation bodies, groups responsible for determining that registration groups meet the guidelines for the purpose of granting accreditation to the registrar to issue ISO certificates.
- Registrars, groups that inspect companies for proper adherence to ISO standards and issue ISO certificates to properly qualified companies. Registrars perform thorough registration audits prior to granting an ISO certificate and two surveillance audits each year that the certificates are effective.

Quality Assurance

ISO 9000 brings together the essential principles common to many different quality management and assurance standards into a single system. The intent of the standard is simply to help a company document and implement a basic quality system so that it has the capability to deliver the quality products and services that its customers request.

The ISO 9000 series covers the entire range of business processes from the moment the order is placed, through the entire production or service development process to the actual delivery of the product or service to the customer. It is important to note that ISO 9000 does not certify products or services or guarantee that quality goods or services will be produced. It simply certifies that a quality system is in place that should enable an organization to meet agreed-upon customer requirements and provide more consistent products or services.

As part of the certification process, an organization implements a quality system based on one of three models relevant to the nature of its operation: ISO 9001, 9002 or 9003. Then a third party (an accredited quality system certification body) audits the company to certify that the system complies with the standard and that the quality system has been implemented. If the organization is found to be in compliance, a certificate is issued bearing the relevant standard.

Benefits

Among internal benefits of implementing the ISO 9002 standard are the following:

- Contributes to improvement through structure and discipline
- Improves efficiency through better documentation and communication
- Reduces rework
- Increases customer satisfaction and therefore reduces customer complaints
- Improves motivation and employee involvement through all levels of the process
- Improves the training process
- Improves positive management control

The eighth cycle of the ISO Survey of ISO 9000, conducted in 1998, revealed that the standards are growing in popularity in the Caribbean and the rest of the world. The Central and South Americas accounted for nearly 2% of the certificates issued worldwide. Fortyseven of these certificates were issued in Caribbean countries. Trinidad and Tobago accounted for approximately one third of these certified organizations. Jamaica came second with six organizations. Antigua and St Lucia received their first certificates in 1998. As has been experienced in the rest of the world, ISO certifications were more common in the manufacturing sectors compared to service sectors.

Up to October 1998 there were no hospitality service organizations achieving this certification in the Caribbean. Considering the importance of the tourism and hospitality industry to the Caribbean, as well as the large stock of hotel rooms in the Caribbean, this is disappointing. At the turn of the century the accommodation stock in the region had risen to around 250,000 rooms and is predicted to approach 400,000 rooms by the year 2020.

Training to Gain ISO 9002

The key to the success of the training process lies in the commitment of management to developing the process. Factors such as organization size, structure, requirements and culture have proven to be very important at the design stage. By involving the end users in the design, planning and implementation of training, it was easy to build the team spirit, a requirement for successful implementation of an ISO 9002 Quality Management System.

Suggested Foundation Training

For organizations that have not yet made a commitment to implementing a quality management system the following training programmes are suggested. This will usually take a total of eight or nine days.

- ISO 9000 Quality Briefing. Examines the fundamental issues and the achievable and measurable benefits of the standard. (1 day)
- Executive Briefing. Provides a clear understanding of the economic benefits and critical success factors for implementing the standards to busy executives who will influence the decision to implement ISO 9000 within their organization. (half a day)
- ISO 9000 Appreciation and Interpretation. Lays the foundation for those individuals directly involved in implementing and maintaining the system. This course is also suitable to provide general quality awareness to all employees of a smaller organization. Maximum benefit will be gained when the employees are encouraged to participate in the setting up of the system. By extending "ownership" of the quality management system to as many people as possible, one can ensure that the system will work well on a day-to-day basis throughout the organization. (1 day)
- ISO 9000 Implementation. Provides sound, practical guidance on how to set about the task of designing and setting up a quality management system and see it through to a successful conclusion. (2 days)
- Documentation/Procedure Writing for ISO 9000. Provides practical guidance in the design, development and implementation of a workable documentation system. Participants will be able to write user-friendly documents, which are effective and suitable for the intended purpose. (1 day)
- Internal Quality Auditing. Provides practical instruction to all employees involved in this process. An additional day may be added for newly trained auditors to put theory into practice by conducting a live audit of the quality system. (2 days)
- Preparing for the Certification Audit. Ensures that the team has clearly understood the prerequisites for a successful assessment and provides guidance on the final preparation and fine-tuning of the quality system. The most common pitfalls – and how to avoid them – will be clearly identified, so that employees will be fully briefed and ready for assessment. (1 day)

The Training Process

ISO 9002:1994 (E) Clause 4.1.2.2 Resources states: "The supplier shall identify resource requirements and provide adequate resources, including the assignment of trained personnel for management, performance of work and verification activities including internal quality audits".

Clause 4.18 Training states: "The supplier shall establish and maintain documented procedures for identifying training needs and provide for the training of all personnel performing activities affecting quality. Personnel performing specific assigned tasks shall be qualified on the basis of appropriate education, training and/or experience, as required. Appropriate records of training shall be maintained".

All organizations implementing the Quality Management System standard (ISO 9002) must have an effective training process in place to satisfy these requirements. Quality and related training and education provide or enhance the knowledge and skills employees need to do their jobs effectively and efficiently. Job enrichment skills are gained and job rotation can occur, thereby enhancing employees' career opportunities.

A planned, systematic training process is instrumental in helping an organization achieve its quality objectives and improve its capabilities. Training can be seen as a four-step process.

These four steps are represented in the training cycle, where the output of one stage provides the input for the following stage. Each stage must be monitored with the aim of closing the gap between required and existing competence.

Training goals must be established, and later evaluated to determine the extent to which these goals were met. This evaluation process can lead to the identification of new goals, which should be addressed in the design of future training activities.

Definition of Training Needs

The first step in the training process towards ISO 9002 certification involves the conducting of a needs analysis of the organization. There are some useful signs, or symptoms, that may indicate the need for training.

These include:

- Dissatisfied customers
- High labour turnover, low morale
- Failure to attain targets on revenue, gross profit and net profit
- High accident, breakage, or wastage rates
- Conflict between departments, such as restaurant and kitchen, housekeeping and reception
- Absence of the skills required for procedure writing or quality auditing
- Absence of formal management review of the quality system.

The organization's strategic goals, quality objectives, training policy, quality management requirements, resource requirements and process design must also be considered when initiating training to ensure that the organization's needs are satisfied.

The following activities should also be carried out:

- Define and document the competence needed for each task that affects product or service quality (e.g. management verification activities such as internal quality audits). This is done through job analysis.
- Assess the competence of personnel to perform the task.
- Develop plans to close existing competence gaps.

The training policy stands as a symbol of management's commitment to this important activity. It provides guidance for the planning of training as well as a comprehensive guide on all elements of the training cycle. The training policy of Le Meridien Jamaica Pegasus is summarized below as an example.

- *Policy:* It is the policy of Le Meridien Jamaica Pegasus to provide training for new and existing employees, in order to continually improve the workforce skill, product performance and services.
- *Scope:* This covers all employees involved in delivering service to the hotel's clients.
- *Purpose:* To ensure that employees are equipped with the appropriate skills to perform their jobs.
- *Responsibility:* It shall be the responsibility of each departmental manager to ensure that employees have adequate training and experience for the jobs to which they are assigned. The training and quality assurance manager shall be responsible for administering and coordinating the hotel's training plan and activities.
- *Procedure:* Each employee who performs a service related to the customer, product or administration shall receive training in that area.

Competence requirements once set must be reviewed periodically to ensure that they remain relevant to the operation. A variety of internal and external factors may be used to derive competence requirements:

- Organizational and technological change that impacts the company's product
- Data recorded at training programmes
- The organization's performance appraisal system
- Internal and external certification needed for the performance of specific tasks
- Requests from employees identifying opportunities for personal development
- Legislation, regulations, standards and directives

Planning for Training

The training plan should be developed and documented at this stage. Included in the training plan are the objectives and expected outcomes of the training. All constraints should be determined and listed. Typical constraints encountered in the hospitality industry include labour union requirements, human resource policy, financial considerations, timing and scheduling requirements (especially in a shift system), the availability, motivation and ability of the individuals to be trained. Factors such as the availability of in-house trainers to perform the training or the selection of reputable outside experts must be determined at this stage. The training plan specification is important in establishing a clear understanding of the organization's needs, the training requirements and the training objectives.

Typical items to be considered in an organization's training plan are:

- The organization's objectives and requirements
- Specification for training needs
- Training objectives
- Selected trainees
- Training method and content outline
- Duration, dates and milestones
- Schedule of resources such as training materials and staff
- Financial requirements
- Criteria and methods for the evaluation of training outcomes, such as trainee's on the job performance and satisfaction level of customers

Implementation of Training

It is important that the organization provides the necessary training resources to ensure success of the training process. In addition, the organization must support the trainer and the trainee while monitoring the quality of the training delivered. There will be resource and time constraints during the implementation of an ISO 9002 Quality System. These contraints have to be quantified and allowed for by reassigning work, working extra time, or scheduling extra employees. Quality system training should address the following:

- Why a formal quality system is being introduced
- Why total participation in the quality system is necessary
- The quality policy of the company
- The documents making up the quality system – quality assurance manuals, procedures, work instructions – and their accessibility to workers.
- Use of forms and other records built into the quality system
- The role of internal auditors
- Corrective and preventive action
- Management review

Evaluation of Training

Evaluation aims to determine the effectiveness of the training process. The organizational and training objectives that were set must be examined to confirm that they have been met. The documents to be examined during the training evaluation are the training specification, training plan and records of the delivery of training.

Training results often cannot be fully analysed and validated until the trainee can be observed and tested on the job. A specified time period (after completion of training) should be agreed within which the evaluations will take place, in order to verify the level of competence achieved.

The evaluation process should include the collection of data and the preparation of an evaluation report analysing the data collected and making recommendations for improvement as required. All training must be documented in training records.

In quality management, reward systems recognize individuals as well as team contributions. A variety of tangible objects may be used to reward superior performance, including days off with pay, badges and medals. Awards functions may be held where recipients are lauded for their achievements. In the hospitality industry benchmarking tours of outstanding properties may be arranged.

The review of the training process should identify any further opportunities for improving the effectiveness of any stage of the training process. A commitment to continuous improvement lies at the heart of a quality management system, modelled from the ISO 9000 Standard.

Quality in Hotels

Ad hoc training and quality control have been common in hotels for centuries. Systematic training, as explained in the previous section, is a prerequisite to implementing a quality assurance management system. Ad hoc training is merely unplanned training and ad hoc quality control is mostly a post-process checking action. These are not adequate to ensure quality standards to achieve ISO 9002 certification. A few hotels have, in the past, implemented steps to introduce "quality circles", essentially a Japanese concept with proven results in Japanese or similar cultures.

Dube et al. (2000) carried out an extensive review of the quality of lodging operations in the United States and noted that functional areas such as human resources, operations, corporate management and marketing receive more attention from management of hotels. They also noted that in the deluxe segment of hotels, the majority of best practices involved operations and human resources. Enz and Siguan (2000) examined thirteen champions in the lodging industry and analysed their best practices. The service-quality "champions" employed a variety of approaches, frequently in combination. Some of the "champions", for example, worked on weaving key tenets into the fabric of the organization in an effort to disseminate service excellence standards and ingrain employees with them. Others focused on empowering employees to provide whatever service the employee deemed necessary to create guest satisfaction. Ritz-Carlton Hotels, for example, empowers all employees to spend up to US$2,000 to solve a guest problem, if needed. Although such initiatives are noted from hotels in different parts of the world to ensure quality service to guests, the popularity of ISO 9002 in the global hospitality industry has not been a phenomenal success. Up to late 1998, only 865 ISO 9002 certificates were issued to hotels and restaurants worldwide (ISO, 1998).

Hotel Operations

Maintaining standardization and required quality in the hospitality industry is very complex. A usual hotel has two main operations: rooms division (bell desk, guest services, reception, business centre, telephone switchboard, rooms, suites, laundry, public areas, etc.) and food and beverage operations (kitchen, restaurant, bars, night clubs, banquet and conference facilities, room service, minibars, kitchen stewarding, etc.). The other departments (marketing, finance, human resources, engineering, security, computer systems, etc.) provide essential support services to rooms division and food and beverage operations. It is generally accepted that food and beverage operation is the most complex operation in a hotel. This is because it includes departments and sections where the quality of products and services is more visible, more difficult to maintain and can easily affect a hotel's image.

Apart from the quality of food and beverage products, longer operating hours, better quality linen, cutlery, crockery, glassware, design, wider choice of food and beverage items, better quality print of menu cards and beverage lists, more tasteful décor, better operating equipment, better tailored uniforms and better calibre of staff (in general) can be noticed in restaurants situated in five-star hotels in comparison with hotels of lower grades. The food and beverage service in five-star hotels has become more complex and challenging owing to the important fact that this class of clientele certainly pay much more money and in return expect a different and better service/product.

A survey carried out a few years ago revealed that waiting staff thought that expert serving techniques were the most important features of their work. The customers surveyed, on the other hand, indicated that what they valued most in a waiter was a smiling, agreeable, welcoming blend of social qualities. This does not mean that techniques are not important, since many guests appreciate a high level of practical skills and expect a fully professional service. However, the waiting staff who merchandise a "meal experience" must cultivate friendliness, good manners and the relevant social skills.

The quality of food and beverage service is a combination of predictions and characteristics on which an individual assesses whether the service will give satisfaction each time it is used, based on the guest's own set of values. A quality standard in food and beverage operations is a combination of characteristics accepted by the consensus of market segments as being appropriate to provide satisfaction for their particular purposes. Therefore, it is important to base policy decisions with regard to quality standards of food and beverage service in a hotel or restaurant on identified and anticipated specific customer needs through research. Hospitality organizations seeking to ensure the continuous quality of their service processes should embark on quality assurance management systems. Only through a systematic process can a hotel achieve a globally accepted quality standard.

Quality Assurance

Terms such as five-star, deluxe, high standards, good service, and fair value for money mean totally different things to different people and are therefore meaningless until they are defined in clear, precise terms. Yet expensive hotel investments and crucial marketing decisions are often described with these phrases. Potential quality can be affected by technical and behavioural factors within organizations and from the environment. It is important to determine the variables that can be manipulated to control these factors, such as design of service process, selection, training, supervision, communication, peer relationships and rewards to ensure sustained quality assurance in hotels.

A Case Study

Le Meridien Jamaica Pegasus Hotel

In October 1998, the largest and premier business hotel in Jamaica, Le Meridien Jamaica Pegasus, became the first hotel in the Caribbean to achieve certification to ISO 9002 Quality Management Standards. This property, referred to as the Pegasus, has 350 rooms and at that time had 400 employees. A unique characteristic of the hotel is the exceptionally long years of service by many senior employees. In 1998 the average length of service to the Pegasus was sixteen years by the first line managers and nine years by the second line managers.

The hotel has four restaurants, two bars, a large ballroom, nine meeting rooms, a gym, two tennis courts, two swimming pools, a jogging track and a shopping arcade. The Pegasus opened in 1972 and has been managed by the same hotel company, Forte Plc. in the United Kingdom, for the last twenty-nine years. During this period, owing to changes within the managing company, the Pegasus underwent two name changes; in 1992 as "Forte Grand" and in 1997 as "Le Meridien". The second rebranding was more crucial, as to reach Le Meridien standards the hotel had to do considerable upgrading and staff training.

In addition to the challenging rebranding process in 1997, the hotel was also faced with a financial problem triggered by an increase of four-star hotel rooms in Kingston by 42% and a decrease of tourist arrivals to Kingston. The occupancy level was around 60% for a few years, but owing to the increase in room capacity in the city, a price war had started. This resulted in the average room rate falling from US$100 to around US$83. Giving in to union demands and agreeing to above-inflation salary increases in the past had resulted in payroll cost (as a percentage of revenue) increasing from 22% in 1995 to 32% in 1997. The bottom line impact of these challenges was that the profitability of the hotel gradually dropped from 22% in 1993 to an alarming 8% in 1997.

As a survival strategy the management was compelled to restructure the operations. While there is nothing new to the downsizing phenomenon, the incidence of organization downsizing has increased considerably in recent years. Commentators warn of the potentially damaging effects of downsizing and redundancy programmes on the survivors and the culture of downsized organizations. The management decided to make 18% of the permanent staff redundant. A bold counterproposal of an unprecedented wage freeze was sent to the union who were demanding a 40% wage increase. The climate was not appropriate for introducing a quality management system that required high labour moral, motivation and commitment. However, the rebranding to Le Meridien and upgrading of the hotel had been committed with the owners. An official launching of "Le Meridien" (by the prime minister of Jamaica) for the end of 1997 had been confirmed.

In this context, the management decided to go ahead with the following during the 1997/1998 financial year:

- Redundancy of fifty-one employees
- Not changing the wage freeze stand in union negotiations
- Frequent frank dialogue with the employees with regards to the financial problems faced by the company and working together in "quality circles" to solve operational problems
- Internal marketing and public relations to convince the employees that quality assurance is the key to solving the financial problems
- Implementing the planned product upgrade
- Completion of the rebranding process by the end of 1997
- Introducing the ISO 9002 Quality Management system as a foundation for the future
- Reviewing the possibility of obtaining four-diamond grading by the American Automobile Association (AAA) and the Green Globe Award within three years

Vision for the Future

The management decided to pay special attention to training and development of a quality culture at the Pegasus. The vision was that this culture would be the backbone of the future quality standards achievements. It was considered important for this backbone to be strengthened with strategic inputs and quality inputs of the desired standards. At the same time this backbone (quality culture) should be strong enough to hold the present (organizational culture) and the future (vision) together.

Quality Policy

The labour dispute at that time arose as a result of the union's refusal to accept a proposal for a moratorium by the management. In spite of the labour dispute, the management won the support of the employees for the quality vision and 300 employees signed a quality policy, which has been displayed in the lobby of the Pegasus for the last four years. The policy, which was developed with input from the 300 employees, states:

Le Meridien Jamaica Pegasus is committed to being the best up market business hotel in the Caribbean; by consistently delivering Le Meridien quality product and service standards, satisfying guest expectations, whilst building employee morale and achieving profit objectives.

The agreed slogan is, "The Best Is Getting Better".

Quality Action

The following ten "commandments" related to the quality policy were developed with input from the 300 employees:

1. Make decisions based on findings from internal quality audits, guest surveys, employee surveys and Le Meridien quality audits.
2. Communicate the company policies and business objectives to all employees.
3. Employ skilled, committed and service oriented people with warm and friendly attitudes.
4. Train, develop, empower, reward and facilitate employees to achieve quality objectives.
5. Analyse productivity of the departments and take timely action to improve efficiency and profitability.
6. Satisfy shareholders by increasing the stock value.
7. Implement good public relations with all segments of the community.
8. Hold regular employee meetings to encourage innovative and creative thinking that will challenge conventional thoughts and practices.
9. Ensure that international standards with a European flavour, blended with the local culture, are implemented.
10. Implement ISO 9002 standards, receive and retain certification over the years.

The framed quality policy and quality actions are displayed in each department, section and office of the Pegasus.

Communication

Communication is the key to success in any process of change. For twelve months, quality and ISO 9002 became items on the agenda of many regular meetings, such as:

- Morning briefing (20 minutes – standing) – five times a week with all departmental managers
- Le Meridien/quality meeting (60 minutes) – once a week with departmental managers

- Purchasing/project meeting (40 minutes) – once a week with five executives
- All managers meeting (60 minutes) – once a month
- Managers and union delegates meeting (60 minutes) – once a month

The Le Meridien/quality meeting was a new meeting created to coordinate rebranding and implementing ISO 9002 during the 1997/1998 financial year.

Quality Analysis

Qualitative analysis of all corrective action forms (for every guest complaint) has to be done once a month as part of the ISO 9002 system. Corrective action forms are discussed at the morning briefings and with the use of a log, follow-up action is monitored by the general manager. The commitment from the general manager is essential for the system to work effectively and productively. Guest questionnaires, too, are analysed and distributed to all managers and departments once a month.

Foundation for the Future

The key hotel activities and external factors that had an impact on the hotel's performance from April 1997 to March 1998 are summarized below.

People

- A Le Meridien trainer from Paris trained thirty employees as on-the-job trainers and a series of training programmes for other employees was conducted by the trainers and management using Le Meridien manuals as guidelines.
- Twenty-three employees were trained as quality auditors to audit the quality of the operations of other departments.
- Good relationships were maintained with the union and employees in spite of prolonged wage negotiations and resulting industrial actions.
- Seven managers underwent brief training/exposure at Le Meridien New Orleans in the United States.
- Employees of the year were sent to Paris and London to join other employees of the year from seventy-three Le Meridien hotels on an award tour of exposure.
- The executive chef won an award "For Excellence in Food Preparation, Delivery and Presentation" during 1997, from the Jamaica Observer newspaper.

Product

- Le Meridien image, service and product standards were introduced and the hotel was rebranded as Le Meridien Jamaica Pegasus on October 9, 1997 with the prime minister of Jamaica as the guest of honour.

- Various projects were undertaken to implement the essential upgrading. These included complete refurbishment of two bedroom floors, installation of a new chiller, installation of a new fire alarm system, painting the building exterior, upgrading of tennis courts, upgrading of gardens and public areas, etc.
- Food and beverage concepts were changed. The coffee shop was upgraded and a section was air-conditioned, the gourmet restaurant concept was fine-tuned to blend with the historic significance of Port Royal and the wine club was transformed into a pizza cellar. All menus were changed.
- The ISO 9002 Quality Management system was introduced. The hotel developed a quality policy with input from most of its employees.
- The hotel continued to be the focal point of social activities in Kingston, often being chosen as the location for major banquets. The hotel continued organizing food festivals and other major events, including 101 holiday events during the last 38 days in 1997.
- The hotel won the Jamaica Observer newspaper's first ever "Table talk" food award for the "Food Event of the Year".
- The Le Meridien mystery guest programme, with a 1,000 point checklist, was introduced by internally arranged monthly mystery guests.

Promotions

- Room reservations, banquet bookings, sales, public relations and advertising were combined and a new marketing department was created with the objective of being more aggressive in marketing.
- The start of the twenty-fifth year of operations of the hotel was celebrated with the governor general of Jamaica as the guest of honour.
- Management sales calls to local clients were accelerated.
- The hotel continued to be the focal point during the Jamaica Carnival. A "wet-feete" was held at the hotel as part of the carnival celebrations.
- A major wedding expo was held.
- Le Meridien promoted the hotel in its regional and worldwide publications, sales and advertising campaigns.
- The hotel continued to be in the limelight through planned public relations and publicity.
- Familiarization tours were arranged for Le Meridien vice president–sales, sales director, and reservation agents, to Washington, D.C., New York and London.
- Frequent participation in Le Meridien sales conferences and planned sales trips to North America, South America and Europe.
- Participation in Le Meridien sales promotion activities.

Profit

- Towards the end of the financial year, British Airways reduced the allotment of thirty-four rooms per day to six rooms per day as most crew members were provided accommodation in Montego Bay instead of Kingston.
- The number of rooms in Kingston was increased by 32% and the four-star category rooms were increased by 42% within a year. At the same period, the arrivals to Kingston were reduced by 2%. With the supply of rooms in Kingston greatly exceeding the demand, the hotel experienced revenue problems. The hotel undertook major restructuring and re-engineering, affecting fifty-one job positions (18% of the total permanent workforce), which were made redundant. The hotel spent J$11 million as redundancy payments, but was able to recover this within eight months from the savings on labour cost.
- For seven months, the hotel held its position of a wage freeze against the union demand for a 40% wage increase for year one and a 35% increase for year two, for line employees. After two "sit ins" and a strike, the matter was referred to the Industrial Disputes Tribunal and a 7.5% wage increase for year one and a 7.5% increase for year two were awarded. This is a "landmark" award in the Jamaican hotel industry as salary increases in hotels had been in the range of 30% to 60% for many years prior to this award. As a result of this award, a single-digit wage increase has become the norm in the Jamaican hotel industry today.

7

Business Tourism and Foreign Exchange

AN OVERVIEW

Authorised dealers may remit foreign exchange upto a reasonable limit, at the request of a traveller towards his hotel accommodation, tour arrangements, etc., in the countries proposed to be visited by him, provided it is out of the foreign exchange purchased by the traveller from an authorised person (including exchange drawn for private travel abroad) in accordance with the Rules, Regulations and Directions in force.

Authorised dealers may effect remittances at the request of agents in India who have tie up arrangements with hotels/agents, etc., abroad for providing hotel accommodations or making other tour arrangements for travellers from India provided the authorised dealer is satisfied that the remittance is being made out of the foreign exchange purchased by the concerned traveller from an authorised person (including exchange drawn for private travel abroad) in accordance with the Rules, Regulations and Directions in force.

Authorised dealer may open foreign currency accounts in the name of agents in India who have tie up arrangements with hotels/agents, etc., abroad for providing hotel accommodations or making other tour arrangements for travellers from India provided:

- The credits to the account are by way of depositing
- Collections made in foreign exchange from travellers, and
- Refunds received from outside India on account of cancellation of bookings/tour arrangements, etc., and
- the debits in foreign exchange are for making payments towards hotel accommodation, tour arrangements, etc., outside India, in accordance with (ii) above.

An Act to consolidate and amend the law relating to foreign exchange with the objective of facilitating external trade and payments and for promoting the orderly development and maintenance of foreign exchange market in India.

SHORT TITLE, EXTENT, APPLICATION AND COMMENCEMENT

- This Act may be called the Foreign Exchange Management Act, 1999.
- It extends to the whole of India.
- It shall also apply to all branches, offices and agencies outside India owned or controlled by a person resident in India and also to any contravention thereunder committed outside India by any person to whom this Act applies.
- It shall come into force on such date as the Central Government may, by notification in the Official Gazette, appoint: Provided that different dates may be appointed for different provisions of this Act and any reference in any such provision to the commencement of this Act shall be construed as a reference to the coming into force of that provision.

  In this Act, unless the context otherwise requires:
  - "Adjudicating Authority" means an officer authorised under sub-section (1) of section 16;
  - "Appellate Tribunal" means the Appellate Tribunal for Foreign Exchange established under section 18;
  - "Authorised person" means an authorised dealer, money changer, off-shore banking unit or any other person for the time being authorised under sub-section (1) of section 10 to deal in foreign exchange or foreign securities;
  - "Bench" means a Bench of the Appellate Tribunal;
  - "capital account transaction" means a transaction which alters the assets or liabilities, including contingent liabilities, outside India of persons resident in India or assets or liabilities in India of persons resident outside India, and includes transactions referred to in sub-section (3) of section 6;
  - "Chairperson" means the Chairperson of the Appellate Tribunal;
  - "Chartered accountant" shall have the meaning assigned to it in clause (b) of sub-section (1) of section 2 of the Chartered Accountants Act, 1949 (38 of 1949);
  - "Currency" includes all currency notes, postal notes, postal orders, money orders, cheques, drafts, travellers cheques, letters of credit, bills of exchange and promissory notes, credit cards or such other similar instruments, as may be notified by the Reserve Bank;
  - "Currency notes" means and includes cash in the form of coins and bank notes;
  - "Current account transaction" means a transaction other than a capital account transaction and without prejudice to the generality of the foregoing such transaction includes:

i. Payments due in connection with foreign trade, other current business, services, and short-term banking and credit facilities in the ordinary course of business,
ii. Payments due as interest on loans and as net income from investments,
iii. Remittances for living expenses of parents, spouse and children residing abroad, and
iv. Expenses in connection with foreign travel, education and medical care of parents, spouse and children;

- "Director of Enforcement" means the Director of Enforcement appointed under sub-section (1) of section 36;
- "Export", with its grammatical variations and cognate expressions, means—
  i. The taking out of India to a place outside India any goods,
  ii. Provision of services from India to any person outside India;
- "Foreign currency" means any currency other than Indian currency;
- "Foreign exchange" means foreign currency and includes—
  i. Deposits, credits and balances payable in any foreign currency,
  ii. Drafts, travellers cheques, letters of credit or bills of exchange, expressed or drawn in Indian currency but payable in any foreign currency,
  iii. Drafts, travellers cheques, letters of credit or bills of exchange drawn by banks, institutions or persons outside India, but payable in Indian currency;
- "Foreign security" means any security, in the form of shares, stocks, bonds, debentures or any other instrument denominated or expressed in foreign currency and includes securities expressed in foreign currency, but where redemption or any form of return such as interest or dividends is payable in Indian currency;
- "Import", with its grammatical variations and cognate expressions, means bringing into India any goods or services;
- "Indian currency" means currency which is expressed or drawn in Indian rupees but does not include special bank notes and special one rupee notes issued under section 28A of the Reserve Bank of India Act, 1934 (2 of 1934);
- "Legal practitioner" shall have the meaning assigned to it in clause,
  i. Sub-section (1) of section 2 of the Advocates Act, 1961 (25 of 1961);
- "Member" means a Member of the Appellate Tribunal and includes the Chairperson thereof;

- "Notify" means to notify in the Official Gazette and the expression "notification" shall be construed accordingly;
- *"Person" includes*:
  i. An individual,
  ii. A Hindu undivided family,
  iii. A company,
  iv. A firm,
  v. An association of persons or a body of individuals, whether incorporated or not,
  vi. Every artificial juridical person, not falling within any of the preceding sub-clauses, and
  vii. Any agency, office or branch owned or controlled by such person;

• *"Person resident in India" means*:
- A person residing in India for more than one hundred and eighty-two days during the course of the preceding financial year but does not include—
  i. A person who has gone out of India or who stays outside India, in either case—
    a. For or on taking up employment outside India, or
    b. For carrying on outside India a business or vocation outside India, or
    c. For any other purpose, in such circumstances as would indicate his intention to stay outside India for an uncertain period;
  ii. A person who has come to or stays in India, in either case, otherwise than—
    a. For or on taking up employment in India, or
    b. For carrying on in India a business or vocation in India, or
    c. For any other purpose, in such circumstances as would indicate his intention to stay in India for an uncertain period;
  iii. Any person or body corporate registered or incorporated in India,
  iv. An office, branch or agency in India owned or controlled by a person resident outside India,
  v. An office, branch or agency outside India owned or controlled by a person resident in India;
- "Person resident outside India" means a person who is not resident in India;
- "Prescribed" means prescribed by rules made under this Act;
- "Repatriate to India" means bringing into India the realised foreign exchange and—

i. The selling of such foreign exchange to an authorised person in India in exchange for rupees, or

ii. The holding of realised amount in an account with an authorised person in India to the extent notified by the Reserve Bank, and includes use of the realised amount for discharge of a debt or liability denominated in foreign exchange and the expression "repatriation" shall be construed accordingly;

– "Reserve Bank" means the Reserve Bank of India constituted under sub-section (1) of section 3 of the Reserve Bank of India Act, 1934 (2 of 1934);

i. "Security" means shares, stocks, bonds and debentures, Government securities as defined in the Public Debt Act, 1944 (18 of 1944), savings certificates to which the Government Savings Certificates Act, 1959 (46 of 1959) applies, deposit receipts in respect of deposits of securities and units of the Unit Trust of India established under sub-section (1) of section 3 of the Unit Trust of India Act, 1963 (52 of 1963) or of any mutual fund and includes certificates of title to securities, but does not include bills of exchange or promissory notes other than Government promissory notes or any other instruments which may be notified by the Reserve Bank as security for the purposes of this Act; (zb) "service" means service of any description which is made available to potential users and includes the provision of facilities in connection with banking, financing, insurance, medical assistance, legal assistance, chit fund, real estate, transport, processing, supply of electrical or other energy, boarding or lodging or both, entertainment, amusement or the purveying of news or other information, but does not include the rendering of any service free of charge or under a contract of personal service; (zc) "Special Director (Appeals)" means an officer appointed under section 18; (zd) "specify" means to specify by regulations made under this Act and the expression "specified" shall be construed accordingly; (ze) "transfer" includes sale, purchase, exchange, mortgage, pledge, gift, loan or any other form of transfer of right, title, possession or lien.

REGULATION AND MANAGEMENT OF FOREIGN EXCHANGE

Save as otherwise provided in this Act, rules or regulations made thereunder, or with the general or special permission of the Reserve Bank, no person shall:

- Deal in or transfer any foreign exchange or foreign security to any person not being an authorised person;
- Make any payment to or for the credit of any person resident outside India in any manner;
- Receive otherwise through an authorised person, any payment by order or on behalf of any person resident outside India in any manner;

  Explanation: For the purpose of this clause, where any person in, or resident in, India receives any payment by order or on behalf of any person resident outside India through any other person (including an authorised person) without a corresponding inward remittance from any place outside India, then, such person shall be deemed to have received such payment otherwise than through an authorised person;
- Enter into any financial transaction in India as consideration for or in association with acquisition or creation or transfer of a right to acquire, any asset outside India by any person.

  Explanation: For the purpose of this clause, "financial transaction" means making any payment to, or for the credit of any person, or receiving any payment for, by order or on behalf of any person, or drawing, issuing or negotiating any bill of exchange or promissory note, or transferring any security or acknowledging any debt.

HOLDING OF FOREIGN EXCHANGE

Save as otherwise provided in this Act, no person resident in India shall acquire, hold, own, possess or transfer any foreign exchange, foreign security or any immovable property situated outside India.

CURRENT ACCOUNT TRANSACTIONS

Any person may sell or draw foreign exchange to or from an authorised person if such sale or drawal is a current account transaction: Provided that the Central Government may, in public interest and in consultation with the Reserve Bank, impose such reasonable restrictions for current account transactions as may be prescribed.

CAPITAL ACCOUNT TRANSACTIONS

- Subject to the provisions of sub-section
- Any person may sell or draw foreign exchange to or from an authorised person for a capital account transaction.
- *The Reserve Bank may, in consultation with the Central Government, specify*:
  - Any class or classes of capital account transactions which are permissible;
  - The limit up to which foreign exchange shall be admissible for such transactions:

Provided that the Reserve Bank shall not impose any restriction on the drawal of foreign exchange for payments due on account of amortization of loans or for depreciation of direct investments in the ordinary course of business.

- Without prejudice to the generality of the provisions of sub-section (2), the Reserve Bank may, by regulations, prohibit, restrict or regulate the following:
  - Transfer or issue of any foreign security by a person resident in India;
  - Transfer or issue of any security by a person resident outside India;
  - Transfer or issue of any security or foreign security by any branch, office or agency in India of a person resident outside India;
  - Any borrowing or lending in foreign exchange in whatever form or by whatever name called;
  - Any borrowing or lending in rupees in whatever form or by whatever name called between a person resident in India and a person resident outside India;
  - Deposits between persons resident in India and persons resident outside India;
  - Export, import or holding of currency or currency notes;
  - Transfer of immovable property outside India, other than a lease not exceeding five years, by a person resident in India;
  - Acquisition or transfer of immovable property in India, other than a lease not exceeding five years, by a person resident outside India;
  - Giving of a guarantee or surety in respect of any debt, obligation or other liability incurred:
    i. By a person resident in India and owed to a person resident outside India; or
    ii. By a person resident outside India.
- A person resident in India may hold, own, transfer or invest in foreign currency, foreign security or any immovable property situated outside India if such currency, security or property was acquired, held or owned by such person when he was resident outside India or inherited from a person who was resident outside India.
- A person resident outside India may hold, own, transfer or invest in Indian currency, security or any immovable property situated in India if such currency, security or property was acquired, held or owned by such person when he was resident in India or inherited from a person who was resident in India.
- Without prejudice to the provisions of this section, the Reserve Bank may, by regulation, prohibit, restrict, or regulate

establishment in India of a branch, office or other place of business by a person resident outside India, for carrying on any activity relating to such branch, office or other place of business.

EXPORT OF GOODS AND SERVICES

- *Every exporter of goods shall:*
  - Furnish to the Reserve Bank or to such other authority a declaration in such form and in such manner as may be specified, containing true and correct material particulars, including the amount representing the full export value or, if the full export value of the goods is not ascertainable at the time of export, the value which the exporter, having regard to the prevailing market conditions, expects to receive on the sale of the goods in a market outside India;
  - Furnish to the Reserve Bank such other information as may be required by the Reserve Bank for the purpose of ensuring the realisation of the export proceeds by such exporter.
- The Reserve Bank may, for the purpose of ensuring that the full export value of the goods or such reduced value of the goods as the Reserve Bank determines, having regard to the prevailing market conditions, is received without any delay, direct any exporter to comply with such requirements as it deems fit.
- Every exporter of services shall furnish to the Reserve Bank or to such other authorities a declaration in such form and in such manner as may be specified, containing the true and correct material particulars in relation to payment for such services.

REALISATION AND REPATRIATION OF FOREIGN EXCHANGE

Save as otherwise provided in this Act, where any amount of foreign exchange is due or has accrued to any person resident in India, such person shall take all reasonable steps to realise and repatriate to India such foreign exchange within such period and in such manner as may be specified by the Reserve Bank.

EXEMPTION FROM REALISATION AND REPATRIATION IN CERTAIN CASES

The provisions of sections 4 and 8 shall not apply to the following, namely:

- Possession of foreign currency or foreign coins by any person up to such limit as the Reserve Bank may specify;
- Foreign currency account held or operated by such person or class of persons and the limit up to which the Reserve Bank may specify;
- Foreign exchange acquired or received before the 8th day of July, 1947 or any income arising or accruing thereon which is held

outside India by any person in pursuance of a general or special permission granted by the Reserve Bank;

- Foreign exchange held by a person resident in India up to such limit as the Reserve Bank may specify, if such foreign exchange was acquired by way of gift or inheritance from a person referred to in clause *(c)*, including any income arising therefrom;
- Foreign exchange acquired from employment, business, trade, vocation, services, honourarium, gifts, inheritance or any other legitimate means up to such limit as the Reserve Bank may specify; and
- Such other receipts in foreign exchange as the Reserve Bank may specify.

Authorised Person

- The Reserve Bank may, on an application made to it in this behalf, authorise any person to be known as authorised person to deal in foreign exchange or in foreign securities, as an authorised dealer, money changer or off-shore banking unit or in any other manner as it deems fit.
- An authorisation under this section shall be in writing and shall be subject to the conditions laid down therein.
- An authorisation granted under sub-section (1) may be revoked by the Reserve Bank at any time if the Reserve Bank is satisfied that:
  - It is in public interest so to do; or
  - The authorised person has failed to comply with the condition subject to which the authorisation was granted or has contravened any of the provisions of the Act or any rule, regulation, notification, direction or order made thereunder: Provided that no such authorisation shall be revoked on any ground referred to in clause (b) unless the authorised person has been given a reasonable opportunity of making a representation in the matter.
- An authorised person shall, in all his dealings in foreign exchange or foreign security, comply with such general or special directions or orders as the Reserve Bank may, from time to time, think fit to give, and, except with the previous permission of the Reserve Bank, an authorised person shall not engage in any transaction involving any foreign exchange or foreign security which is not in conformity with the terms of his authorisation under this section.
- An authorised person shall, before undertaking any transaction in foreign exchange on behalf of any person, require that person to make such declaration and to give such information as will reasonably satisfy him that the transaction will not involve, and is

not designed for the purpose of any contravention or evasion of the provisions of this Act or of any rule, regulation, notification, direction or order made thereunder, and where the said person refuses to comply with any such requirement or makes only unsatisfactory compliance therewith, the authorised person shall refuse in writing to undertake the transaction and shall, if he has reason to believe that any such contravention or evasion as aforesaid is contemplated by the person, report the matter to the Reserve Bank.

- Any person, other than an authorised person, who has acquired or purchased foreign exchange for any purpose mentioned in the declaration made by him to authorised person under sub-section (5) does not use it for such purpose or does not surrender it to authorised person within the specified period or uses the foreign exchange so acquired or purchased for any other purpose for which purchase or acquisition of foreign exchange is not permissible under the provisions of the Act or the rules or regulations or direction or order made thereunder shall be deemed to have committed contravention of the provisions of the Act for the purpose of this section.

RESERVE BANK'S POWERS TO ISSUE DIRECTIONS TO AUTHORISED PERSON

- The Reserve Bank may, for the purpose of securing compliance with the provisions of this Act and of any rules, regulations, notifications or directions made thereunder, give to the authorised persons any direction in regard to making of payment or the doing or desist from doing any act relating to foreign exchange or foreign security.
- The Reserve Bank may, for the purpose of ensuring the compliance with the provisions of this Act or of any rule, regulation, notification, direction or order made thereunder, direct any authorised person to furnish such information, in such manner, as it deems fit.
- Where any authorised person contravenes any direction given by the Reserve Bank under this Act or fails to file any return as directed by the Reserve Bank, the Reserve Bank may, after giving reasonable opportunity of being heard, impose on the authorised person a penalty which may extend to ten thousand rupees and in the case of continuing contravention with an additional penalty which may extend to two thousand rupees for every day during which such contravention continues.

POWER OF RESERVE BANK TO INSPECT AUTHORISED PERSON

- The Reserve Bank may, at any time, cause an inspection to be made, by any officer of the Reserve Bank specially authorised in writing by the Reserve Bank in this behalf, of the business of any authorised person as may appear to it to be necessary or expedient for the purpose of:

- Verifying the correctness of any statement, information or particulars furnished to the Reserve Bank;
- Obtaining any information or particulars which such authorised person has failed to furnish on being called upon to do so;
- Securing compliance with the provisions of this Act or of any rules, regulations, directions or orders made thereunder.

- It shall be the duty of every authorised person, and where such person is a company or a firm, every director, partner or other officer of such company or firm, as the case may be, to produce to any officer making an inspection under sub-section (1), such books, accounts and other documents in his custody or power and to furnish any statement or information relating to the affairs of such person, company or firm as the said officer may require within such time and in such manner as the said officer may direct.

CONTRAVENTION AND PENALTIES

- If any person contravenes any provision of this Act, or contravenes any rule, regulation, notification, direction or order issued in exercise of the powers under this Act, or contravenes any condition subject to which an authorisation is issued by the Reserve Bank, he shall, upon adjudication, be liable to a penalty up to thrice the sum involved in such contravention where such amount is quantifiable, or up to two lakh rupees where the amount is not quantifiable, and where such contravention is a continuing one, further penalty which may extend to five thousand rupees for every day after the first day during which the contravention continues.
- Any Adjudicating Authority adjudging any contravention under sub-section (1), may, if he thinks fit in addition to any penalty which he may impose for such contravention direct that any currency, security or any other money or property in respect of which the contravention has taken place shall be confiscated to the Central Government and further direct that the foreign exchange holdings, if any of the persons committing the contraventions or any part thereof, shall be brought back into India or shall be retained outside India in accordance with the directions made in this behalf.

  Explanation: For the purposes of this sub-section, "property" in respect of which contravention has taken place, shall include:

  - Deposits in a bank, where the said property is converted into such deposits;

- Indian currency, where the said property is converted into that currency; and
- Any other property which has resulted out of the conversion of that property.

Enforcement of the orders of Adjudicating Authority.

- Subject to the provisions of sub-section (2) of section 19, if any person fails to make full payment of the penalty imposed on him under section 13 within a period of ninety days from the date on which the notice for payment of such penalty is served on him, he shall be liable to civil imprisonment under this section.
- No order for the arrest and detention in civil prison of a defaulter shall be made unless the Adjudicating Authority has issued and served a notice upon the defaulter calling upon him to appear before him on the date specified in the notice and to show cause why he should not be committed to the civil prison, and unless the Adjudicating Authority, for reasons in writing, is satisfied:
  - That the defaulter, with the object or effect of obstructing the recovery of penalty, has after the issue of notice by the Adjudicating Authority, dishonestly transferred concealed, or removed any part of his property, or
  - That the defaulter has, or has had since the issuing of notice by the Adjudicating Authority, the means to pay the arrears or some substantial part thereof and refuses or neglects or has refused or neglected to pay the same.
- Notwithstanding anything contained in sub-section (1), a warrant for the arrest of the defaulter may be issued by the Adjudicating Authority if the Adjudicating Authority is satisfied, by affidavit or otherwise, that with the object or effect of delaying the execution of the certificate the defaulter is likely to abscond or leave the local limits of the jurisdiction of the Adjudicating Authority.
- Where appearance is not made pursuant to a notice issued and served under sub-section (1), the Adjudicating Authority may issue a warrant for the arrest of the defaulter.
- A warrant of arrest issued by the Adjudicating Authority under sub-section (3) or sub-section
- May also be executed by any other Adjudicating Authority within whose jurisdiction the defaulter may for the time being be found.
- Every person arrested in pursuance of a warrant of arrest under this section shall be brought before the Adjudicating Authority issuing the warrant as soon as practicable and in any event within twenty-four hours of his arrest (exclusive of the time required for the journey): Provided that, if the defaulter pays the amount entered in the warrant of arrest as due and the costs of the arrest to the officer arresting him, such officer shall at once release him.

Explanation: For the purposes of this sub-section, where the defaulter is a Hindu undivided family, the *karta* thereof shall be deemed to be the defaulter.

- When a defaulter appears before the Adjudicating Authority pursuant to a notice to show cause or is brought before the Adjudicating Authority under this section, the Adjudicating Authority shall give the defaulter an opportunity showing cause why he should not be committed to the civil prison.
- Pending the conclusion of the inquiry, the Adjudicating Authority may, in his discretion, order the defaulter to be detained in the custody of such officer as the Adjudicating Authority may think fit or release him on his furnishing the security to the satisfaction of the Adjudicating Authority for his appearance as and when required.
- Upon the conclusion of the inquiry, the Adjudicating Authority may make an order for the detention of the defaulter in the civil prison and shall in that event cause him to be arrested if he is not already under arrest: Provided that in order to give a defaulter an opportunity of satisfying the arrears, the Adjudicating Authority may, before making the order of detention, leave the defaulter in the custody of the officer arresting him or of any other officer for a specified period not exceeding fifteen days, or release him on his furnishing security to the satisfaction of the Adjudicating Authority for his appearance at the expiration of the specified period if the arrears are not satisfied.
- When the Adjudicating Authority does not make an order of detention under sub-section (9), he shall, if the defaulter is under arrest, direct his release.
- Every person detained in the civil prison in execution of the certificate may be so detained,—
  - Where the certificate is for a demand of an amount exceeding rupees one crore, up to three years, and
  - *In any other case, up to six months*: Provided that he shall be released from such detention on the amount mentioned in the warrant for his detention being paid to the officer-in-charge of the civil prison.
- A defaulter released from detention under this section shall not, merely by reason of his release, be discharged from his liability for the arrears, but he shall not be liable to be arrested under the certificate in execution of which he was detained in the civil prison.
- A detention order may be executed at any place in India in the manner provided for the execution of warrant of arrest under the Code of Criminal Procedure, 1973 (2 of 1974).

POWER TO COMPOUND CONTRAVENTION

- Any contravention under section 13 may, on an application made by theperson committing such contravention, be compounded within one hundred and eighty days from the date of receipt of application by the Director of Enforcement or such other officers of the Directorate of Enforcement and Officers of the Reserve Bank as may be authorised in this behalf by the Central Government in such manner as may be prescribed.
- Where a contravention has been compounded under sub-section (1), no proceeding or further proceeding, as the case may be, shall be initiated or continued, as the case may be, against the person committing such contravention under that section, in respect of the contravention so compounded.

APPOINTMENT OF ADJUDICATING AUTHORITY

- For the purpose of adjudication under section 13, the Central Government may, by an order published in the Official Gazette, appoint as many officers of the Central Government as it may think fit, as the Adjudicating Authorities for holding an inquiry in the manner prescribed after giving the person alleged to have committed contravention under section 13, against whom a complaint has been made under sub-section
- Hereinafter in this section referred to as the said person a reasonable opportunity of being heard for the purpose of imposing any penalty: Provided that where the Adjudicating Authority is of opinion that the said person is likely to abscond or is likely to evade in any manner, the payment of penalty, if levied, it may direct the said person to furnish a bond or guarantee for such amount and subject to such conditions as it may deem fit.
- The Central Government shall, while appointing the Adjudicating Authorities under sub-section (1), also specify in the order published in the Official Gazette, their respective jurisdictions.
- No Adjudicating Authority shall hold an enquiry under sub-section (1) except upon a complaint in writing made by any officer authorised by a general or special order by the Central Government.
- The said person may appear either in person or take the assistance of a legal practitioner or a chartered accountant of his choice for presenting his case before the Adjudicating Authority.
- Every Adjudicating Authority shall have the same powers of a civil court which are conferred on the Appellate Tribunal under sub-section (2) of section 28 and:
  - All proceedings before it shall be deemed to be judicial proceedings within the meaning of sections 193 and 228 of the Indian Penal Code (45 of 1860);

- Shall be deemed to be a civil court for the purposes of sections 345 and 346 of the Code of Criminal Procedure, 1973 (2 of 1974).

- Every Adjudicating Authority shall deal with the complaint under sub-section (2) as expeditiously as possible and endeavour shall be made to dispose of the complaint finally within one year from the date of receipt of the complaint: Provided that where the complaint cannot be disposed off within the said period, the Adjudicating Authority shall record periodically the reasons in writing for not disposing off the complaint within the said period.

APPEAL TO SPECIAL DIRECTOR (APPEALS)

- The Central Government shall, by notification, appoint one or more Special Directors (Appeals) to hear appeals against the orders of the Adjudicating Authorities under this section and shall also specify in the said notification the matter and places in relation to which the Special Director (Appeals) may exercise jurisdiction.
- Any person aggrieved by an order made by the Adjudicating Authority, being an Assistant Director of Enforcement or a Deputy Director of Enforcement, may prefer an appeal to the Special Director (Appeals).
- Every appeal under sub-section (1) shall be filed within forty-five days from the date on which the copy of the order made by the Adjudicating Authority is received by the aggrieved person and it shall be in such form, verified in such manner and be accompanied by such fee as may be prescribed: Provided that the Special Director (Appeals) may entertain an appeal after the expiry of the said period of forty-five days, if he is satisfied that there was sufficient cause for not filing it within that period.
- On receipt of an appeal under sub-section (1), the Special Director (Appeals) may after giving the parties to the appeal an opportunity of being heard, pass such order thereon as he thinks fit confirming, modifying or setting aside the order appealed against.
- The Special Director (Appeals) shall send a copy of every order made by him to the parties to appeal and to the concerned Adjudicating Authority.
- The Special Director (Appeals) shall have the same powers of a civil court which are conferred on the Appellate Tribunal under sub-section (2) of section 28 and:
  - All proceedings before him shall be deemed to be judicial proceedings within the meaning of sections 193 and 228 of the Indian Penal Code (45 of 1860);
  - Shall be deemed to be a civil court for the purposes of sections 345 and 346 of the Code of Criminal Procedure, 1973 (2 of 1974).

ESTABLISHMENT OF APPELLATE TRIBUNAL

The Central Government shall, by notification, establish an Appellate Tribunal to be known as the Appellate Tribunal for Foreign Exchange to hear appeals against the orders of the Adjudicating Authorities and the Special Director (Appeals) under this Act.

APPEAL TO APPELLATE TRIBUNAL

- Save as provided in sub-section (2), the Central Government or any person aggrieved by an order made by an Adjudicating Authority, other than those referred to sub-section (1) of section 17, or the Special Director (Appeals), may prefer an appeal to the Appellate Tribunal: Provided that any person appealing against the order of the Adjudicating Authority or the Special Director (Appeals) levying any penalty, shall while filing the appeal, deposit the amount of such penalty with such authority as may be notified by the Central Government: Provided further that where in any particular case, the Appellate Tribunal is of the opinion that the deposit of such penalty would cause undue hardship to such person, the Appellate Tribunal may dispense with such deposit subject to such conditions as it may deem fit to impose so as to safeguard the realisation of penalty.
- Every appeal under sub-section (1) shall be filed within a period of forty-five days from the date on which a copy of the order made by the Adjudicating Authority or the Special Director (Appeals) is received by the aggrieved person or by the Central Government and it shall be in such form, verified in such manner and be accompanied by such fee as may be prescribed: Provided that the Appellate Tribunal may entertain an appeal after the expiry of the said period of forty-five days if it is satisfied that there was sufficient cause for not filing it within that period.
- On receipt of an appeal under sub-section (1), the Appellate Tribunal may, after giving the parties to the appeal an opportunity of being heard, pass such orders thereon as it thinks fit, confirming, modifying or setting aside the order appealed against.
- The Appellate Tribunal shall send a copy of every order made by it to the parties to the appeal and to the concerned Adjudicating Authority or the Special Director (Appeals), as the case may be.
- The appeal filed before the Appellate Tribunal under sub-section (1) shall be dealt with by it as expeditiously as possible and endeavour shall be made by it to dispose of the appeal finally within one hundred and eighty days from the date of receipt of the appeal: Provided that where any appeal could not be disposed of within the said period of one hundred and eighty days, the Appellate

Tribunal shall record its reasons in writing for not disposing of the appeal within the said period.

- The Appellate Tribunal may, for the purpose of examining the legality, propriety or correctness of any order made by the Adjudicating Authority under section 16 in relation to any proceeding, on its own motion or otherwise, call for the records of such proceedings and make such order in the case as it thinks fit.

COMPOSITION OF APPELLATE TRIBUNAL

- The Appellate Tribunal shall consist of a Chairperson and such number of Members as the Central Government may deem fit.
- *Subject to the provisions of this Act,*:
  - The jurisdiction of the Appellate Tribunal may be exercised by Benches thereof;
  - A Bench may be constituted by the Chairperson with one or more Members as the Chairperson may deem fit;
  - The Benches of the Appellate Tribunal shall ordinarily sit at New Delhi and at such other places as the Central Government may, in consultation with the Chairperson, notify;
  - The Central Government shall notify the areas in relation to which each Bench of the Appellate Tribunal may exercise jurisdiction.
- Notwithstanding anything contained in sub-section (2), the Chairperson may transfer a Member from one Bench to another Bench.
- If at any stage of the hearing of any case or matter it appears to the Chairperson or a Member that the case or matter is of such a nature that it ought to be heard by a Bench consisting of two Members, the case or matter may be transferred by the Chairperson or, as the case may be, referred to him for transfer, to such Bench as the Chairperson may deem fit.

QUALIFICATIONS FOR APPOINTMENT

- *A person shall not be qualified for appointment as the Chairperson or a Member unless he*:
  - In the case of Chairperson, is or has been, or is qualified to be, a Judge of a High Court; and
  - In the case of a Member, is or has been, or is qualified to be, a District Judge.
- *A person shall not be qualified for appointment as a Special Director (Appeals) unless he*:
  - Has been a member of the Indian Legal Service and has held a post in Grade I of that Service; or
  - Has been a member of the Indian Revenue Service and has held a post equivalent to a Joint Secretary to the Government of India.

TERM OF OFFICE

The Chairperson and every other Member shall hold office as such for a term of five years from the date on which he enters upon his office: Provided that no Chairperson or other Member shall hold office as such after he has attained,:

- In the case of the Chairperson, the age of sixty-five years;
- In the case of any other Member, the age of sixty-two years.

TERMS AND CONDITIONS OF SERVICE

The salary and allowances payable to and the other terms and conditions of service of the Chairperson, other Members and the Special Director (Appeals) shall be such as may be prescribed: Provided that neither the salary and allowances nor the other terms and conditions of service of the Chairperson or a Member shall be varied to his disadvantage after appointment.

VACANCIES

If, for reason other than temporary absence, any vacancy occurs in the office of the Chairperson or a Member, the Central Government shall appoint another person in accordance with the provisions of this Act to fill the vacancy and the proceedings may be continued before the Appellate Tribunal from the stage at which the vacancy is filled.

RESIGNATION AND REMOVAL

- The Chairperson or a Member may, by notice in writing under his hand addressed to the Central Government, resign his office: Provided that the Chairperson or a Member shall, unless he is permitted by the Central Government to relinquish his office sooner, continue to hold office until the expiry of three months from the date of receipt of such notice or until a person duly appointed as his successor enters upon his office or until the expiry of term of office, whichever is the earliest.
- The Chairperson or a Member shall not be removed from his office except by an order by the Central Government on the ground of proved misbehaviour or incapacity after an inquiry made by such person as the President may appoint for this purpose in which the Chairperson or a Member concerned has been informed of the charges against him and given a reasonable opportunity of being heard in respect of such charges.

MEMBER TO ACT AS CHAIRPERSON IN CERTAIN CIRCUMSTANCES

- In the event of the occurrence of any vacancy in the office of the Chairperson by reason of his death, resignation or otherwise, the senior-most Member shall act as the Chairperson until the date on which a new Chairperson, appointed in accordance with the provisions of this Act to fill such vacancy, enters upon his office.

- When the Chairperson is unable to discharge his functions owing to absence, illness or any other cause, the senior most Member shall discharge the functions of the Chairperson until the date on which the Chairperson resumes his duties.

STAFF OF APPELLATE TRIBUNAL AND SPECIAL DIRECTOR (APPEALS)

- The Central Government shall provide the Appellate Tribunal and the Special Director (Appeals) with such officers and employees as it may deem fit.
- The officers and employees of the Appellate Tribunal and office of the Special Director (Appeals) shall discharge their functions under the general superintendence of the Chairperson and the Special Director (Appeals), as the case may be.
- The salaries and allowances and other conditions of service of the officers and employees of the Appellate Tribunal and office of the Special Director (Appeals) shall be such as may be prescribed.

PROCEDURE AND POWERS OF APPELLATE TRIBUNAL AND SPECIAL DIRECTOR

- The Appellate Tribunal and the Special Director (Appeals) shall not be bound by the procedure laid down by the Code of Civil Procedure, 1908 (5 of 1908) but shall be guided by the principles of natural justice and, subject to the other provisions of this Act, the Appellate Tribunal and the Special Director (Appeals) shall have powers to regulate its own procedure.
- The Appellate Tribunal and the Special Director (Appeals) shall have, for the purposes of discharging its functions under this Act, the same powers as are vested in a civil court under the Code of Civil Procedure, 1908 (5 of 1908); while trying a suit, in respect of the following matters, namely:
  - Summoning and enforcing the attendance of any person and examining him on oath;
  - Requiring the discovery and production of documents;
  - Receiving evidence on affidavits;
  - Subject to the provisions of sections 123 and 124 of the Indian Evidence Act, 1872 (1 of 1872) requisitioning any public record or document or copy of such record or document from any office;
  - Issuing commissions for the examination of witnesses or documents;

  - Reviewing its decisions;
  - Dismissing a representation of default or deciding it *ex parte;*
  - Setting aside any order of dismissal of any representation for default or any order passed by it *ex parte;* and
  - Any other matter which may be prescribed by the Central Government.
- An order made by the Appellate Tribunal or the Special Director (Appeals) under this Act shall be executable by the Appellate Tribunal or the Special Director (Appeals) as a decree of civil court and, for this purpose, the Appellate Tribunal and the Special Director (Appeals) shall have all the powers of a civil court.
- Notwithstanding anything contained in sub-section (3), the Appellate Tribunal or the Special Director (Appeals) may transmit any order made by it to a civil court having local jurisdiction and such civil court shall execute the order as if it were a decree made by that court.
- All proceedings before the Appellate Tribunal and the Special Director (Appeals) shall be deemed to be judicial proceedings within the meaning of sections 193 and 228 of the Indian Penal Code (45 of 1860) and the Appellate Tribunal shall be deemed to be a civil court for the purposes of sections 345 and 346 of the Code of Criminal Procedure, 1973 (2 of 1974)

DISTRIBUTION OF BUSINESS AMONGST BENCHES

Where Benches are constituted, the Chairperson may, from time to time, by notification, make provisions as to the distribution of the business of the Appellate Tribunal amongst the Benches and also provide for the matters which may be dealt with by each Bench.

POWER OF CHAIRPERSON TO TRANSFER CASES

On the application of any of the parties and after notice to the parties, and after hearing such of them as he may desire to be heard, or on his own motion without such notice, the Chairperson may transfer any case pending before one Bench, for disposal, to any other Bench.

DECISION TO BE BY MAJORITY

If the Members of a Bench consisting of two Members differ in opinion on any point, they shall state the point or points on which they differ, and make a reference to the Chairperson who shall either hear the point or points himself or refer the case for hearing on such point or points by one or more of the other Members of the Appellate Tribunal and such point or points shall be decided according to the opinion of the majority of the Members of the Appellate Tribunal who have heard the case, including those who first heard it.

Right of appellant to take assistance of legal practitioner or chartered accountant and of Government, to appoint presenting officers.

- A person preferring an appeal to the Appellate Tribunal or the Special Director (Appeals) under this Act may either appear in person or take the assistance of a legal practitioner or a chartered accountant of his choice to present his case before the Appellate Tribunal or the Special Director (Appeals), as the case may be.
- The Central Government may authorise one or more legal practitioners or chartered accountants or any of its officers to act as presenting officers and every person so authorised may present the case with respect to any appeal before the Appellate Tribunal or the Special Director (Appeals), as the case may be.

MEMBERS, ETC. TO BE PUBLIC SERVANTS

The Chairperson, Members and other officers and employees of the Appellate Tribunal, the Special Director (Appeals) and the Adjudicating Authority shall be deemed to be public servants within the meaning of section 21 of the Indian Penal Code (45 of 1860).

CIVIL COURT NOT TO HAVE JURISDICTION

No civil court shall have jurisdiction to entertain any suit or proceeding in respect of any matter which an Adjudicating Authority or the Appellate Tribunal or the Special Director (Appeals) is empowered by or under this Act to determine and no injunction shall be granted by any court or other authority in respect of any action taken or to be taken in pursuance of any power conferred by or under this Act.

APPEAL TO HIGH COURT

Any person aggrieved by any decision or order of the Appellate Tribunal may file an appeal to the High Court within sixty days from the date of communication of the decision or order of the Appellate Tribunal on any question of law arising out of such order: Provided that the High Court may, if it is satisfied that the appellant was prevented by sufficient cause from filing the appeal within the said period, allow it to be filed within a further period not exceeding sixty days.

- *Explanation*: In this section "High Court" means,
  - The High Court within the jurisdiction of which the aggrieved party ordinarily resides or carries on business or personally works for gain; and
  - Where the Central Government is the aggrieved party, the High Court within the jurisdiction of which the respondent, or in a case where there are more than one respondent, any of the respondents, ordinarily resides or carries on business or personally works for gain.

DIRECTORATE OF ENFORCEMENT

- The Central Government shall establish a Directorate of Enforcement with a Director and such other officers or class of officers as it thinks fit, who shall be called officers of Enforcement, for the purposes of this Act.
- Without prejudice to provisions of sub-section (1), the Central Government may authorise the Director of Enforcement or an Additional Director of Enforcement or a Special Director of Enforcement or a Deputy Director of Enforcement to appoint officers of Enforcement below the rank of an Assistant Director of Enforcement.
- Subject to such conditions and limitations as the Central Government may impose, an officer of Enforcement may exercise the powers and discharge the duties conferred or imposed on him under this Act.

POWER OF SEARCH, SEIZURE, ETC

- The Director of Enforcement and other officers of Enforcement, not below the rank of an Assistant Director, shall take up for investigation the contravention referred to in section 13.
- Without prejudice to the provisions of sub-section (1), the Central Government may also, by notification, authorise any officer or class of officers in the Central Government, State Government or the Reserve Bank, not below the rank of an Under Secretary to the Government of India to investigate any contravention referred to in section 13.
- The officers referred to in sub-section (1) shall exercise the like powers which are conferred on income-tax authorities under the Income-tax Act, 1961 (43 of 1961) and shall exercise such powers, subject to such limitations laid down under that Act.

EMPOWERING OTHER OFFICERS

- The Central Government may, by order and subject to such conditions and limitations as it thinks fit to impose, authorise any officer of customs or any central excise officer or any police officer or any other officer of the Central Government or a State Government to exercise such of the powers and discharge such of the duties of the Director of Enforcement or any other officer of Enforcement under this Act as may be stated in the order.
- The officers referred to in sub-section (1) shall exercise the like powers which are conferred on the income-tax authorities under the Income-tax Act, 1961 (43 of 1961), subject to such conditions and limitations as the Central Government may impose.

PRESUMPTION AS TO DOCUMENTS IN CERTAIN CASES

Where any document:

- Is produced or furnished by any person or has been seized from the custody or control of any person, in either case, under this Act or under any other law; or
- Has been received from any place outside India (duly authenticated by such authority or person and in such manner as may be prescribed) in the course of investigation of any contravention under this Act alleged to have been committed by any person, and such document is tendered in any proceeding under this Act in evidence against him, or against him and any other person who is proceeded against jointly with him, the court or the Adjudicating Authority, as the case may be, shall—
  - Presume, unless the contrary is proved, that the signature and every other part of such document which purports to be in the handwriting of any particular person or which the court may reasonably assume to have been signed by, or to be in the handwriting of, any particular person, is in that person's handwriting, and in the case of a document executed or attested, that it was executed or attested by the person by whom it purports to have been so executed or attested;
  - Admit the document in evidence notwithstanding that it is not duly stamped, if such document is otherwise admissible in evidence;
  - In a case falling under clause *(i)*, also presume, unless the contrary is proved, the truth of the contents of such document.

SUSPENSION OF OPERATION OF THIS ACT

- If the Central Government is satisfied that circumstances have arisen rendering it necessary that any permission granted or restriction imposed by this Act should cease to be granted or imposed, or if it considers necessary or expedient so to do in public interest, the Central Government may, by notification, suspend or relax to such extent either indefinitely or for such period as may be notified, the operation of all or any of the provisions of this Act.
- Where the operation of any provision of this Act has under sub-section (1) been suspended or relaxed indefinitely, such suspension or relaxation may, at any time while this Act remains in force, be removed by the Central Government by notification.
- Every notification issued under this section shall be laid, as soon as may be after it is issued, before each House of Parliament, while it is in session, for a total period of thirty days which may be

comprised in one session or in two or more successive sessions, and if, before the expiry of the session immediately following the session or the successive sessions aforesaid, both Houses agree in making any modification in the notification or both Houses agree that the notification should not be issued, the notification shall thereafter have effect only in such modified form or be of no effect, as the case may be; so, however, that any such modification or annulment shall be without prejudice to the validity of anything previously done under that notification.

POWER OF CENTRAL GOVERNMENT TO GIVE DIRECTIONS

For the purposes of this Act, the Central Government may, from time to time, give to the Reserve Bank such general or special directions as it thinks fit, and the Reserve Bank shall, in the discharge of its functions under this Act, comply with any such directions.

CONTRAVENTION BY COMPANIES

- Where a person committing a contravention of any of the provisions of this Act or of any rule, direction or order made thereunder is a company, every person who, at the time the contravention was committed, was in charge of, and was responsible to, the company for the conduct of the business of the company as well as the company, shall be deemed to be guilty of the contravention and shall be liable to be proceeded against and punished accordingly: Provided that nothing contained in this sub-section shall render any such person liable to punishment if he proves that the contravention took place without his knowledge or that he exercised due diligence to prevent such contravention.
- Notwithstanding anything contained in sub-section (1), where a contravention of any of the provisions of this Act or of any rule, direction or order made thereunder has been committed by a company and it is proved that the contravention has taken place with the consent or connivance of, or is attributable to any neglect on the part of, any director, manager, secretary or other officer of the company, such director, manager, secretary or other officer shall also be deemed to be guilty of the contravention and shall be liable to be proceeded against and punished accordingly.

  Explanation: For the purposes of this section,
  - "Company" means any body corporate and includes a firm or other association of individuals; and
  - "Director", in relation to a firm, means a partner in the firm.

Death or Insolvency in Certain Cases

Any right, obligation, liability, proceeding or appeal arising in relation to the provisions of section 13 shall not abate by reason of death or insolvency of the person liable under that section and upon such death or insolvency such rights and obligations shall devolve on the legal representative of such person or the official receiver or the official assignee, as the case may be: Provided that a legal representative of the deceased shall be liable only to the extent of the inheritance or estate of the deceased.

BAR OF LEGAL PROCEEDINGS

No suit, prosecution or other legal proceeding shall lie against the Central Government or the Reserve Bank or any officer of that Government or of the Reserve Bank or any other person exercising any power or discharging any functions or performing any duties under this Act, for anything in good faith done or intended to be done under this Act or any rule, regulation, notification, direction or order made thereunder.

REMOVAL OF DIFFICULTIES

- If any difficulty arises in giving effect to the provisions of this Act, the Central Government may, by order, do anything not inconsistent with the provisions of this Act for the purpose of removing the difficulty: Provided that no such order shall be made under this section after the expiry of two years from the commencement of this Act.
- Every order made under this section shall be laid, as soon as may be after it is made, before each House of Parliament.

POWER TO MAKE RULES

- The Central Government may, by notification, make rules to carry out the provisions of this Act.
- Without prejudice to the generality of the foregoing power, such rules may provide for,:
  - The imposition of reasonable restrictions on current account transactions under section 5;
  - The manner in which the contravention may be compounded under sub-section (1) of section 15;
  - The manner of holding an inquiry by the Adjudicating Authority under sub-section (1) of section 16;
  - The form of appeal and fee for filing such appeal under sections 17 and 19;
  - The salary and allowances payable to and the other terms and conditions of service of the Chairperson and other Members of the Appellate Tribunal and the Special Director (Appeals) under section 23;
  - The salaries and allowances and other conditions of service of the officers and employees of the Appellate Tribunal and the office of the Special Director (Appeals) under sub-section (3) of section 27;

  - The additional matters in respect of which the Appellate Tribunal and the Special Director (Appeals) may exercise the powers of civil court under clause *(i)* of sub-section (2) of section 28;
  - The authority or person and the manner in which any document may be authenticated under clause *(ii)* of section 39; and
  - Any other matter which is required to be, or may be, prescribed.

POWER TO MAKE REGULATIONS

- The Reserve Bank may, by notification, make regulations to carry out the provisions of this Act and the rules made thereunder.
- Without prejudice to the generality of the foregoing power, such regulations may provide for,:
  - The permissible classes of capital account transactions, the limits of admissibility of foreign exchange for such transactions, and the prohibition, restriction or regulation of certain capital account transactions under section 6;
  - The manner and the form in which the declaration is to be furnished under clause *(a)* of sub-section (1) of section 7;
  - The period within which and the manner of repatriation of foreign exchange under section 8;
  - The limit up to which any person may possess foreign currency or foreign coins under clause (a) of section 9;
  - The class of persons and the limit up to which foreign currency account may be held or operated under clause *(b)* of section 9;
  - The limit up to which foreign exchange acquired may be exempted under clause (d) of section 9;
  - The limit up to which foreign exchange acquired may be retained under clause (e) of section 9;
  - Any other matter which is required to be, or may be, specified.

RULES AND REGULATIONS TO BE LAID BEFORE PARLIAMENT

Every rule and regulation made under this Act shall be laid, as soon as may be after it is made, before each House of Parliament, while it is in session for a total period of thirty days which may be comprised in one session or in two or more successive sessions, and if, before the expiry of the session immediately following the session or the successive sessions aforesaid, both Houses agree in making any modification in the rule or regulation, or both Houses agree that the rule or regulation should not be made, the rule or regulation shall thereafter have effect only in such modified form or be of no effect, as the case may be; so, however, that any such modification or annulment shall be without prejudice to the validity of anything previously done under that rule or regulation.

REPEAL AND SAVING

- The Foreign Exchange Regulation Act, 1973 (46 of 1973) is hereby repealed and the Appellate Board constituted under sub-section (1) of section 52 of the said Act (hereinafter referred to as the repealed Act) shall stand dissolved.
- On the dissolution of the said Appellate Board, the person appointed as Chairman of the Appellate Board and every other person appointed as Member and holding office as such immediately before such date shall vacate their respective offices and no such Chairman or other person shall be entitled to claim any compensation for the premature termination of the term of his office or of any contract of service.
- Notwithstanding anything contained in any other law for the time being in force, no court shall take cognizance of an offence under the repealed Act and no adjudicating officer shall take notice of any contravention under section 51 of the repealed Act after the expiry of a period of two years from the date of the commencement of this Act.
- Subject to the provisions of sub-section (3) all offences committed under the repealed Act shall continue to be governed by the provisions of the repealed Act as if that Act had not been repealed.
- *Notwithstanding such repeal,:*
  - Anything done or any action taken or purported to have been done or taken including any rule, notification, inspection, order or notice made or issued or any appointment, confirmation or declaration made or any licence, permission, authorization or exemption granted or any document or instrument executed or any direction given under the Act hereby repealed shall, in so far as it is not inconsistent with the provisions of this Act, be deemed to have been done or taken under the corresponding provisions of this Act;
  - Any appeal preferred to the Appellate Board under sub-section (2) of section 52 of the repealed Act but not disposed of before the commencement of this Act shall stand transferred to and shall be disposed of by the Appellate Tribunal constituted under this Act;
  - Every appeal from any decision or order of the Appellate Board under sub-section (3) or sub-section (4) of section 52 of the repealed Act shall, if not filed before the commencement of this Act, be filed before the High Court within a period of sixty days of such commencement: Provided that the High Court may entertain such appeal after the expiry of the said period of sixty days if it is satisfied that the appellant was

prevented by sufficient cause from filing the appeal within the said period.

- Save as otherwise provided in sub-section (3), the mention of particular matters in sub-sections (2), (4) and (5) shall not be held to prejudice or affect the general application of section 6 of the General Clauses Act, 1897 (10 of 1897) with regard to the effect of repeal.

THE CONSERVATION OF FOREIGN EXCHANGE

- Short title, extent and commencement—(1) This Act may be called the Conservation of Foreign Exchange and Prevention of Smuggling Activities Act, 1974.
  - It extends to the whole of India.
  - It shall come into force on such date as the Central Government may, by notification in the Official Gazette, appoint.
- *Definitions-In this Act, unless the context otherwise requires,:*
  - "Appropriate Government" means, as respects a detention order made by the Central Government or by an officer of the Central Government or a person detained under such order, the Central Government, and as respects a detention order made by a State Government or by an officer of a State Government or a person detained under such order, the State Government;
  - "Detention order" means an order made under section 3;
  - "Foreigner" has the same meaning as in the Foreigners Act, 1946 (31 of 1946);
  - "Indian customs waters" has the same meaning as in clause (28) of the Customs Act, 1962 (52 of 1962);
  - "Smuggling" has the same meanings as in clause (39) of section 2 of the Customs Act, 1962, and all its grammatical variations and cognate expressions shall be construed accordingly;
  - "State Government", in relation to a Union territory, means the Administrator thereof;
  - Any reference in this Act to a law which is not in force in the State of Jammu and Kashmir shall, in relation to that State, be construed as a reference to the corresponding law, if any, in force in that State.
- *Power to make orders detaining certain persons*:
  - The Central Government or the State Government or any officer of the Central Government, not below the rank of a Joint Secretary to that Government, specially empowered for the purposes of this section by that Government, or any officer of the State Government, not below the rank of a Secretary to

that Government, specially empowered for the purposes of this section by that Government, may, if satisfied, with respect to any person (including a foreigner), that, with a view to preventing him from acting in any manner prejudicial to the conservation or augmentation of foreign exchange or with a view to preventing him from

i. Smuggling goods, or
ii. Abetting the smuggling of goods, or
iii. Engaging in transporting or concealing or keeping smuggled goods, or
iv. Dealing in smuggled goods otherwise than by engaging in transporting or concealing or keeping smuggled goods, or
v. Harbouring persons engaged in smuggling goods or in abetting the smuggling of goods, it is necessary so to do, make an order directing that such person be detained:

- Provided that no order of detention shall be made on any of the grounds specified in this sub-section on which an order of detention may be made under section 3 of the Prevention of Illicit Traffic in Narcotic Drugs and Psychotropic Substances Act, 1988 or under section 3 of the Jammu and Kashmir Prevention of Illicit Traffic in Narcotic Drugs and Psychotropic Substances ordinance, 1988..
- When any order of detention is made by a State Government or by an officer empowered by a State Government, the State Government shall, within ten days, forward to the Central Government a report in respect of the order.
- For the purposes of clause (5) of article 22 of the Constitution, the communication to a person detained in pursuance of a detention order of the grounds on which the order has been made shall be made as soon as may be after the detention, but ordinarily not later than five days, and in exceptional circumstances and for reasons to be recorded in writing, not later than fifteen days, from the date of detention.

- Execution of detention orders-A detention order may be executed at any place in India in the manner provided for the execution of warrants of arrest under the Code of Criminal Procedure, 1973 (2 of 1974).
- Power to regulate place and conditions of detention-Every person in respect of whom a detention order has been made shall be liable:
  - To be detained in such place and under such conditions including conditions as to maintenance, interviews or communication with others, discipline and punishment for breaches of discipline, as the appropriate Government may, by general or special order, specify; and

- To be removed from one place of detention to another place of detention, whether within the same State or in another State by order of the appropriate Government;
  Provided that no order shall be made by a State Government under clause (b) for the removal of a person from one State to another State except with the consent of the Government of that other State.
- *Grounds of detention severable*: Where a person has been detained in pursuance of an order of detention under sub-section (1) which has been made on two or more grounds, such order of detention shall be deemed to have been made separately on each of such grounds and accordingly:
  a. Such order shall not be deemed to be invalid or inoperative merely because one or some of the grounds is or are:
  i. Vague,
  ii. Non-existent,
  iii. Not relevant,
  iv. Not connected or not proximately connected with such person, or
  v. Invalid for any other reason whatsoever, and it is not, therefore, possible to hold that the Government or officer making such order would have been satisfied as provided in sub-section (1) of section 3 with reference to the remaining ground or grounds and made the order of detention;
- The Government or officer making the order of detention shall be deemed to have made the order of detention under the said sub-section (1) after being satisfied as provided in that sub-section with reference to the remaining ground or grounds.]

• Detention order not to be invalid or inoperative on certain grounds- No detention order shall be invalid or inoperative merely by reason:
  - That the person to be detained thereunder is outside the limited of the territorial jurisdiction of the Government or the officer making the order of detention, or
  - That the place of detention of such person is outside the said limits.

• Powers in relation to absconding persons (1) If the appropriate Government has reason to believe that a person in respect of whom a detention order has been made has absconded or is concealing himself so that the order cannot be executed, the Government may:
  - Make a report in writing of the fact to a Metropolitan Magistrate or a Magistrate of the first class having jurisdiction in the place where the said person ordinarily resides; and thereupon the provisions of sections 82, 83, 84 and 85 of the Code of Criminal Procedure, 1973 (2 of 1974), shall apply in respect of the said

person and his property as if the order directing that he be detained were a warrant issued by the Magistrate;

- By order notified in the Official Gazette direct the said person to appear before such officer, at such place and within such period as may be specified in the order; and if the said person fails to comply with such direction, he shall, unless he proves that it was not possible for him to comply therewith and that he had, within the period specified in the order, informed the officer mentioned in the order of the reason which rendered compliance therewith impossible and of his whereabouts, be punishable therewith impossible and of his whereabouts, be punishable with imprisonment for a term which may extend to one year or with fine or with both. (2)
  Nothwithstanding anything contained in the Code of Criminal Procedure, 1973 (2 of 1974), every offence under clause (b) of sub-section (1) shall be cognizable.

- Advisory Board-For the purposes of sub-clause (a) of clause (c) of clause (7) of article 22 of the Constitution,:
  - The Central Government and each State Government shall, wherever necessary, constitute one or more Advisory Boards each of which shall consist of a Chairman and two other persons possessing the qualifications specified in sub-clause (a) of clause (4) of article 22 of the Constitution;
  - Save as otherwise provided in section 9, the appropriate Government shall, within five weeks from the date of detention of a person under a detention order make a reference in respect thereof to the Advisory Board constituted under clause (a) to enable the Advisory Board to make the report under sub-clause (a) of clause (4) of article 22 of the Constitution;
  - The Advisory Board to which a reference is made under clause (b) shall after considering the reference and the materials placed before it and after calling for such further information as it may deed necessary from the appropriate Government or from any person called for the purpose through the appropriate Government, from the person concerned, and if, in any particular case, it considers it essential so to do or if the person concerned desires to be heard in person, after hearing him person, prepare its report specifying in a separate paragraph thereof its opinion as to whether or not there is sufficient cause for the detention of the person concerned and submit the same within eleven weeks from the date of detention of the person concerned;
  - When there is a difference of opinion among the members forming the Advisory Board the opinion of the majority of such members shall be deemed to be the opinion of the Board;

- A person against whom an order of detention has been made under this Act shall not be entitled to appear by any legal practitioner in any matter connected with the reference to the Advisory Board, and the proceedings of the Advisory Board and its report, excepting that part of the report in which the opinion of the Advisory Board is specified, shall be confidential;
- In every case where the Advisory Board has reported that there is in its opinion sufficient cause for the detention of a person, the appropriate Government may confirm the detention order and continue the detention of the person concerned for such period as it thinks fit and in every case where the Advisory Board has reported that there is in its opinion no sufficient cause for the detention of the person concerned, the appropriate Government shall revoke the detention order and cause the person to be released forthwith.

• Cases in which and circumstances under which persons may be detained for period longer than three months without obtaining the opinion of Advisory Board-(1) Notwithstanding anything contained in this Act, any person (including a foreigner) in respect of whom an order of detention is made under this Act at any time before the 31st July, 1996, may be detained without obtaining, in accordance with the provisions of sub-clause (a) of clause (4) of article 22 of the Constitution, the opinion of an Advisory Board for a period longer than three months but not exceeding six months from the date of his detention, where the order of detention has been made against such person with a view to preventing him from smuggling goods or abetting the smuggling of goods or engaging in transporting or concealing or keeping smuggled goods and the Central Government or any Officer of the Central Government, not below the rank of an Additional Secretary to that Government, specially empowered for the purpose of this section by that Government, is satisfied that such person—
  - Smuggles or is likely to smuggle goods into, out of or through any area highly vulnerable to smuggling; or
  - Abets or is likely to abet the smuggling of goods into, out of or through any area highly vulnerable to smuggling; or
  - Engages or is likely to engage in transporting or concealing or keeping smuggled goods in any area highly vulnerable to smuggling, and makes a declaration to that effect within five weeks of the detention of such person.

  Explanation 1: In this sub-section, "area highly vulnerable to smuggling" means,:

  i. The Indian customs waters, contiguous to the State of Goa, Gujarat, Karnataka, Kerala, Maharashtra, Tamil Nadu and the Union territories of Daman and Diu and Pondicherry;

ii. The Inland area fifty kilometres in width from the coast of India falling within the territories of the States of Goa, Gujarat, Karnataka, Kerala, Maharashtra, Tamil Nadu and the Union territories of Daman and Diu and Pondicherry;
iii. The inland area fifty kilometres in width from the India-Pakistan border in the State of Gujarat, Jammu and Kashmir, Punjab and Rajasthan;
iv. The customs air port of Delhi; and
v. Such further or other Indian customs waters, or inland area not exceeding one hundred kilometres in width from any other coast or border of India, or such other customs station, as the Central Government may, having regard to the vulnerability of such waters, area or customs station, as the case may be, to smuggling, by notification in the Official Gazette, specify in this behalf.

Explanation 2:

1. For the purposes of Explanation 1, "customs airport" and "customs station" shall have the same meaning as in clauses (10) and (13) of section 2 of the Customs Act, 1962 (52 of 1962), respectively.
2. In the case of any person detained under a detention order to which the provisions of sub-section (1) apply, section 8 shall have effect subject to the following modifications, namely:
    i. In clause (b), for the words "shall, within five weeks", the words "shall, within four months and two weeks" shall be substituted;
    ii. In clause (c),:
        1. For the words "the detention of the person concerned", the words "the continued detention of the person concerned" shall be substituted;
        2. For the words "eleven weeks", the words "five months and three weeks" shall be substituted;
    iii. In clause (f), for the words "for the detention", at both the places where they occur, the words "for the continued detention" shall be substituted.

- *Maximum period of detention*: The maximum period for which any person may be detained in pursuance of any detention order to which the provisions of section 9 do not apply and which has been confirmed under clause (f) of section 8 shall be a period of one year from the date of detention or the specified period, whichever period expires late and the maximum period for which any person may be detained in pursuance of any detention order to which the provisions of section 9 apply and which has been confirmed under clause (f) of section 8 read with sub-section (2) of section 9 shall be a period of two years from the date of detention or the specified period, whichever period expires later;

Provided that nothing contained in this section shall affect the power of the appropriate Government in neither case to revoke or modify the detention order at any earlier time. Explanation In this section and section 10A-"specified period" means the period during which the Proclamation of Emergency issued under clause (1) of article 352 of the Constitution on the 3rd day of December, 1971 and the Proclamation of Emergency issued under that clause on the 25th day of June, 1975, are both in operation.

– *Extension of period of detention*:

i. Notwithstanding anything contained in any other provision of this Act, the detention of every person detained under a detention order which has been confirmed under clause (f) of section 8 before the commencement of the Conservation of Foreign Exchange and Prevention of Smuggling Activities (Amendment) Act, 1976, and which is in force immediately before such commencement shall, unless his detention has been continued by the appropriate Government under the said clause for a period shorter than one year from the date of his detention, continue until the expiry of a period of one year from the date of his detention under such order or until the expiry of the specified period, whichever period expires later: Provided that nothing contained in this sub-section shall affect the power of the appropriate Government to revoke or modify such detention order at any earlier time.

ii. Notwithstanding anything contained in any other provision of this Act, the detention of every person detained under a detention order which has been confirmed under clause (f) of section 8 read with sub-section (2) of section 9 before the commencement of the Conservation of Foreign Exchange and Prevention of Smuggling Activities (Amendment) Act, 1976, and which is in force immediately before such commencement, shall, unless his detention has been continued by the appropriate Government under the said clause (f) read with the said sub-section (2) for a period shorter than two years from the date of his detention, continue until the expiry of a period of two years from the date of his detention under such order or until the expiry of the specified period, whichever period expires later: Provided that nothing contained in this sub-section shall affect the power of the appropriate Government to revoke or modify such detention order at any earlier time.

- *Revocation of detention orders*:
  - Without prejudice to provisions of section 21 of the General Clauses Act, 1897 (10 of 1897), a detention order may, at any time, be revoked or modified:
    i. Notwithstanding that the order has been made by an officer of a State Government, by that State Government or by the Central Government;
    ii. Notwithstanding that the order has been made by an officer of the Central Government or by a State Government, by the Central Government.
  - The revocation of a detention order shall not bar the making of another detention order under section (3) against the same person.
- *Temporary release of persons detained*:
  - The Central Government may, at any time, direct that any person detained in pursuance of a detention order made by that Government or an officer subordinate to that Government or by a State Government or by an officer subordinate to a State Government, may be released for any specified period either without conditions or upon such conditions specified in the directions as that person accepts, and may, at any time, cancel his release.
    i. A State Government may, at any time, direct that any person detained in pursuance of a detention order made by that Government or by an officer subordinate to that Government may be released for any specified period either without conditions or upon such conditions specified in the direction as that person accepts, and may, at any time, cancel his release.
  - In directing the release of any person under sub-section (1) or sub-section (1A) the Government directing the release may require him to enter into a bond with sureties for the due observance of the conditions specified in the direction.
  - Any person released under sub-section (1) or sub-section (1A) shall surrender himself at the time and place, and to the authority, specified in the order directing his release or cancelling his release, as the case may be.
  - If any person fails without sufficient cause to surrender himself in the manner specified in sub-section(3) he shall be punishable

with imprisonment for a term which may extend to two years, or with fine, or with both.

- If any person released under sub-section(1) or sub-section(1A) fails to fulfill any of the conditions imposed upon him under the said sub-section or in the bond entered into by him, the bond shall be declared to be forfeited and any person bound thereby shall be liable to pay the penalty thereof.
- Notwithstanding anything contained in any other law and save as otherwise provided in this section, no person against whom a detention order made under this Act is in force shall be released whether on bail or bail bond or otherwise.

• Special provisions for dealing with emergency-(1) Notwithstanding anything contained in this Act or any rules of natural justice, the provisions of this section shall have effect during the period of operation of the Proclamation of Emergency issued under clause

  - Article 352 of the Constitution on the 3rd day of December, 1971, or the Proclamation of Emergency issued under that clause on the 25th day of June, 1975, or a period of twenty four months from the 25th day of June, 1975, whichever period is the shortest.
  - When making an order of detention under this Act against any person after the commencement of the Conservation of Foreign and Prevention of Smuggling Activities (Amendment) Act, 1975, the Central Government or the State Government or, as the case may be, the officer making the order of detention shall consider whether the detention of such person under this Act is necessary for dealing effectively with the emergency in respect of which the Proclamations referred to in sub-section (1) have been issued (hereafter in this section referred to as the emergency) and if, on such consideration, the Central Government or the State Government or, as the case may be, the officer is satisfied that it is necessary to detain such person for effectively dealing with the emergency, that Government or officer may make a declaration to that effect and communicate a copy of the declaration to the person concerned: Provided that where such declaration is made by an officer, it shall be reviewed by the appropriate Government within fifteen days from the date of making of the declaration and such declaration shall cease to have effect unless it is confirmed by that Government, after such review, within the said period of fifteen days.
  - The question whether the detention of any person in respect of whom a declaration has been made under sub-section (2) continues to be necessary for effectively dealing with the emergency shall be reconsidered by the appropriate Government

within four months from the date of such declaration and thereafter at intervals not exceeding four months, and if, one such reconsideration, it appears to the appropriate Government that the detention of the person is no longer necessary for effectively dealing with the emergency, the Government may revoke the declaration.

- In making any consideration, review or reconsideration under sub-section (2) or (3) the appropriate Government or officer may, if such Government or officer considers it to be against the public interest to do otherwise, act on the basis of the information and materials in its or his possession without disclosing the facts or giving an opportunity of making a representation to the person concerned.
- It shall not be necessary to disclose to any person detained under a detention order to which the provisions of sub-section (2) apply, the grounds on which the order has been made during the period the declaration made in respect of such person under that sub-section is in force, and, accordingly, such period shall not be taken into account for the purpose of sub-section (3) of section 3
- In the case of every person detained under a detention order to which the provisions of sub-section (2) apply, being a person in respect of whom a declaration has been made thereunder, the period during which such declaration is in force shall not be taken into account for the purpose of computing:
    i. The periods specified in clauses (b) and (c) of section 8
    ii. The periods of "one year" and "five weeks" specified in sub-section (1), the period of "one year" specified in sub-section (2)(i), and the period of "six months" specified in sub-section (3), of section 9.

- Protection of action taken in good faith-No suit or other legal proceeding shall lie against the Central Government or a State Government, and no suit, prosecution or other legal proceedings shall lie against any person, for anything in good faith done or intended to be done in pursuance of this Act.
- *Repeal*: The Maintenance of Internal Security (Amendment) Ordinance, 1974 (11 of 1974), shall, on the commencement of this Act, stand repealed and accordingly the amendments made in the Maintenance of Internal Security Act, 1971 (26 of 1971), by the said Ordinance shall, on such commencement, cease to have effect.

CUSTOMS VALUATION

In exercise of the powers conferred by Section 156 of the Customs Act,

1962 (52 of 1962), read with Section 22 of the General Clauses Act, 1897 (10 of 1897), and in supersession of the Customs Valuation Rules, 1963 except as respect things done or omitted to be done before such super session, the Central Government hereby makes the following rules, namely:

- *Short title, commencement and application*:
  - These rules may be called the Customs Valuation (Determination of Price of Imported Goods) Rules, 1988.
  - They shall come into force on the 16th August, 1988.
  - They shall apply imported goods where a duty of customs is chargeable by reference to their value.
- *Definitions*: (1) In these rules, unless the context otherwise requires,-
  - "Computed value" means the value of imported goods determined in accordance with rule 7A of these rules; (aa) " deductive value" means the value determined in accordance with rule 7 of these rules;
  - "Goods of the same class or kind", means imported goods that are within a group of range of imported goods produced by a particular industry of industrial sector and includes identical goods of similar goods;
  - *"Identical goods" means imported goods*:
    i. Which are same in all respects, including physical characteristics, quality and reputation as the goods being valued except for minor differences in appearance that do not affect the value of the goods;
    ii. Produced in the country in which the goods being valued were produced; and
    iii. produced by the same person who produced the goods, or where no such goods are available, goods produced by a different person, but shall not include imported goods where engineering, development work, art work, design work, plan or sketch undertaken in India were completed directly or indirectly by the buyer on these imported goods free of charge or at a reduced cost for use in connection with the production and sale for export of these imported goods;
  - "Produced" includes grown, manufactured and mined;
  - "Similar goods" means imported goods –
    i. Which although not alike in all respects, have like characteristics and like component materials which enable them to perform the same functions and to be commercially intercha-ngeable with the goods being valued having regard to the quality, reputation and the existence of trade mark;

ii. Produced in the country in which the goods being valued were produced; and

iii. Produced by the same person who produced the goods being valued, or where no such goods are available, goods produced by a different person, but shall not include imported goods where engineering, development work, art work, design work, plan or sketch undertaken in India were completed directly or indirectly by the buyer on these imported goods free of charge or at a reduced cost for use in connection with production and sale for export of these imported goods;

- "Transaction value" means the value determined in accordance with Rule 4 of these rules. (2) For the purpose of these rules, persons shall be deemed to be " related " only if –
  i. They are officers or directors of one another's businesses;
  ii. They are legally recognized partners in business;
  iii. They are employer and exployee;
  iv. Any person directly or indirectly owns, controls or holds 5 per cent or more of the outstanding voting stock or shares of both of them;
  v. One of them directly or indirectly controls the other;
  vi. Both of them are directly or indirectly controlled by a third person;
  vii. Together they directly or indirectly control a third person; or
  viii. They are members of the same family.
- *Explanation* I: The term " person" also includes legal persons.
- *Explanation* II: Persons who are associated in the business of one another in that one is the sole agent or sole distributor or sole concessionaire, however described, of the other shall be deemed to be related for the purpose of these rules, if they fall within the criteria of this sub-rule.

- *Determination of the method of valuation—For the purpose of these rules*:
  i. The value of imported goods shall be the transaction value;
  ii. If the value cannot be determined under the provisions of clause (i) above, the value shall be determined by proceeding sequentially through Rules 5 to 8 of these rules.
     1. *Transaction value*: (1) The transaction value of imported goods shall be the price actually paid or payable for the goods when sold for export to India, adjusted in accordance with the provisions of Rule 9 of these rules.
     2. The transaction value of imported goods under sub-rule (1) above shall be accepted provided that:

a. There are no restrictions as to the disposition or use of the goods by the buyer other than restrictions which are imposed or required by law or by the public authorities in India; or

- Limit the geographical area in which the goods may be resold; or
- Do not substantially affect the value of the goods;
  - The sale or price is not subject to same condition or consideration for which a value cannot be determined in respect of the goods being valued;
  - No part of the proceeds of any subsequent resale, disposal or use of the goods by the buyer will accrue directly or indirectly to the seller unless an appropriate adjustment can be made in accordance with the provisions of Rule 9 of these rules; and
  - the buyer and seller are not related, or where the buyer and seller are related, that transaction value is acceptable for customs purposes under the provisions of sub-rule below.
    a. Where the buyer and seller are related, the transaction value shall be accepted provided that the examination of the circumstances of the sale of the imported goods indicate that the relationship did not influence the price.
    b. In a sale between related persons, the transaction value shall be accepted, whenever the importer demonstrates that the declared value of the goods being valued, closely approximates to one of the following values ascertained at or about the same time:
       i. The transaction value of identical goods, or of similar goods, in sales to unrelated buyers in India;
       ii. The deductive value for identical goods or similar goods;
       iii. The computed value for identical goods or similar goods.
       Provided that in applying the values used for comparison, due account shall be taken of demonstrated difference in commercial levels, quantity levels, adjustments in accordance with the provisions of Rule 9 of these rules and cost incurred by the seller in sales in which he and the buyer are not related;
    c. Substitute values shall not be established under the provisions of clause (b) of this sub-rule.
  - Transaction of value of identical goods.
    i. Subject to the provisions of Rule 3 of these rules, the value of imported goods shall be the transaction value of identical goods sold for export to India and imported at or about the same time as the goods being valued.

ii. In applying this rule, the transaction value of identical goods in a sale at the same commercial level and in substantially the same quantity as the goods being valued shall be used to determine the value of imported goods.

iii. Where no sale referred to in clause (b) of sub-rule (1) of this rule, is found, the transaction value of identical goods sold at a different commercial level or in different quantities or both, adjusted to take account of the difference attributable to commercial level or to the quantity or both, shall be used, provided that such adjustments shall be made on the basis of the demonstrated evidence which clearly establishes the reasonableness and accuracy of the adjustments, whether such adjustment leads to an increase or decrease in the value.

(2) Where the cost and charges referred to in sub-rule (2) of Rule 9 of these rules are included in the transaction value of identical goods, an adjustment shall be made, if there are significant differences in such costs and charges between the goods being valued and the identical goods in question arising from differences in distances and means of transport.

(3) In applying this rule, if more than one transaction value of identical goods is found; the lowest such value shall be used to determine the value of imported goods.

- *Transaction value of similar goods*:
  1. Subject to the provisions of Rule 3 of these rules, the value of imported goods shall be the transaction value of similar goods sold for export to India and imported at or about the same time as the goods being valued.
  2. The provisions of clauses (b) and (c) of sub-rule (1), sub-rule (2) and sub-rule(3),of Rule 5 of these rules shall, mutatis mutandis, also apply in respect of similar goods.

  Determination of value when transaction values is not available—If the value of imported goods cannot be determined under the provisions of rules 4, 5and 6, the value shall be determined under the provisions of rule 7 or, when the value cannot be determined under that rule, under rule 7A: Provided that at the request of the importer, and with the approval of the proper officer, the order of application of rules 7 and 7A shall be reversed.]
- Deductive value—
  - Subject to the provisions of Rule 3 of these rules, if the goods being valued or identical or similar imported goods are sold in India, in the condition as imported at or about the time at which the declaration for determination of value is presented,

the value of imported goods shall be based on the unit price at which the imported goods or identical or similar imported goods are sold in the greatest aggregate quantity to persons who are not related to the sellers in India, subject to the following deductions:—

i. Either the commission usually paid or agreed to be paid or the additions usually made for profits and general expenses in connection with sales in India of imported goods of the same class or kind;
ii. The usual costs of transport and insurance and associated costs incurred within India;
iii. The customs duties and other taxes payable in India by reason of importation or sale of the goods.

- If neither the imported goods nor identical nor similar imported goods are sold at or about the same time of importation of the goods being valued, the value of imported goods shall, subject otherwise to the provisions of sub-rule (1) of this rule, be based on the unit price at which the imported goods or identical or similar imported goods are sold in India, at the earliest date after importation but before the expiry of ninety days after such importation.
  (a) If neither the imported goods not identical nor similar imported goods are sold in India in the conditions as imported, then, the value shall be based on the unit price at which the imported goods, after further processing, are sold in the greatest aggregate quantity to persons who are not related to the seller in India
  (b) In such determination, due allowance shall be made for the value added by processing and the deductions, provided for in items (i) to (iii) of sub-rule (1) of this rule.
- *Computed value*: Subject to the provisions of rule 3, the value of imported goods shall be based on a computed value, which shall consist of the sum of:
  a. The cost of value of materials and fabrication or other processing employed in producing the imported goods;
  b. An amount for profit and general expenses equal to that usually reflected in sales of goods of the same class or kind as the goods being valued which are made by producers in the country of exportation for export to India;
  c. Rhe cost or value of all other expenses under sub-rule (2) of rule 9 of these rules.

• Residual method—(1) Subject to the provisions of Rule 3 of these rules, where the value of imported goods cannot be determined under the provisions of any of the preceding rules, the value shall be determined using reasonable means consistent with the principles and general provisions of these rules and sub-section (1) of Section 14 of the Customs Act, 1962 (52 of 1962) and on the basis of data available in India. (2) No value shall be determined under the provisions of (5) this rule on the basis of-

i. The selling price in India of the goods produced in India;
ii. A system which provides for the acceptance for customs purposes \ of the highest of the two alternative values;
iii. The price of the goods on the domestic market of country of exportation; [(iii a) the cost of production other than computed values which have been determined for identical or similar goods in accordance with the provisions of rule 7A.
iv. The price of the goods for the export to a country other than India;
v. Minimum customs values; or
vi. Arbitrary or fictitious values.

- *Cost and services:*
  1. In determining the transaction value, there shall be added to the price actually paid or payable for the imported goods,-
     - The following cost and services, to the extent they are incurred by the buyer but are not included in the price actually paid or payable for the imported goods, namely:

  i. Commissions and brokerage, except buying commissions;
  ii. The cost of containers which are treated as being one for customs purposes with the goods in question;
  iii. The cost of packing whether for labour or materials;
     - The value, apportioned as appropriate, of the following goods and services where supplied directly or indirectly by the buyer free of charge or at reduced cost for use in connection with the production and sale for export of imported goods, to the extent that such value has not been included in the price actually paid of payable, namely:

  i. Materials, components, parts and similar items incorporated in the imported goods;
  ii. Tools, dies, moulds and similar items used in the production of the imported goods;
  iii. Materials consumed in the production of the imported goods;
  iv. Engineering, development, art work, design work, and and plans and sketches undertaken elsewhere than in India and necessary for the production of the imported goods;
     - Royalties and license fees related to the imported goods that the buyer is required to pay, directly or indirectly, as a condition of the sale of the goods being valued, to the extent

that such royalties and fees are not included in the price actually paid or payable.

- The value of any part of the proceeds of any subsequent resale, disposal or use of the imported goods that accrues, directly or indirectly, to the seller;
- All other payments actually made or to be made as a condition of sale of the imported goods, by the buyer to the seller, or by the buyer to a third party to satisfy an obligation of the seller to the extent that such payments are not included in the price actually paid of payable.

2. For the purposes of sub-section (1) and sub section (1A) of section14 of the Customs Act, 1962 (52 of 1962) and these rules, the value of the imported goods shall be the value of such goods, for delivery at the time and place of importation and shall include:
   a. The cost of transport of the imported goods to the place of importation;
   b. Loading, unloading and handling charges associated with the delivery of the imported goods at the place of importation; and
   c. The cost of insurance:
      i. Where the coast of transport referred to in clause (a) is not ascertainable, such cost shall be twenty per cent of the free on board value of the goods;
      ii. The charges referred to in clause (b) shall be one per cent of the free on board value of the goods plus the coast of transport referred to in clause (a) plus the coast of insurance referred to in clause (c);
      iii. Where the coast referred to in clause (c) is not ascertainable, such cost shall be 1.125% of free on board value of the goods;

         Provided further that in the case of goods imported by air, where the cost referred to in clause (a) is ascertainable, such cost shall not exceed twenty per cent of free on board value of the goods: Provided also that where the free on board value of the goods is not ascertainable, the coasts referred to in clause (a) shall be twenty per cent of the free on board value of the goods plus cost of insurance for clause (i) above and the cost referred to in clause (c) shall be 1.125% of the free on board value of the goods plus cost of transport for clause (iii) above.
3. Additions to the price actually paid or payable shall be made under this rule on the bases of objective and quantifiable data.

4. No addition shall be made to the price actually paid or payable in determining the value of the imported goods except as provided for in this rule.

- *Declaration by the importer:*
  1. *The importer or his agent shall furnish:*
     a. A declaration disclosing full and accurate details relating to the value of imported goods; and
     b. Any other statement, information or document including an invoice of the manufacturer or producer of the imported goods where the oops are imorted from or through a person other than the manufacturer or producer, as considered necessary by the proper officer for determination of the value of imported goods under these rule.
  2. Nothing contained in these rules shall be construed as restricting or calling into question the right of the proper officer of customs to satisfy himself as to the truth or accuracy of any statement, information, document or declaration presented for valuation purposes.
  3. The provisions of the Customs Act, 1962 (52 of 1962) relating to confiscation, penalty and prosecution shall apply to cases where wrong declaration, information, statement or documents are furnished under these rules.
- Rejection of declared value – (1) When the proper officer has reason to doubt the truth or accuracy of the value declared in relation to any imported goods, he may ask the importer of such goods to furnish further information including documents or other evidence and if, after receiving such further information, or in the absence of a response of such importer, the proper officer still has reasonable doubt about the truth or accuracy of the value so declared, it shall be deemed that the value of such imported goods cannot be determined under the provisions of sub-rule (1) of rule 4.(2) At the request of and importer, the proper officer, shall intimate the importer in writing the grounds for doubting the truth or accuracy of the value declared in relation to goods imported by such importer and provide a reasonable opportunity of being heard, before taking a final decision under sub-rule (1).]
- *Settlement of dispute*: In case of dispute between the importer and the proper officer of customs valuing the goods, the same shall be resolved consistent with the provisions contained in sub-section (1) of Section 14 of the Customs Act, 1962 (52 of 1962).
- *Interpretative Notes*: The interpretative notes specified in the Schedule to these rules shall apply for the interpretation of these rules.
  – Substituted by M.F. (D.R) Notification No.26/95-Cus.(N.T.),dated 24-4-1995.

- Inserted by M.F.(D.R.) Notification No.26/95-Cus,(N.T.), dated 24-4-1995.
- Inserted by M.F.(D.R.) Notification No.26/95-Cus.(N.T.), dated 24-4-1995.
- Inserted by M.F.(D.R.) Notification No.26/95-Cus.(N.T.),dated 24-4-1995
- Substituted by M.F.(D.R.)F.No.528/167/88-Cus.,(TV)/ICD, dated 6-9-1988.
- Inserted by M.F.(D.R.)Notification No.26/95-Cus.(N.T.),dated 24-4-95
- Substituted by M.F.(D.R.)Notification No.39/90(N.T.)-Cus., dated 5-7-1990
- Substituted (w.e.f.1-10-1991) by M.F.(D.R.) Notification No.67/91 Cus. (N.T.), dated 1-10-1991.
- Inserted by M.F.(D.R.)Notification No.10/98-Cus.(N.T.),dated 19-2-1998.

THE SCHEDULE

General Note:

Use of generally accepted accounting principles:

- " Generally accepted accounting principles" refer to the recognized consensus or substantial authoritative support within a country at a particular time as to which economic resources and obligations shall be recorded as assets and liabilities, which changes in assets and liabilities should be recorded, how the assets and liabilities and changes in them should be measured, what information should be disclosed and how it should be disclosed and which financial statements should be prepared. These standards may be broad guidelines of general application as well as detailed practices and procedures.

Notes to Rules

In Rule 2(2) (v), for the purposes of these rules, one person shall be deemed to control another when the former is legally or operationally in a position to exercise restraint or direction over the latter.

Note to Rule 4

Price Actually Paid or Payable

The price actually paid or payable is the total payment made or to be made by the buyer to or for the benefit of the seller for the imported goods. The payment need not necessarily take the form of a transfer of money. Payment may be made way of letters of credit or negotiable instruments.

Payment may be made directly or indirectly. An example of an indirect payment would be the settlement by the buyer, whether in whole or in part, of a debt owed by the seller.

Activities undertaken by the buyer on his own account, other that those for which an adjustment is provided in Rule 9, are not considered to be and indirect payment to the seller, even though they might be regarded as of benefit to the seller. The costs of such activities shall not, therefore, be added to the price actually paid or payable in determining the value of imported goods. The value of imported goods shall not include the following charges or costs provided that they are distinguished from the price actually paid or payable for the imported goods: Charges for construction, erection, assembly, maintenance or technical assistance, undertaken after importation on imported goods such as industrial plant, machinery or equipment;

- The cost of transport after importation;
- Duties and taxes in India.

The price actually paid or payable refers to the price for the imported goods. Thus the flow of dividends or other payments from the buyer to the seller that do not relate to the imported goods are not part of the customs value.

Rule 4(2)(a)(iii)

Among restrictions which would not render a price actually paid or payable unacceptable are restrictions which do not substantially affect the value of the goods. An example of such restrictions would be the case where a seller requires a buyer of automobiles no to sell or exhibit them prior to a fixed date which represents the beginning of a model year.

Rule 4(2)(b)

If the sale or price is subject to some condition or consideration for which a value cannot be determined with respect to the goods being valued, the transaction value shall not be acceptable for customs purposes.

Some examples of this include:

- The seller establishes the price of the imported goods on condition that the buyer will also buy other goods in specified quantities;
- The price of the imported goods is dependent upon the price or prices at which the buyer of the imported goods sells other goods to the seller of the imported goods;
- The price is established on the basis of a form of payments extraneous to the imported goods, such as where the imported goods are semi-finished goods which have been provided by the seller on condition that he will receive a specified quantity of the finished goods.

However, conditions or considerations relating to the production or marketing of the imported goods shall to result in rejection of the transaction value. For example, the fact that the buyer furnishes the seller with engineering and plans undertaken in India shall not result in rejection of the transaction value for the purposes of Rule 4. Likewise, if the buyer undertakes on his own account, even though by agreement with the seller, activities relating to the marketing or the imported goods, the value of these activities is not part of the value of imported goods nor shall such activities result in rejection of the transaction value.

Rule 4(3)

- Rule 4(3) (a) and Rule 4(3) (b) provide different means of establishing the acceptability of a transaction value.
- Rule 4(3) (a) provides that where the buyer and the seller are related, the circumstances surrounding the sale shall be examined and the transaction value shall be accepted as the value of imported goods provided that the relationship did not influence the price. It is not intended that there should be an examination of the circumstances in all cases where the buyer and the seller are related. Such examination will only be required where there are doubts about the acceptability of the price. Where the proper officer of customs has no doubts about the acceptability of the price, it should be accepted without requesting further information from the importer. For example, the proper officer of customs may have previously examined the relationship, or he may already have detailed information concerning the buyer and the seller, and may already be satisfied from such examination or information that the relationship did not influence the price.
- Where the proper officer of customs is unable to accept the transaction value without further inquiry, he should give the importer an opportunity to supply such further detailed information as may be necessary to enable him to examine the circumstances surrounding the sale. In this context, the proper officer of customs should be prepared to examine relevant aspects of the transaction, including the way in which the buyer and seller organize their commercial relations and the way in which the price in question was arrived at, in order to determine whether the relationship influenced the price. Where it can be shown that the buyer and seller, although related under the provisions of Rule 2(2), buy from and sell to each other as if they were not related, this would demonstrate that the price had not been influenced by the relationship. As example of this, if the price had been settled in a manner consistent with the normal pricing practices of the industry in question or with the way the seller settles prices for sales to buyers who are not related to him, this would demonstrate that the price had not been influenced by the relationship. As a further example, where it is shown that the price is adequate to ensure

recovery of all costs plus a profit which is representative of the firm's overall profit realised over a representative period of time (*e.g.* on an annual basis) in sales of goods of the same class or kind, this would demonstrate that the price had not been influenced.

- Rule 4(3)(b) provides an opportunity for the importer to demonstrate that the transaction value closely approximates to a "test" value previously accepted by the proper offer of customs and is therefore acceptable under the provisions of rule 4. Where a test under rule 4(3)(b) is met, it is not necessary to examine the question of influence under [Rule 4(3)(a)]. If the proper officer of customs has already sufficient information to be satisfied, without further detailed inquiries, that one the tests provided in rule 4(3)(b) has been met, there is no reason for him to require the importer to demonstrate that the test can be met. In rule 4(3)(b) the term " unrelated buyers" means buyers who are not related to the seller in any particular case.

Rule 4(3)(b)

A number of factors must be taken into consideration in determining whether one value " closely approximates" to another value. These factors include the nature of the imported goods, the nature of the industry itself, the season in which the goods are imported, and whether the difference in value is commercially significant. Since these factors may vary from case to case, it would be impossible to apply a uniform standard such as a fixed percentage, in each case. For example, a small difference in value in a case involving one type of goods could be unacceptable while a large difference in a case involving another type of goods might be acceptable in determining whether the transaction value closely approximates to the "test" values set forth in rule 4(3)(b).

Notes to Rule 5

- In applying rule 5, the proper officer of customs shall, wherever possible, use a sale of identical goods at the same commercial level and in substantially the same quantities as the goods being valued. Where no such sale is found, a sale of identical goods that takes place under any one of the following three conditions may be used:
  - A sale at the same commercial level but in different quantities;
  - A sale at a different commercial level but in substantially the same quantities; or
  - A sale at a different commercial level and in different quantities.
- Having found a sale under any one of these three conditions adjustments will then be made, as the case may be, for:
  a. Quantity factors only;
  b. Commercial level factors only; or
  c. Both commercial level and quantity factors.

- For the purposes of rule 5, the transaction value of identical imported goods means a value, adjusted as provided for in rule 5(1)(b) and (c) and rule 5(2), which has already been accepted under rule 4.
- A condition for adjustment because of different commercial levels or different quantities is that such adjustment, whether it leads to an increase or a decrease in the value, be made only on the basis of demonstrated evidence that clearly establishes the reasonableness and accuracy of the adjustment, *e.g.* valid price lists containing prices referring to different levels or different quantities. As an example of this, if the imported goods being valued consist of a shipment of 10 units and the only identical imported goods for which a transaction value exists involved a sale of 500 units, and it is recognized that the seller grants quantity discounts, the required adjustment may be accomplished by resorting to the seller's price list and using that price applicable to a sale of 10 units. This does not require that a sale had to have been made in quantities of 10 as long as the price list has been established as being bona fide through sales at other quantities. In the absence of such an objective measure, however, the determination of a value under the provisions of rule 5 is not appropriate.

Note to Rule 6

- In applying rule 6, the proper officer of customs shall, wherever possible, use a sale of similar goods at the same commercial level and in substantially the same quantities as the goods being valued. For the purpose of rule 6, the transaction value of similar imported goods means the value of imported goods, adjusted as provided for in rule 6(2) which has already been accepted under rule 4.
- All other provisions contained in note to rule 5 shall mutatis mutandis also apply in respect of similar goods.

Note to Rule 7

- The term "unit/price at which.... Goods are sold in the greatest aggregate quantity" means the price at which the greatest number of units is sold in sales to persons who are not related to the persons from whom they buy such goods at the first commercial level after importation at which such sales take place.
- As an example of this, goods are sold from a price list which grants favourable unit prices for purchases made in larger quantities.

Sale quantity Unit price Number of sales Total quantity sold at each price1-10 units 100 10 sales of 5 units, 65.5 sales of 3 units 11-25 units 95 5 sales of 11 units. 55 over 25 units 90 1 sale of 30 units 80

1 Sale of 50 Units

The greatest number of units sold at a price is 80, therefore, the unit price in the greatest aggregate quantity is 90.

- As another example of this, two sales occur, in the first sale 500 units are sold at a price of 95 currency units each. In the second sale 400 units are sold at a price of 90 currency units each. In this example, the greatest number of units sold at a particular price is 500, therefore, the unit price n the greatest aggregate quantity is 95.
- A third example would be the following situation where various quantities are sold at various prices.
  - Sales sale quantity Unit price
    40 units 100 30 units 90
    15 units 100 50 units 95
    25 units 105 35 units 90
    5 units 100
  - Total quantity sold Unit price
    65 90 50 95
    60 100 25 105

In this example, the greatest number of units sold at a particular price is 65, therefore, the unit price in the greatest aggregate quantity is 90.

- Any sale in India, as described in paragraph 1 above to a person who supplies directly or indirectly free of charge or at reduced cost for use in connection with the production and sale for export of the imported goods any of the elements specified in rule 9(1) (b), should not be taken into account in establishing the unit price for the purposes of rule 7.
- It should be noted that "profit and general expenses" referred to in rule 7(1) should be taken as a whole. The figure for the purposes of this deduction should be determined on the basis of information supplied by or on behalf of the importer unless his figures are inconsistent with those obtaining in sales in India, of imported goods of the same class or kind. Where the importers figures are inconsistent with such figures, the amount for profit and general expenses may be based upon relevant information other than that supplied by or on behalf of the importer.
- The "general expenses" include the direct and indirect costs of marketing the goods in question.
- Local taxes payable by reason of the sale of the goods for which deduction is not made under the provisions of rule 7(1)(iii) shall be deducted under the provisions of rule 7(1)(i).
- In determining either the commissions or the usual profits and general expenses under the provisions of rule 7(1), the question whether certain

goods are "of the same class or kind" as other goods must be determined on a case-by-case basis by reference to the circumstances involved. Sales in India, of the narrowest group or range of imported goods of the same class or kind, which includes the goods being valued, for which the necessary information can be provided, should be examined. For the purposes of rule 7 "goods of the same class or kind" includes goods imported from the same country as the goods being valued as well as goods imported from other countries.

- For the purposes of rule 7(2) the "earliest date" shall be the date by which sales of the imported goods or of identical or similar imported, goods are made in sufficient quantity to establish the unit price.
- Where the method in rule 7(3) is used, deductions made for the value added by further processing shall be based on objective and quantifiable data relating to the cost of such work. Accepted industry formulas, recipes, methods or construction, and other industry practices would form the basis of the calculations.
- It is recognized that the method of valuation provided for in rule 7(3) would normally not be applicable when, as a result of the further processing, the imported goods lose their identity. However there can be instances where, although the identity of the imported goods is lose their identity. However there can be instances where, although the identity of the imported goods is lost, the value added by the processing can be determined accurately without unreasonable difficulty. On the other hand, there can also be instances where the imported goods maintain their identity but form such a minor elements in the goods sold in the country of importation that the use of this valuation method would be unjustified. In view of the above, each situation of this type must be considered on a case-by-case basis.

Note to Rule 7A

- As a general rule, value of imported goods is determined under these rules on the basis of information readily available in India. In order to determine a computed value, however, it may be necessary to examine the costs of producing the goods being valued and other information which has to be obtained from outside India. Furthermore, in most cases, the producer of the goods will be outside the jurisdiction of the proper officer. The use of the computed value method will generally be limited to those cases where the buyer and seller are related, and the producer is prepared to supply to the proper officer the necessary costing and to provide facilities for any subsequent verification which may be necessary.
- The "cost or value" referred to in clause (a) of rule 7A is to be determined on the basis of information relating to the production

of the goods being valued supplied by or on behalf of the producer. It is to be based upon the commercial accounts of the producer, provided that such accounts are consistent with the generally accepted accounting principles applied in the country where the goods are produced.

- The "cost or value" shall include the cost of elements specified in clauses (1)(a)(ii) and (1)(a)(iii) of rule 9. It shall also include the value, apportioned as appropriate under the provisions of the relevant note to rule 9, of any element specified in rule 9(1)(b) which has been supplied directly or indirectly by the buyer for use in connection with the production of the imported goods. The value of the elements specified in rule 9(1)(b)(iv) which are undertaken in India shall be included only to the extent that such elements are charged to the producer. It is to be understood that no cost or value of the elements referred to in this paragraph shall be counted twice in determining the computed value.
- The "amount for profit and general expenses" referred to in clause (b) of rule 7A is to be determined on the basis of information supplied by or on behalf of the producer unless the producer's figures are inconsistent with those usually reflected in sales of goods of the same class or kind as the goods being valued which are made by producers in the country of exportation for export to India.
- It should be noted in this context that the "amount for profit and general expenses" has to be taken as a whole. It follows that if, in any particular case, the producer's profit figure is low and his general expenses are high, the producer's profit and general expenses taken together may nevertheless be consistent with that usually reflected in sales of goods of the same class or kind. Such a situation might occur, for example, if a product were being launched in India and the producer accepted a nil or low profit to offset high general expenses associated with the launch. Where the producer can demonstrate a low profit on his sales of the imported goods because of particular commercial circumstances, his actual profit figures should be taken into account provided that he has valid commercial reasons to justify them and his pricing policy reflects usual pricing policies in the branch of industry concerned. Such a situation might occur for example, where producers have been forced to lower prices temporarily because of an unforeseeable drop in demand, or where they sell goods to complement a range of goods being produced in India and accept a low profit to maintain competitivity. Where the producer's own figures for profit and general expenses are not consistent with those usually reflected in sales of goods of the same class or kind as the goods being valued which are made by producers in the country of exportation for export to India, the

amount for profit and general expenses may be based upon relevant information other than that supplied by or on behalf of the producer of the goods.

- The "general expenses" referred to in clause(b) of rule 7A covers the direct and indirect costs of producing and selling the goods for export which are not included under clause (a)of rule 7A.
- Whether certain goods are "of the same class or kind" as other goods must be determined on a case-by-case basis with reference to the circumstances involved. In determining the usual profits and general expenses under the provisions of rule 7A, sales for export to India of the narrowest group or range of goods, which includes the goods being valued, for which the necessary information can be provided, should be examined. For the purposes of rule 7A "goods of the same class or kind" must be from the same country as the goods being valued.

Note to Rule 8

- Value of imported goods determined under the provisions of rule 8 should to the greatest extent possible, be based on previously determined customs values.
- The methods of valuation to be employed under rule 8 may be those laid down in (rules 4 to 7A), inclusive, but a reasonable flexibility in the application of such methods would be in conformity with the aims and provision of rule 8.
- *Some examples of reasonable flexibility are as follows*:
  - *Identical goods*: The requirement that the identical goods should be imported at or about the same time as the goods being valued could be flexibly interpreted; identical imported goods produced in a country other than the country of exportation of the goods being valued could be the basis for customs valuation; customs values of identical imported goods already determined under the provisions of (rules 7 and 7A) could be used.
  - *Similar goods*: The requirement that the similar goods should be imported at or about the same time as the goods being valued could be flexibly interpreted; similar imported goods produced in a country other than the country of exportation of the goods being valued could be the basis for customs valuation; customs values of similar imported goods already determined under the provisions of (rules 7 and 7A) could be used.
  - *Deductive method*: The requirement that the goods shall have been sold in the "condition as imported" in rule 7(1) could be flexibly interpreted; the ninety days requirement could be administered flexibly.

Note to Rule 9

In rule 9(1)(a)(i), the term "buying commissions" means fees paid by an importer to his agent for the service of representing him abroad in the purchase of the goods being valued.

Rule 9(1)(b)(ii)

- There are two factors involved in the apportionment of the elements specified in rule 9(1)(b)(ii) to the imported goods – the value of the element itself and the way in which that value is to be apportioned to the imported goods. The apportionment of these elements should be made in a seasonable manner appropriate to the circumstances and in accordance with generally accepted accounting principles.
- Concerning the value of the element, if the importer acquires the element from a seller not related to him at a given cost, the value of the element is that cost. If the element was produced by the importer or by a person related to him, its value would be the cost of producing it. If the element had been previously used by the importer, regardless of whether it had been acquired or produced by such importer, the original cost of acquisition or production would have to be adjusted downward to reflect its use in order to arrive at the value of the element.
- Once a value has been determined for the element it is necessary to apportion that value to the imported goods. Various possibilities exist. For example, the value might be apportioned to the first shipment if the importer wishes to pay duty on the entire value at one time. As another example, the importer may request that the value be apportioned over the number of units produced up to the time of the first shipment. As a further example, he may request that the value be apportioned over the entire anticipated production where contracts or firm commitments exists for that production. The method of apportionment used will depend upon the documentation provided by the importer.
- As an illustration of the above, an importer provides the producer with a mould to be used in the production of the imported goods and contracts with him to buy 10,000 units. By the time of arrival of the first shipment of 1,000 units the producer has already produced 4,000 units. The importer may request the proper officer of customs to apportion the value of the mould over 1,000 units, 4,000 units or 10,000 units.

Rule 9(1)(b)(iv)

- Additions for the elements specified in rule 9(1)(b)(iv) should be based on objective and quantifiable data. In order to minimize the burden for both the importer and proper officer of customs in determining the values to be added, data readily available in the buyer's commercial record system should be used in so far as possible.

- For those elements supplied by the buyer which were purchased or leased by the buyer, the addition would be the cost of the purchase or the lease. No addition shall be made for those elements available in the public domain, other than the cost of obtaining copies of them.
- The case with which it may be possible to calculate the values to be added will depend on a particular firm's structure and management practice, as well as its accounting methods.
- For example, it is possible that a firm which imports a variety of products from several countries maintains the records of its design centre outside the country of importation in such a way as to show accurately the costs attributable to a given product. In such cases, a direct adjustment may appropriately be made under the provisions of rule 9.
- In another case, a firm may carry the cost of the design centre outside the country of importation as a general overhead expense without allocation to specific products. In this instance, an appropriate adjustment could be made under the provisions of rule 9 with respect to the imported goods by apportioning total design centre costs over total production benefiting from the design centre and adding such apportioned cost on a unit basis to imports.
- Variations in the above circumstances will, of course, require different factors to be considered in determining the proper method of allocation.
- In cases where the production of the element in question involves a number of countries and over a period of time, the adjustment should be limited to the value actually added to that element outside the country of importation.

Rule 9(1)(c)

- The royalties and license fees referred to in rule 9(1) (c) may include among other things, payments in respect to patents, trademarks and copyrights. However, the charges for the right to reproduce the imported goods in the country of importation shall not be added to the price actually paid or payable for the imported goods in determining the customs value.
- Payments made by the buyer for the right to distribute or resell the imported goods shall not be added to the price actually paid or payable for the imported goods if such payments are not a condition of the sale for export to the country of importation of the imported goods.

Rule 9(3)

Where objective and quantifiable data do not exist with regard to the additions required to be made under the provisions of rule 9, the transaction value cannot be determined under the provisions of rule 4. As an illustration of this, a royalty is paid on the basis of the price in a sale in the importing country of a litre of particular product that was imported by the kilogram and made up into a solution after importation. If the royalty is based partially on the imported goods and partially on other factors, which have nothing to do with the imported goods (such as when the imported goods are mixed with domestic ingredients and are no longer separately identifiable, or when the royalty cannot be distinguished from special financial arrangements between the buyer and the seller), it would be inappropriate to attempt to make an addition for the royalty. However, if the amount of this royalty is based only on the imported goods and can be readily quantified, an addition to the price actually paid or payable can be made.

- Substituted by M.F. (D.R.) Letter F.No 528/167/88-Cus.(TU/ICD), dated 28.10.1988.
- Inserted by M.F.(D.R.) Notification No.26/95-Cus.(N.T.),dated 24-4-1995.
- Subsitituted by M.F.(D.R.) Notification No.26/95-Cus.(N.T.),dated 24-4-1995.
- Subsitituted by M.F.(D.R.)Notification No.26/95-Cus.(N.T.),dated 24-4-1995.
- Substituted by M.F.(D.R.)Notification No.26/95-Cus.(N.T.),dated 24-4-95.

SMUGGLERS AND FOREIGN EXCHANGE MANIPULATORS

An Act to provide for the forfeiture of illegally acquired properties of smugglers and foreign exchange manipulators and for matters connected therewith or incidental thereto; Whereas for the effective prevention of smuggling activities and foreign exchange manipulations which are having a deleterious effect on the national economy it is necessary to deprive persons engaged in such activities and manipulations of their ill-gotten gains; And whereas such persons have been augmenting such gains by violations of wealth-tax, income-tax or other laws or by other means and have thereby been increasing their resources for operating in a clandestine manner; And whereas such persons have in many cases been holding the properties acquired by them through such gains in the names of their relatives, associates and confidants. Be it enacted by Parliament in the Twenty-sixth Year of the Republic of India as follows:

Short title, Extent and Commencement

- This act may be called the Smugglers and Foreign Exchange Manipulators (Forfeiture of Property) Act, 1976.

- It extends to the whole of India except the State of Jammu and Kashmir.
- It shall be deemed to have come into force on the 5th day of November, 1975.

Application

- The provisions of this Act shall apply only to the persons specified in sub-section (2).
- The persons referred to in sub-section (1) are the following, namely:
  - *Every person*:
    i. Who has been convicted under the Sea Customs Act, 1878 (8 of 1878), or the Customs Act, 1962 (52 of 1962), of an offence in relation to goods of a value exceeding one lakh of rupees; or
    ii. Who having been convicted under the Sea Customs Act, 1878 (8 of 1878), or the Customs Act, 1962 (52 of 1962), has been convicted subsequently under either of those Acts; or
    iii. Who having been convicted under the Foreign Exchange Regulation Act, 1947 (7 of 1947), or the Foreign Exchange Regulation Act, 1973 (46 of 1973), has been convicted subsequently under either or those Act;
  - Every person in respect of whom an order of detention has been made under the Conservation of Foreign Exchange and Prevention of Smuggling Activities Act, 1974 (52 of 1974):Provided that-
    i. Such order of detention, being an order which the provisions of section 9 or section 12A of the said Act do not apply, has not been revoked on the report of the Advisory Board under section 8 of the said Act or before the receipt of the report of the Advisory Board or before making a reference to the Advisory Board; or
    ii. Such order of detention, being an order to which the provisions of section 9 of the said Act apply, has not been revoked before the expiry of the time for, or on the basis of, the review under sub-section (3) of section 9 or on the report of the Advisory board under section 8, read with sub-section (2) of section 9, of the said Act; or
    iii. Such order of detention, being an order to which the provisions of section 12A of the said Act apply, has not been revoked before the expiry of the time for, or on the basis of, the first review under sub-section (3) of that section, or on the basis of the report of the Advisory Board under section 8, read with sub-section (6) of section 12A, of that Act; or

iv. Such order of detention has not been set aside by a Court of competent jurisdiction;

- Every person who is a relative of person referred to in clause (a) or clause (b);
- Every associate of a person referred to in clause (a) or clause (b);
- Any holder (hereafter in this clause referred to as the present holder) of any property which was at any time previously held by a person referred to in clause (a) or clause (b) unless the present holder or, as the case may be, any one who held such property after such person and before the present holder, is or was a transferee in good faith for adequate consideration.

Explanation 1: For the purposes of sub-clause (i) of clause (a), the value of any goods in relation to which a person has been convicted of an offence shall be the wholesale price of the goods in the ordinary cause of trade in India as on the date of the commission of the offence.

Explanation 2: For the purposes of clause (c), "relative", in relation to a person, means:

i. Spouse of the person;
ii. Brother or sister of the person;
iii. Brother or sister of the spouse of the person;
iv. Any lineal ascendant or descendant of the person;
v. Any lineal ascendant or descendant of the spouse of the person;
vi. Spouse of a person referred to in clause (ii), clause (iii), clause (iv) or clause (v);
vii. Any lineal descendant of a person referred to in clause (ii) or clause (iii).

Explanation 3: For the purposes of clause (d), "associate", in relation to a person, means-

i. Any individual who, had been or is residing in the residential premises (including out-houses) of such person;
ii. Any individual who had been or is managing the affairs or keeping the accounts of such person;
iii. Any association of persons, body of individuals, partnership firm, or private company within the meaning of the Companies Act, 1956 (1 of 1956), of which such person had been or is a member, partner or director;
iv. Any individual who had been or is a member, partner or director of an association of persons, body of individuals, partnership firm or private company referred to in clause (iii) at any time when such person had been or is a member,

partner or director of such association, body, partnership firm or private company;

v. Any person who had been or is managing the affairs, or keeping the accounts, of any association of persons, body of individuals, partnership firm or private company referred to in clause (iii);

vi. The trustee of any trust, where,-

    a. The trust has been created by such person; or

    b. The value of the assets contributed by such person (including the value of the assets, if any, contributed by him earlier) to the trust amounts, on the date on which the contribution is made, to not less than twenty per cent of the value of the assets of the trust on that date;

vii. Where the competent authority, for reasons to be recorded in writing, considers that any properties of such person are held on his behalf by any other person, such other person.

– *Explanation 4*: For the avoidance of doubt, it is hereby provided that the question whether any person is a person to whom the provisions of this Act apply may be determined with reference to any facts, circumstances or events (including any conviction or detention) which occurred or took place before the commencement of this Act

ACT NOT TO APPLY TO CERTAIN PERSONS

On and from the commencement of the provisions of the Narcotic Drugs and Psychotropic Substances Act, 1985 (61 of 1985), the provisions of this Act shall not apply to persons in relation to whom any order, or proceeding, may be made or taken under that Chapter.

Definitions

- In this Act, unless the context otherwise requires, "Appellate Tribunal" means the Appellate Tribunal for Forfeited Property constituted under section 12; "competent authority" means an officer of the Central Government authorised by it under sub-section (1) of section 5 to perform the functions of a competent authority under this Act; "illegally acquired property", in relation to any person to whom this Act applies, means-

i. Any property acquired by such person, whether before or after the commencement of this act, wholly or partly out of or by means of any income, earnings or assets derived or obtained from or attributable to any activity prohibited by or under any law for the time being in force relating to any matter in respect of which Parliament has power to make laws; or

ii. Any property acquired by such person, whether before or after the commencement of this Act, wholly or partly out of or by means of any income, earnings or assets in respect of which any such law has been contravened; or

iii. Any property acquired by such person, whether before or after the commencement of this Act, wholly or partly out of or by means of any income, earnings or assets the source of which cannot be proved and which cannot be shown to be attributable to any act or thing done in respect of any matter in relation to which Parliament has no power to make laws; or

iv. Any property acquired by such person, whether before or after the commencement of this Act, for a consideration, or by any means, wholly or partly traceable to any property referred to in sub-clauses (i) to (iii) or the income or earnings from such property and includes-any property held by such person which would have been, in relation to any previous holder thereof, illegally acquired property under this clause if such previous holder had not ceased to hold it, unless such person or any other person who held the property at any time after such previous holder or, where there are two or more such previous holders, the last of such previous holders is or was a transferee in good faith for adequate consideration; any property acquired by such person, whether before or after the commencement of this Act, for a consideration, or by any means, wholly or partly traceable to any property falling under item (A), or the income or earnings therefrom; "prescribed" means prescribed by rules made under this Act; "property" includes any interest in property, movable or immovable; "trust" includes any other legal obligation. (2) Any reference in this Act to any law which is not in force in any area shall, in relation to that area, be construed as a reference to the corresponding law, if any, in force in that area. (3) Any reference in this Act to any officer or authority shall, in relation to any area in which there is no officer or authority with the same designation, be construed as a reference to such officer or authority as may be specified by the central Government by notification in the Official Gazette.

PROHIBITION OF HOLDING ILLEGALLY ACQUIRED PROPERTY

- As from the commencement of this Act, it shall not be lawful for any person to whom this Act applies to hold any illegally acquired property either by himself or through any other person on his behalf.
- Where any person holds any illegally acquired property in

contravention of the provisions of sub-section (1), such property shall be liable to be forfeited to the Central Government in accordance with the provisions of this Act.

COMPETENT AUTHORITY

- The Central Government may, by order published in the Official Gazette, authorise as many officers of the Central Government (non below the rank of a Joint Secretary to the Government), as it thinks fit, to perform the functions of the competent authority under this Act.
- The competent authorities shall perform their functions in respect of such persons or classes or persons as the Central Government may, by order, direct.

NOTICE OF FORFEITURE

- If, having regard to the value of the properties held by any person to whom this Act applies, either by himself or through any other person on his behalf, his known sources, of income, earnings or assets, and any other information or material available to it as a result of action taken under section 18 or otherwise, the competent authority has reason to believe (the reasons for such belief to be recorded in writing) that all or any of such properties are illegally acquired properties, it may serve a notice upon such person (hereinafter referred to as the person affected) calling upon him within such time as may be specified in the notice, which shall not be ordinarily less than thirty days, to indicate the sources of his income, earnings or assets, out of which or by means of which he has acquired such property, the evidence on which he relies and other relevant information and particulars, and to show cause why all or any of such properties, as the case may be, should not be declared to be illegally acquired properties and forfeited to the Central Government under this Act.
- Where a notice under sub-section (1) to any person specifies any property as being held on behalf of such person by any other person, a copy of the notice shall also be served upon such other person.

FORFEITURE OF PROPERTY IN CERTAIN CASES:

- The competent authority may, after considering the explanation, if any, to the show-cause notice issued under section6, and the materials available before it and after giving to the person affected (and in a case where the person affected holds any property specified in the notice through any other person, to such other person also) a reasonable opportunity of being heard, by order, record a finding whether all or any of the properties in question are illegally acquired properties.

- Where the competent authority is satisfied that some of the properties referred to in the show-cause notice are illegally acquired properties but is not able to identify specifically such properties, then, it shall be lawful for the competent authority to specify the properties which, to the best of its judgment, are illegally acquired properties and record a finding accordingly under sub-section (1).
- Where the competent authority records a finding under this section to the effect that any property is illegally acquired property, it shall declare that such property shall, subject to the provisions of this Act, stand forfeited to the central Government free from all encumbrances.
- Where any shares in a company stand forfeited to the Central Government under this Act, then, the company shall, notwithstanding any thing contained in the Companies Act, 1956 (1 of 1956), or the articles of association of the company, forthwith register the Central Government as the transferee of such shares.

BURDEN OF PROOF

In any proceedings under this Act, the burden of proving that any property specified in the notice served under section 6 in not illegally acquired property shall be on the person affected.

FINE IN LIEU OF FORFEITURE

- Where the competent authority makes declaration that any property stands forfeited to the Central Government under section 7 and it is a case where the source of only a part, being less than one-half, of the income, earnings or assets with which such property was acquired has not been proved to the satisfaction of the competent authority, it shall make an order giving an option to the person affected to pay, in lieu of forfeiture, a fine equal to one and one-fifth times the value of such part.

  Explanation: For the purposes of this sub-section, the value of any part of income, earnings or assets, with which any property has been acquired, shall be,-
  - In the case of any part of income of earnings, the amount of such part of income of earnings;
  - In the case of any part of assets, the proportionate part of the full value of the consideration for the acquisition of such assets.
- Before making an order imposing a fine under sub-section (1), the person affected shall be given a reasonable opportunity of being head.
- Where the person affected pays the fine due under sub-section (1),

within such time as may allowed in that behalf, the competent authority may, by order, revoke the declaration of forfeiture under section 7 and thereupon such property shall stand released.

PROCEDURE IN RELATION TO CERTAIN TRUST PROPERTIES

In the case of any person referred to in clause (vi) of Explanation 3 to sub-section (2) of section 2, if the competent authority, on the basis of the information and materials available to it, has reason to believe (the reasons for such belief to be recorded in writing) that any property held in trusts in illegally acquired property, it may serve a notice upon the author of the trust or, as the case may be, the contributor of the assets out of or by means of which such property was acquired by the trust and the trustees, calling upon them within such time as may be specified in the notice which shall not ordinarily be less than thirty days, to explain the source of the money or other assets out of or by means of which such property was acquired or, as the case may be, the source of the money or other assets which were contributed to the trust for acquiring such property and thereupon such notice shall be deemed to be a notice served under section 6 and all other provisions of this Act shall apply accordingly.

Explanation: For the purposes of this section "illegally acquired property", in relation to any property held in trust, includes:

- Any property which if it had continued to be held by the author of the trust of the contributor of such property to the trust would have been illegally acquired property in relation to such author or contributor;
- Any property acquired by the trust out of any contributions made by any person which would have been illegally acquired property in relation to such person had such person acquired such property out of such contributions.

CERTAIN TRANSFERS TO BE NULL AND VOID

Where after the issue of a notice under section 6 or under section 10, any property referred to in the said notice is transferred by any mode whatsoever such transfer shall, for the purposes of the proceedings under this Act, be ignored and if such property is subsequently forfeited to the Central Government under section 7, then, the transfer of such property shall be deemed to be null and void.

CONSTITUTION OF APPELLATE TRIBUNAL

- The Central Government may, be notification in the Official Gazette, constitute an Appellate Tribunal to be called the Appellate Tribunal for Forfeited Property consisting of a Chairman and such number of other members (being officers of the Central Government not below the rank of a Joint secretary to the Government) as the Central Government thinks fit, to be appointed by that Government for hearing appeals against the orders made under section 7, sub-section (1) of section 9 or section 10.

- The Chairman of the Appellate Tribunal shall be a person who is or has been or is qualified to be a judge of the Supreme Court or of a High Court.
- The terms and conditions of service of the Chairman and other members shall be such as may be prescribed.
- Any person aggrieved by an order of the competent authority made under section 7, sub-section (1) of section 9 or section 10, may, within forty-five days from the date on which the order is served on him, prefer an appeal to the Appellate Tribunal. Provided that the Appellate Tribunal may entertain any appeal after the said period of forty-five days, but not after sixty days, from the date aforesaid if it is satisfied that the appellant was prevented by sufficient cause from filling the appeal in time.
- On receipt of an appeal under sub-section (4), the Appellate Tribunal may, after giving an opportunity to the appellant to be heard, if he so desires, and after making such further enquiry as it deems fit, confirm, modify or set aside the order appealed against.
- The powers and functions of the Appellate tribunal may be exercised and discharged by Benches consisting of three members and constituted by the Chairman of the Appellate Tribunal.
  - Notwithstanding anything contained in sub-section (6), where the Chairman considers it necessary so to do for the expeditious disposal of appeals under this section, he may constitute a Bench of two members and a Bench so constituted may exercise and discharge the powers and functions of the Appellate Tribunal: Provided that if the members of a Bench so constituted differ on any point or points, they shall state the point or points on which they differ and refer the same to a third members (to be specified by the chairman) for hearing on such point or points and such point or points shall be decided according to the opinion of that member.
- The Appellate Tribunal may regulate its own procedure.
- On application to the Appellate Tribunal and on payment of the prescribed fee, the Tribunal may allow a party to any appeal or any person authorised in this behalf by such party to inspect at any time during office hours, any relevant records and registers of the Tribunal and obtain a certified copy of any part thereof.

NOTICE OR ORDER NOT TO BE INVALID FOR ERROR IN DESCRIPTION

No notice issued or served, no declaration made, and no order passed, under this Act shall be deemed to be invalid by reason of any error in the description of the property or person mentioned therein if such property or person is identifiable from the description so mentioned.

BAR OF JURISDICTION

No order passed or declaration made under this Act shall be appealable except as provided therein and no civil court shall have jurisdiction in respect of any matter which the Appellate Tribunal or any competent authority is empowered by or under the Act to determine, and no injunction shall be granted by any Court or other authority in respect of any action taken or to be taken in pursuance of any power conferred by or under this Act.

COMPETENT AUTHORITY AND APPELLATE TRIBUNAL TO HAVE POWERS OF CIVIL COURT

The competent authority and the Appellate tribunal shall have all the powers of a civil court while trying a suit under the Code of Civil Procedure, 1908 (5 of 1908), in respect of the following maters, namely:

- Summoning and enforcing the attendance of any person and examining him on oath;
- Requiring the discovery and production of documents;
- Receiving evidence on affidavits;
- Requisitioning any public record or copy thereof from any court or office;
- Issuing commissions for examination of witnesses or documents;
- Any other matter which may be prescribed.

INFORMATION TO COMPETENT AUTHORITY

- Notwithstanding anything contained in any other law, the competent authority shall have power to require any officer or authority of the central Government or a State Government of a local authority to furnish information in relation to such persons, points or matters as in the opinion of the competent authority will be useful for, or relevant to, the purposes of this Act.
- Any officer of the Income-tax Department, the Customs Department or the Central Excise Department or any officer of Enforcement appointed under the Foreign Exchange Regulation Act, 1973 (46 of 1973), may furnish suo motu any information available with him to the competent authority if in the opinion of the officer such information will be useful to the competent authority for the purposes of this Act.

CERTAIN OFFICERS TO ASSIST COMPETENT AUTHORITY AND APPELLATE TRIBUNAL

For the purposes of any proceedings under this Act, the following officers are hereby empowered and required to assist the competent authority and the Appellate Tribunal, namely:

- Officers of the Customs Department;
- Officers of the Central Excise Department;
- Officers of the Income-tax Department;
- Officers of Enforcement appointed under the Foreign Exchange Regulation Act, 1973 (46 of 1973);
- Officers of Police;
- Such other officers of the Central of State Government as are specified by the Central Government in this behalf by notification in the Official Gazette.

POWER OF COMPETENT AUTHORITY TO REQUIRE CERTAIN OFFICERS TO EXERCISE CERTAIN POWERS

- For the purposes of any proceedings under this Act or the initiation of any such proceedings, the competent authority shall have power to cause to be conducted any inquiry, investigation or survey in respect of any person, place, property, assets, documents, books of account or any other relevant matters.
- For the purposes referred to in sub-section (1), the competent authority may, having regard to the nature of the inquiry, investigation or survey, require an officer of the Income-tax Department to conduct or cause to be conducted such inquiry, investigation or survey.
- Any officer of the Income-tax Department who is conducting or is causing to be conducted any inquiry, investigation or survey required to be conducted under sub-section (2), may, for the purpose of such inquiry, investigation or survey, exercise any power (including the power to authorise the exercise of any power) which may be exercised by him for any purpose under the Income-tax Act, 1961 (43 of 1961), and the provisions of the said Act shall, so far as may be, apply accordingly.

POWER TO TAKE POSSESSION

- Where any property has been declared to be forfeited to the Central Government under this Act, or where the person affected has failed to pay the fine due under sub-section (1) of section 9 within the time allowed therefore under sub-section (3) of the section, the competent authority may order the person affected as well as any other person who may be in possession of the property to surrender or deliver possession thereof to the competent authority or to any person duly authorised by it in this behalf within thirty days of the service of the order.

- If any person refuses or fails to comply with an order made under sub-section (1), the competent authority may take possession of the property and may for that purpose use such force as may be necessary.
- Notwithstanding anything contained in sub-section (2), the competent authority may, for the purpose of taking possession of any property referred to in sub-section (1), requisition the service of any police officer to assist the competent authority and it shall be the duty of such officer to comply with such requisition.

RECTIFICATION OF MISTAKES

With a view to rectifying any mistakes apparent from the record, the competent authority or the Appellate Tribunal, as the case may be, may amend any order made by it within a period of one year from the date of the order: Provided that if any such amendment is likely to affect any person prejudicially, it shall not be made without giving to such person a reasonable opportunity of being heard.

FINDINGS UNDER OTHER LAWS NOT CONCLUSIVE FOR PROCEEDINGS UNDER THIS ACT

No finding of any officer of authority under any other law shall be conclusive for the purposes of any proceedings under this act.

SERVICE OF NOTICES AND ORDERS

Any notice or order issued or make under this Act shall be served:

- By tendering the notice or order or sending it by registered post to the person for whom it is intended or to his agent;
- If the notice or order cannot be served in the manner provided in clause (a), by affixing it on a conspicuous place in the property in relation to which the notice or order is issued or made, or on some conspicuous part of the premises in which the person for whom it is intended is known to have last resided or carried on business or personally worked for gain.

PROTECTION OF ACTION TAKEN IN GOOD FAITH

No suit, prosecution or other proceeding shall lie against the Central Government or any Officer of the Central or State Government for any thing which is done, or intended to be done, in good faith, in pursuance of this Act or the rules made thereunder.

ACT TO HAVE OVERRIDING EFFECT

The provisions of this Act shall have effect notwithstanding any thing inconsistent therewith contained in any other law for the time being in force.

PROVISIONS OF THE ACT NOT TO APPLY TO CERTAIN PROPERTIES HELP IN TRUST

Nothing contained in this Act shall apply in relation to any property held by a trust or an institution created or established wholly for public, religious or charitable purposes if:

- Such property has been so held by such trust or institution from a date prior to the commencement of this Act.
- Such property is wholly traceable to any property held by such trust or institution prior to the commencement of this Act.

POWER TO MAKE RULES

- The Central Government may, by notification in the Official Gazette, make rules to carry out the provisions of this Act.
- In particular and without prejudice to the generality of the foregoing power, such rules may provide for all or any of the following matters, namely:
  - The terms and conditions of service of the chairman and other members of the Appellate Tribunal under sub-section (3) of section 12;
    i. The fees which shall be paid for the inspection of the records and registers of the Appellate Tribunal or for obtaining a certified copy of any part thereof under sub-section (8) of section 12;
  - The powers of a civil court that may be exercised by the competent authority and the Appellate Tribunal under clause (f) of section 15;
  - Any other matter which has to be, or may be, prescribed.

Index